Manifest Civility

Westphalia Press Civility Series

westphaliapress.org

Volume 1
Revolutionary Civility
Rules of Decent Behavior in Company and Conversation

Volume 2
Expansive Civility
The American Chesterfield

Volume 3
Manifest Civility
The Young Man's Own Book

Volume 4
Industrial Civility
The Primer of Politeness

Volume 5
Progressive Civility
Wehman's Etiquette and Politeness

Volume 6
Civility and the Great War
The Stakes of Diplomacy

Volume 7
Postwar Civility
On Kindness

Manifest Civility

The Young Man's Own Book

by Anonymous

Volume 3 in the Westphalia Press Civility Series

WESTPHALIA PRESS
An imprint of Policy Studies Organization

Westphalia Press
An imprint of Policy Studies Organization
1527 New Hampshire Ave., NW
Washington, D.C. 20036
dgutierrezs@ipsonet.org

ISBN-13: 978-1935907732
ISBN-10: 1935907735

Cover design by Taillefer Long at Illuminated Stories:
www.illuminatedstories.com

Updated material and comments on this edition
can be found at the Westphalia Press website:
www.westphaliapress.org

In Search of Civility

An archaic meaning of civility was 'study of the humanities,' and as a word it appears in the sixteenth century. The years have not blunted its importance; it is one of the guiding principles of *Wikipedia*, which informs readers that, "The civility policy is a standard of conduct that sets out how *Wikipedia* editors should interact. Stated simply, editors should always treat each other with consideration and respect. In order to keep the focus on improving the encyclopedia and to help maintain a pleasant editing environment, editors should behave politely, calmly and reasonably, even during heated debates."

Other voices also have been raised about the need to consider civility as a priority in an increasingly abrasive modern society. The Institute for Civility in Government in Houston, ably led by Cassandra Dahnke and Tomas Spath, has for many years hosted Washington seminars and blogs on the subject. Profesor J.M. Forni at Johns Hopkins has made a life's work out of studying the ramifications of civility. In the Hopkins alumni magazine he sums the current situation up when he writes:

E

We do have our manners. What we have lost are the manners of past generations. That we have manners, however, does not mean we ought to be perfectly happy with the manners we have. In fact, many Americans think that civility and manners are in decline, that this decline has increased in the past several years, and that there is a causal connection between incivility and violence. Does reality match the perception of a decline? Yes and no. There is little doubt that we are losing established forms of deference and respect. On the other hand, new forms of respect take the place of those becoming obsolete. A pregnant woman may not easily find a youngster willing to give her his seat on a bus. But the number of men willing to treat the same woman as an intellectual peer on the job is higher today than it was yesterday.

This does not mean that we should ignore the coarsening of social interaction that we have been witnessing in recent years. Our manners inevitably suffer when:

1. We are poorly trained in self-restraint.

2. We are used to seeing others as means to the satisfaction of our desires rather than ends in themselves.

3. We are overly concerned about financial gain and professional achievement.

4. We are constantly besieged by stress and fatigue.

5. We are surrounded by strangers who will remain strangers.

When some or all of these factors are at work, it becomes difficult to be considerate — and consideration is the ethical requirement of manners that are really good.

Clearly we need more people to take an interest in the topic rather than less. The Westphalia Press Civility Series demonstrates that the topic has many aspects, including etiquette and diplomacy. My friend Ambassador Mark Hambley suggests that there even might be some connection between the decline of cursive writing and the decline of civility. Unfortunately the current lack of civility in Washington is as noticeable or more noticeable than the state of the nation's handwriting. While politics has always been a competitive sport, common consensus is that the political life in the capital recently has become far more contentious than in recent memory.

The Westphalia Press Civility Series presents manners, etiquette, diplomacy, decent behavior, and politeness as fruit in the same orchard. The books are intended to be an accessible resource for studying facets of a subject that we think contributes to the current policy anxiety that has paralyzed decision making.

The subject has a universal aspect. Although we relish including George Washington as author of one of the titles in the collection, he actually found many of the maxims in his *Rules of Civility* in the literature of French Jesuits of the 1590s that was rendered in English by Francis Hawkins in London in 1640. By all account he was a man of manners no matter what the circumstances, and so we respectfully dedicate this series to his memory, in hopes that present day leaders will reflect on his example.

Paul Rich
President, Policy Studies Organization
Garfield House, Washington, D.C.

G

H

THE
YOUNG MAN'S
OWN BOOK

PHILADELPHIA:

DESILVER THOMAS & Co,

EDWARD C. BIDDLE.

Make it an object to spend some portion of your leisure time
in the company of intelligent and virtuous ladies   Page 115.

THE

YOUNG MAN'S

OWN BOOK:

A MANUAL OF POLITENESS, INTELLECTUAL IM
PROVEMENT, AND MORAL DEPORTMENT,

CALCULATED

TO FORM THE CHARACTER ON A SOLID BASIS,
AND TO INSURE RESPECTABILITY
AND SUCCESS IN LIFE.

Sui cuique mores fingunt fortunam.—*Corn. Nepos.*
It is a man's manners that make his fortune.

Philadelphia:
DESILVER, THOMAS, AND Co.
253 MARKET STREET.

1835.

PREFACE.

In the outset of life, every young man needs a friendly adviser, who shall give him some leading hints concerning the line of conduct which he should adopt, in order to insure success and respectability. Sometimes one is fortunate enough to find such a monitor in a father, guardian, or elder brother; and seldom does a youth enter upon this momentous and responsible career without some real or pretended friend, who volunteers his advice. But few are so fortunate as to have a living adviser who is at hand on all occasions; or who is qualified to give counsel on all the subjects in which a young man may require it.

In coming forward to offer his services as a guide and mentor, the author of the "Young Man's Own Book" presents himself with a degree of confidence which he would not feel, if he had relied entirely on his own observation and experience. This he has by no means presumed to do. On the contrary, in pointing out the means of mental improvement, in laying down maxims of worldly prudence and moral wisdom, in offering counsel concerning manners and behavior, amusements, occupations, the conduct of domestic life, and the pursuit of business, he has had recourse to the writings and opinions of those whose authority is undisputed; and has only introduced his own remarks where the particular situation of affairs, or the peculiar tone of manners in this country seemed to require them.

By this course, he trusts that he has produced a manual which every young man may safely take as a guide in all those particulars in which it professes to offer advice—a volume to which he may repair with confidence, and on whose authority he may rely with safety—which may properly be his companion at home and abroad, in the daily conduct of life, and on those important emergencies when good advice is of more value than fine gold.

CONTENTS.

ADVICE WITH RESPECT TO MANNERS AND

THE

Young Man's Own Book.

NECESSITY OF BEING WELL INFORMED.

The young are apt to disregard the value of knowledge, partly, we fear, from the pertinacious constancy with which teachers, parents, and guardians endeavor to impress them with its inestimable worth. "Knowledge better than House and Lands," is the title of one of the first picture books presented to a child, and it is the substance of ten thousand precepts which are constantly dinned in his ears from infancy upwards; so that, at last, the truth becomes tiresome and almost detested.

Still it is a sober truth, of which every young man should feel the force—that, with the single exception of a good conscience, no possession can be so valuable as a good stock of information. Some portion of it is always coming into use; and there is hardly any kind of information which may not become useful in the course of an active life.

When we speak of information, we do not mean that merely which has direct reference to a man's trade, profession or business. To be skilful in these is a matter of absolute necessity; so much so, that we often see, for example, a merchant beginning the world with no other stock than a good character and a thorough knowledge of business, and speedily acquiring wealth and respectability, while another, who is not well informed in his business, begins with a fortune, fails in every thing he undertakes, causes loss and disgrace to all who are connected with him, and goes on blundering to the end of the chapter.

But a thorough knowledge of one's business or profession is not enough, of itself, to constitute what is properly called a well-informed man. On the contrary, one who possesses this kind of information only, is generally regarded as a mere machine, unfit for society or rational enjoyment. A man should possess a certain amount of liberal and scientific information, to which he should always be adding something as long as he lives, and in this free country he should make himself acquainted with his own political and legal rights.

"Keep a thing seven years and you will have use for it," is an old motto which will apply admirably well to almost any branch of knowledge. Learn almost any science, language or art, and in a few years you will find it of service to you. This truth is so important that I would add to it by way of commentary, "Employ that leisure, which others waste in idle and corrupting pursuits, in the acquisition of those branches of knowledge which serve to amuse as well as instruct; natural history, for example, or chemistry, or astronomy, or drawing, or any of the numerous kindred branches of study."

MEANS OF ACQUIRING INFORMATION.

THERE are five eminent means or methods whereby the mind is improved in the knowledge of things, and these are observation, reading, instruction by lectures, conversation, and meditation ; which last, in a most peculiar manner, is called study. Let us survey the general definitions or descriptions of them all.

I. Observation is the notice that we take of all occurrences in human life, whether they are sensible or intellectual, whether relating to persons or things, to ourselves or others. It is this that furnishes us, even from our infancy, with a rich variety of ideas, words and phrases : it is by this we know that fire will burn, that the sun gives light, that a horse eats grass, that an acorn produces an oak, that man is a being capable of reasoning and discourse, that our judgment is weak, that our mistakes are many, that our sorrows are great, that our bodies die and are carried to the grave, and that one generation succeeds another. All those things which we see, which we hear or feel, which we perceive by sense or consciousness, or which we know in a direct manner, with scarce any exercise of our reflecting faculties, or our reasoning powers, may be included under the general name of observation.

When this observation relates to any thing that immediately concerns ourselves, and of which we are conscious, it may be called experience. So I am said to know or experience that I have in myself a power of thinking, fearing, loving, &c., that I have appetites and passions working in me, and that many personal occurrences have attended me in this life.

Observation therefore includes all that Locke means by sensation and reflection.

When we are searching out the nature or properties of any thing by various methods of trial, or when we apply some active powers, or set some causes to work to observe what effects they would produce, this sort of observation is called experiment. So when I throw a bullet into water, I find it sinks; and when I throw the same bullet into quicksilver, I see it swims: but if I beat out this bullet [into a thin hollow shape, like a dish, then it will swim in the water too. So when I strike two flints together, I find they produce fire: when I throw a seed into the earth, it grows up into a plant.

All these belong to the first method of know ledge: which we shall call observation.

II. Reading is that means or method of knowledge whereby we acquaint ourselves with what other men have written, or published to the world in their writings. The arts of reading and writing are of infinite advantage; for by them we are made partakers of the sentiments, observations, reasonings, and improvements of all the learned world, in the most remote nations, and in former ages almost from the beginning of mankind.

III. Public or private lectures are such verbal instructions as are given by a teacher while the learners attend in silence. This is the way of learning religion from the pulpit; or of philosophy or theology from the professor's chair; or of mathematics, by a teacher showing us various theorems or problems, i. e. speculations or practices by de.

monstration and operation, with all the instruments of art necessary to those operations.

IV. Conversation is another method of improving our minds, wherein, by natural discourse and inquiry, we learn the sentiments of others, as well as communicate our sentiments to others in the same manner. Sometimes indeed, though both parties speak by turns, yet the advantage is only on one side, as when a teacher and a learner meet and discourse together: but frequently the profit is mutual. Under this head of conversation we may also rank disputes of various kinds.

V. Meditation or study includes all those exercises of the mind, whereby we render all the former methods useful for our increase in true knowledge and wisdom. It is by meditation we come to confirm our memory of things that pass through our thoughts in the occurrences of life, in our own experiences, and in the observations we make. It is by meditation that we draw various inferences, and establish in our minds general principles of knowledge. It is by meditation that we compare the various ideas which we derive from our senses, or from the operations of our mental faculties, and join them in propositions. It is by meditation that we fix in our memory whatsoever we learn, and form our own judgment of the truth or falsehood, the strength or weakness, of what others speak or write. It is meditation or study that draws out long chains of argument, and searches and finds deep and difficult truths which before lay concealed in darkness.

It would be a needless thing to prove, that our own solitary meditations, together with the few observations that the most part of mankind are capable of making, are not sufficient, of themselves, to lead us into the attainment of any considerable proportion of knowledge, at least in an age so much improved as ours is, without the assistance of conversation and reading, and other proper instructions that are to be attained in our days. Yet all these five methods have their peculiar advantages, whereby they assist each other; and their peculiar defects, which have need to be supplied by the other's assistance. Let us trace over some of the particular advantages of each.

OBSERVATION.

I. One method of improving the mind is observation, and the advantages of it are these:

1. It is owing to observation, that our mind is furnished with the first simple and complex ideas. It is this lays the groundwork and foundation of all knowledge, and makes us capable of using any of the other methods for improving the mind: for if we did not attain a variety of sensible and intellectual ideas by the sensations of outward objects, by the consciousness of our own appetites and passions, pleasures and pains, and by inward experience of the actings of our own faculties, it would be impossible either for men or books to teach us any thing. It is observation that must give us our first ideas of things, as it includes in it sense and consciousness.

2. All our knowledge derived from observation, whether it be of single ideas or of propositions, is knowledge gotten at first hand. Hereby we see and know things as they are, or as they appear to us; we take the impressions of them on our minds from the original objects themselves, which give a clearer and stronger conception of things:

these ideas are more lively, and the propositions (at least in many cases) are much more evident. Whereas, what knowledge we derive from lectures, reading, and conversation, is but the copy of other men's ideas, that is, the picture of a picture; and it is one remove farther from the original.

3. Another advantage of observation is, that we may gain knowledge all the day long, and every moment of our lives; and every moment of our existence we may be adding something to our intellectual treasures thereby, except only while we are asleep.

READING.

II. The next way of improving the mind is by reading, and the advantages of it are such as these :

1. By reading we acquaint ourselves in a very extensive manner, with the affairs, actions, and thoughts of the living and the dead, in the most remote nations, and most distant ages, and that with as much ease as though they lived in our own age and nation. By reading of books we may learn something from all parts of mankind; whereas by observation we learn all from ourselves, and only what comes within our own direct cognizance; by conversation we can only enjoy the assistance of a very few persons, viz. those who are near us, and live at the same time when we do, that is, our neighbors and contemporaries; but our knowledge is much more narrowed still, if we confine ourselves merely to our own solitary reasonings, without much observation or reading : for then all our improvement must arise only from our own inward powers and meditations.

B

2. By reading we learn not only the actions and the sentiments of different nations and ages, but we transfer to ourselves the knowledge and improvements of the most learned men, the wisest and the best of mankind, when or wheresoever they lived: for though many books have been written by weak and injudicious persons, yet the most of those books which have obtained great reputation in the world are the products of great and wise men in their several ages and nations : whereas we can obtain the conversation and instruction of those only who are within the reach of our dwelling, or our acquaintance, whether they are wise or unwise ; and sometimes that narrow sphere scarce affords any person of great eminence in wisdom or learning, unless our instructor happen to have this character. And as for our own study and meditations, even when we arrive at some good degrees of learning, our advantage for farther improvement in knowledge by them· is still far more contracted than what we may derive from reading.

3. When we read good authors, we learn the best, the most labored, and most refined sentiments, even of those wise and learned men ; for they have studied hard, and have committed to writing their maturest thoughts, and the result of their long study and experience : whereas by conversation, and in some lectures, we obtain many times only the present thoughts of our tutors or friends, which (though they may be bright and useful) yet at first perhaps may be sudden and indigested, and are mere hints which have risen to no maturity.

4. It is another advantage of reading, that we

may review what we have read ; we may consult the page again and again, and meditate on it, at successive seasons, in our serenest and retired hours, having the book always at hand : but what we obtain by conversation and in lectures, is oftentimes lost again as soon as the company breaks up, or at least when the day vanishes, unless we happen to have the talent of a good memory, or quickly retire and note down whatever remarkable we have found in those discourses. And for the same reason, and for the want of retiring and writing, many a learned man has lost several useful meditations of his own, and could never recall them again.

LECTURES.

III. The advantages of verbal instructions by public or private lectures are these :

1. There is something more sprightly, more delightful and entertaining in the living discourse of a wise, learned, and well-qualified teacher, than there is in the silent and sedentary practice of reading. The very turn of voice, the good pronunciation, and the polite and alluring manner which some teachers have attained, will engage the attention, keep the soul fixed, and convey and insinuate into the mind the ideas of things in a more lively and forcible way, than the mere reading of books in the silence and retirement of the closet.

2. A tutor or instructor, when he paraphrases and explains other authors, can mark out the precise point of difficulty or controversy, and unfold it. He can show you which paragraphs are of

greatest importance, and which are of less moment. He can teach his hearers what authors, or
what parts of an author, are best worth reading
on any particular subject, and thus save his disciples much time and pains, by shortening the labors of their closet and private studies. He can
show you what were the doctrines of the ancients,
in a compendium which perhaps would cost much
labor and the perusal of many books to attain. He
can inform you what new doctrines or sentiments
are arising in the world, before they come to be
public; as well as acquaint you with his own private thoughts, and his own experiments and observations, which never were, and perhaps never
will be, published to the world, and yet may be
very valuable and useful.

3. A living instructor can convey to our senses
those notions with which he would furnish our
minds, when he teaches us natural philosophy, or
most parts of mathematical learning. He can
make the experiments before our eyes. He can
describe figures and diagrams, point to the lines
and angles, and make out the demonstration in a
more intelligible manner by sensible means, which
cannot so well be done by mere reading, even
though we should have the same figures lying in
a book before our eyes. A living teacher, therefore, is a most necessary help in these studies.

We might add also, that even where the subject
of discourse is moral, logical, or rhetorical, &c.,
and which does not directly come under the notice
of our senses, a tutor may explain his ideas by
such familiar examples, and plain or simple simil-
itudes, as seldom find place in books and writings.

4. When an instructor in his lectures delivers
any matter of difficulty, or expresses himself in

such a manner as seems obscure, so that you do not take up his ideas clearly or fully, you have an opportunity, at least when the lecture is finished, or at other proper seasons, to inquire how such a sentence should be understood, or how such a difficulty may be explained and removed.

If there be permission given to free converse with the tutor, either in the midst of the lecture, or rather at the end of it, concerning any doubts or difficulties that occur to the hearer, this brings it very near to conversation or discourse.

CONVERSATION.

IV. Conversation is the next method of improvement, and it is attended with the following advantages :

1. When we converse familiarly with a learned friend, we have his own help at hand to explain to us every word and sentiment that seems obscure in his discourse, and to inform us of his whole meaning ; so that we are in much less danger of mistaking his sense : whereas in books, whatsoever is really obscure may also abide always obscure without remedy, since the author is not at hand, that we may inquire his sense.

If we mistake the meaning of our friend in conversation, we are quickly set right ; but in reading, we many times go on in the same mistake, and are not capable of recovering ourselves from it. Thence it comes to pass that we have so many contests in all ages about the meaning of ancient authors, and especially the sacred writers. Happy should we be, could we but converse with Moses, Isaiah, and St. Paul, and consult the prophets and apostles, when we meet with a difficult text! but that glorious conversation is reserved for the ages of future blessedness.

2. When we are discoursing upon any theme with a friend, we may propose our doubts and objections against his sentiments, and have them solved and answered at once. The difficulties that arise in our minds may be removed by one enlightening word; whereas in reading, if a difficulty or question arise in our thoughts, which the author has not happened to mention, we must be content without a present answer or solution of it.

3. Not only the doubts which arise in the mind upon any subject of discourse are easily proposed and solved in conversation, but the very difficulties we meet with in books, and in our private studies, may find a relief by friendly conference We may pore upon a knotty point in solitary meditation many months without a solution, because perhaps we have gotten into a wrong tract of thought; and our labor (while we are pursuing a false scent) is not only useless and unsuccessful, but it leads us perhaps into a long train of error for want of being corrected in the first step. But if we note down this difficulty when we read it, we may propose it to an ingenious friend when we see him; we may be relieved in a moment, and find the difficulty vanish: he beholds the object perhaps in a different view, sets it before us in quite another light, leads us at once to evidence and truth, and that with a delightful surprise.

4. Conversation calls out into light what has been lodged in all the recesses and secret chambers of the soul: by occasional hints and incidents it brings old useful notions into remembrance; it

unfolds and displays the hidden treasures of knowledge with which reading, observation, and study
had before furnished the mind.   By mutual discourse, the mind is awakened and allured to bring
forth its hoards of knowledge, and it learns how
to render them most useful to mankind.   A man
of vast reading without conversation is like a
miser, who lives only to himself.

5. In free and friendly conversation, our intel
lectual powers are more animated, and our faculties
act with a superior vigor in the quest and pursuit
of unknown truths.   There is a sharpness and
sagacity of thought that attends conversation, be
yond what we find whilst we are shut up reading
and musing in our retirements.   Our minds may
be serene in solitude, but not sparkling, though
perhaps we are employed in reading the works of
the brightest writers.   Often has it happened in
free discourse, that new thoughts are strangely
struck out, and the seeds of truth sparkle and
blaze through the company, which in calm and
silent reading would never have been excited.   By
conversation you will both give and receive this
benefit; as flints, when put into motion, and striking against each other, produce living fire on both
sides, which would never have arisen from the
same hard materials in a state of rest.

6. In generous conversation, amongst ingenious
and learned men, we have a great advantage of
proposing our private opinions, and of bringing
our own sentiments to the test, and learning in a
more compendious and safer way what the world
will judge of them, how mankind will receive
them, what objections may be raised against them,
what defects there are in our scheme, and how
to correct our own mistakes; which advantages

are not so easy to be obtained by our own private meditations : for the pleasure we take in our own notions, and the passion of self-love, as well as the narrowness of our views, tempt us to pass too favorable an opinion on our own schemes; whereas the variety of genius in our several associates will give happy notices how our opinions will stand in the view of mankind.

7. It is also another considerable advantage of conversation, that it furnishes the student with the knowledge of men and the affairs of life, as reading furnishes him with book learning. A man who dwells all his days among books, may have amassed together a vast heap of learning; but he may be a mere scholar, which is a contemptible sort of character in the world. A hermit, who has been shut up in his cell in a college, has contracted a sort of mould and rust upon his soul, and all his airs of behavior have a certain awkwardness in them; but these awkward airs are worn away by degrees in company: the rust and the mould are filed and brushed off by polite conversation. The scholar now becomes a citizen or a gentleman, a neighbor and a friend; he learns how to dress his sentiments in the most pleasing colors, as well as to set them in the strongest light. Thus he brings out his opinions with honor; he makes some use of them in the world, and improves the theory by the practice.

But before we proceed too far in finishing a bright character by conversation, we should consider that something else is necessary besides an acquaintance with men and books; and therefore we add,

STUDY.

V. Mere lectures, reading, and conversation, without thinking, are not sufficient to make a man of knowledge and wisdom. It is our own thought and reflection, study and meditation, which must attend all the other methods of improvement, and perfect them. It carries these advantages with it :

1. Though observation and instruction, reading and conversation, may furnish us with many ideas of men and things, yet it is our own meditation, and the labor of our own thoughts, that must form our judgment of things. Our own thoughts should join or disjoin these ideas in a proposition for ourselves; it is our own mind that must judge for ourselves concerning the agreement or disagreement of ideas, and form propositions of truth out of them. Reading and conversation may acquaint us with many truths, and with many arguments to support them ; but it is our own study and reasoning that must determine whether these propositions are true, and whether these arguments are just and solid.

It is confessed there are a thousand things which our eyes have not seen, and which would never come within the reach of our personal and immediate knowledge and observation, because of the distance of times and places : these must be known by consulting other persons; and that is done either in their writings or in their discourses. But after all, let this be a fixed point with us, that it is our own reflection and judgment which must determine how far we should receive that which books or men inform us of, and how far they are worthy of our assent and credit.

2. It is meditation and study that transfer and

convey the notions and sentiments of others to ourselves, so as to make them properly our own. It is our own judgment upon them, as well as our memory of them, that makes them become our own property. It does as it were concoct our intellectual food, and turns it into a part of ourselves; just as a man may call his limbs and his flesh his own, whether he borrowed the materials from the ox or the sheep, from the lark or the lobster: whether he derived it from corn or milk, the fruits of the trees, or the herbs and roots of the earth; it is all now become one substance with himself, and he wields and manages those muscles and limbs for his own proper purposes, which once were the substance of other animals, or of vegetables; that very substance which last week was grazing in the field or swimming in the sea, floating in the milk-pail, or growing in the garden, is now become part of the man.

3. By study and meditation we improve the hints that we have acquired by observation, conversation, and reading: we take more time in thinking, and by the labor of the mind we penetrate deeper into the themes of knowledge, and carry our thoughts sometimes much farther on many subjects, than we ever met with, either in the books of the dead or discourses of the living. It is our own reasoning that draws out one truth from another, and forms a whole scheme or science from a few hints which we borrowed elsewhere.

By a survey of these things we may justly conclude, that he who spends all his time in hearing lectures, or poring over books, without observation, meditation, or converse, will have but a mere historical knowledge of learning, and be able only to tell what others have known or said on the subject: he that lets all his time flow away in conversation, without due observation, reading, or study, will gain but a slight and superficial knowledge, which will be in danger of vanishing with the voice of the speaker: and he that confines himself merely to his closet, and his own narrow observation of things, and is taught only by his own solitary thoughts, without instruction by lectures, reading, or free conversation, will be in danger of a narrow spirit, a vain conceit of himself, and an unreasonable contempt of others; and, after all, he will obtain but a very limited and imperfect view and knowledge of things, and he will seldom learn how to make that knowledge useful.

These five methods of improvement should be pursued jointly, and go hand in hand, where our circumstances are so happy as to find opportunity and conveniency to enjoy them all: though we must give our opinion that two of them, viz. reading and meditation, should employ much more of our time than public lectures, or conversation and discourse. As for observation, we may be always acquiring knowledge that way, whether we are alone or in company.

READING USELESS WITHOUT REFLECTION.

In directing your attention to books for knowledge, says Hopkinson, in earnestly pressing upon you to consult with assiduity the great oracles of wisdom and taste, whose works have endured through many generations, receiving their succes-

sive sanction, you must not understand us to recommend that you should content yourselves with
learning by rote their reasoning; or adopting,
without examination, their opinions. Indeed, if
every opinion uttered were true, and every argument logical and sound, you would, by a servile
acquiescence in them, obtain but a part of the
uses of reading and study. You might become
possessed of a large and rich stock of facts; of
many true and excellent deductions from them;
of just and elevated sentiments, and sublime ima-
ginings; but they would lie on your memory as
in the books from which you derived them, unless,
by the exercise of your own understanding, you
make them your own. You must pass them into
the circulation of your own thoughts; test them
by your own experience, and apply them to practical use. If you suffer the knowledge you have
obtained from your books to rest upon the memory
as it came there, it might as well, for any practical
purpose, have remained on your shelves, to be
taken down, as occasion might demand. The food
we take into the stomach, will contribute nothing
to our nourishment, health, and strength, unless
it be digested, and, passing into the different parts
of the body, become part of ourselves—without
this process and distribution, it is rather a weight
upon the organs of life; an oppression upon the
elasticity of the system. So it is with learning
remaining on the memory in the crude masses
in which it was received. (Reflection is the di-
gestive power of the mind; by this we prove
what we have read and heard; we separate it
into various parts; we modify conclusions that
are too strong; we narrow principles that are too
universal, and extend those that are too much re-

stricted, to new objects and relations. We select and retain what is good and valuable, and reject the unsound and unprofitable. We thus extract from that we have learned from others, all its nutritious juices; we strengthen and enrich the soil of our own intellect; making it capable, in return, of producing fruit and food for others.)

Another evil consequence of depending wholly on authority for our opinions on all subjects, and shrinking from the use of our own understanding, is, that we remain in a mental, helpless childhood, all our lives; becoming, indeed, more timid and servile than children. We lose all modest confidence in ourselves; we give up that independence of thought and action, which is the noblest privilege of a rational being—we sink into mere machines, automata, worked by a thousand springs and wires drawing us sometimes in one direction and then in another—we fear to move a step without our leading string; or to speak not " in verbo magistri." The perceptions and conclusions of our own judgment are altogether neglected and disregarded; and we refer, perpetually, and often absurdly, to what has been said or done on the question a century or more ago. Such readers may be truly called *Bookworms*, who devour words, but never touch an idea. The faculties bestowed upon us by nature, are of no other use than to register the judgments of other minds; and where we have no such authority at hand, we stand, lost, confounded, and unable to advance or retreat. We decide nothing for ourselves; the will becomes torpid by inaction, and, like a palsied arm, can be moved only by extrinsic force. Who would expect to make his limbs and muscles strong, active, and adroit, without exercise and a constant application of them to their uses? or hope to excel in athletic feats by studying, without practising, the means and preparations employed by the great masters of the art. It has been well said, that "although we may be learned by the help of others, we can never be wise but by our own wisdom." The practical application of knowledge will make us wise; we thus enlarge our views of every subject that is interesting to us as individuals, or parts of the great family of mankind; we multiply our ideas; correct errors; erase prejudices; purify our principles, and settle down upon the everlasting foundations of truth in all things. This is the true use and value of all we can acquire and know from the examples of the great, or the lessons of the learned. If we make not this use of it, it is worthless lumber; or, rather, the source and aliment of pride, selfishness, and conceit. It produces in us pedantic dullness and ridiculous ostentation; it unfits us for social intercourse and rational recreation, and makes us disagreeable companions in all the relations of life.

PRACTICE OF OBSERVATION.

THOUGH observation, in the strict sense of the word, and as it is distinguished from meditation and study, is the first means of improvement, and in its strictest sense does not include in it any reasonings of the mind upon the things which we observe, or inferences drawn from them; yet the operations of the mind are so exceeding swift, that it is hardly possible for a thinking man to gain experience or observation without making some secret and short reflections upon them : and therefore, in giving a few directions concerning this method of improvement, we shall not so narrowly confine ourselves to the first mere impression of objects on the mind by observation; but include also some hints which relate to the first, most easy, and obvious reflections or reasoning which arise from them.

1. Let the enlargement of your knowledge be one constant view and design in life : since there is no time or place, no transactions, occurrences, or engagements in life, which exclude us from this method of improving the mind. When we are alone, even in darkness and silence, we may converse with our own hearts, observe the working of our own spirits, and reflect upon the inward motions of our own passions in some of the latest occurrences in life ; we may acquaint ourselves with the powers and properties, the tendencies and inclinations both of body and spirit, and gain a more intimate knowledge of ourselves. When we are in company, we may discover something more of human nature, of human passions and follies, and of human affairs, vices, and virtues, by conversing with mankind, and observing their conduct. Nor is there any thing more valuable than the knowledge of ourselves, and the knowledge of men, except it be the knowledge of God who made us, and our relation to him as our Governor.

When we are in the house or the city, wheresoever we turn our eyes, we see the works of men : when we are abroad in the country, we behold more of the works of God. The skies and the ground, above and beneath us, and the animal and

vegetable world round about us, may entertain our
observation with ten thousand varieties.

Endeavor therefore to derive some instruction
or improvement of the mind from every thing
which you see or hear, from every thing which occurs in human life, from every thing within you
or without you.

Bring down some knowledge from the clouds,
the stars, the sun, the moon, and the revolutions
of all the planets. Dig and draw up some valuable meditations from the depths of the earth, and
search them through the watery depths. Extract
some intellectual improvements from the minerals
and metals; from the wonders of nature among
the vegetables, the herbs, trees and flowers. Learn
some lessons from the birds and the beasts, and the
meanest insect. Read the wisdom of God, and his
admirable contrivance in them all; read his al-
mighty power, his rich and various goodness, in
all the works of his hands.

From the day and the night, the hours and the
flying minutes, learn a wise improvement of time,
and be watchful to seize every opportunity to increase in knowledge.

From the vicissitudes and revolutions of nations
and families, and from the various occurrences of
the world, learn the instability of mortal affairs, the
uncertainty of life, the certainty of death. From
a coffin and a funeral, learn to meditate upon your
own departure.

From the vices and the follies of others, observe
what is hateful in them; consider how such a
practice looks in another person, and remember
that it looks as ill or worse in yourself. From the
virtue of others, learn something worthy of your
imitation.

From the deformity, the distress, or calamity of others derive lessons of thankfulness to God, and hymns of grateful praise to your Creator, Governor, and Benefactor, who has formed you in a better mould, and guarded you from those evils. Learn also the sacred lesson of contentment, in your own estate, and compassion to your neighbor under his miseries.

From your natural powers, sensations, judgment, memory, hands, feet, &c. make this inference, that they were not given you for nothing, but for some useful employment to the honor of your Maker, and for the good of your fellow-creatures, as well as for your own best interest and final happiness.

From the sorrows, the pains, the sicknesses, and sufferings that attend you, learn the evil of sin, and the imperfection of your present state. From your own sins and follies, learn the goodness of God toward you, and the practice of love toward God and man.

Thus from every appearance in nature, and from every occurrence of life, you may derive natural, moral,, and religious observations, to entertain your minds, as well as rules of conduct in the affairs relating to this life and that which is to come.

II. In order to furnish the mind with a rich variety of ideas, the laudable curiosity of young people should be indulged and gratified, rather than discouraged. It is a very hopeful sign in young persons, to see them curious in observing, and inquisitive in searching into the greatest part of things that occur; nor should such an inquiring temper be frowned into silence, nor be rigorously restrained, but should rather be satisfied by proper answers given to all those queries.

For this reason also, where time and fortune allow it, young people should be led into company at proper seasons, should be carried abroad to see the fields, and the woods, and the rivers, the buildings, towns, and cities distant from their own dwelling; they should be entertained with the sight of strange birds, beasts, fishes, insects, vegetables, and productions both of nature and art of every kind, whether they are the products of their own or foreign nations: and in due time, where Providence gives opportunity, they may travel under a wise inspector or tutor to different parts of the world for the same end, that they may bring home treasures of useful knowledge.

III. Among all these observations write down what is most remarkable and uncommon: reserve these remarks in store for proper occasions, and at proper seasons take a review of them. Such a practice will give you a habit of useful thinking; this will secure the workings of your mind from running to waste; and by this means even your looser moments will turn to happy account both here and hereafter.

And whatsoever useful observations may have been made, let them be at least some part of the subject of your conversation among your friends at your next meeting.

Let the circumstances or situations in life be what or where they will, a man should never neglect this improvement which may be derived from observation. Let him rove through the earth or the seas, for his own humor as a traveller, or pursue his diversions in what part of the world he pleases as a gentleman: let prosperous or adverse fortune call him to the most distant parts of the globe: still let him carry on his knowledge and

the improvement of his mind by wise observations.
In due time, by this means, he may render himself some way useful to the societies of mankind.

Theobaldino, in his younger years, visited the
forests of Norway on the account of trade and
timber, and besides his proper observations of the
growth of trees on these northern mountains, he
learned there was a sort of people called Fins, in
those confines which border upon Sweden, whose
habitation is in the woods ; and he lived afterwards to give a good account of them and some
of their customs to the Royal Society for the improvement of natural knowledge. Puteoli was
taken captive into Turkey in his youth, and travelled with his master in their holy pilgrimage to
Mecca, whereby he became more intelligent in
the forms, ceremonies, and fooleries of the Ma-
hometan worship, than perhaps any Briton ever
did before; and by his manuscripts we are made
more acquainted in this last century with the
Turkish ceremonies than any one had ever informed us.

IV. Let us keep our minds as free as possible
from passions and prejudices ; for these will give
a wrong turn to our observations both on persons
and things. The eyes of a man affected with the
jaundice, give a yellow hue to all he looks upon ;
and the mind tinctured with any passion or prejudice, diffuses a false color over the real appearances of things, and disguises many of the common occurrences of life; it never beholds things
in a true light, nor suffers them to appear as they
are. Whensoever, therefore, you would make
proper observations, let self, with all its influences,
stand aside as far as possible : abstract your own
interest and your own concern from them, and

bid all friendships and enmities stand aloof and keep out of the way in the observations that you make relating to persons and things.

If this rule were well obeyed, we should be much better guarded against those common kinds of misconduct in the observations of men, viz. the false judgments of pride and envy. How ready is envy to mingle with the notices which we take of other persons! How often is mankind prone to put an ill sense upon the actions of their neighbors, to take a survey of them in an evil position, and in an unhappy light! And by this means we form a worse opinion of our neighbors than they deserve; while at the same time pride and self flattery tempt us to make unjust observations on ourselves in our own favor. In all the favorable judgments we pass concerning ourselves, we should allow a little abatement on this account.

V. In making your observations on persons, take care of indulging that busy curiosity which is ever inquiring into private and domestic affairs, with an endless itch of learning the secret history of families. It is but seldom that such a prying curiosity attains any valuable ends; it often begets suspicions, jealousies, and disturbances in households, and it is a frequent temptation to persons to defame their neighbors: some persons cannot help telling what they know: a busy-body is most liable to become a tattler upon every occasion.

VI. Let your observation, even of persons and their conduct, be chiefly designed in order to lead you to a better acquaintance with things, particularly with human nature; and to inform you what to imitate and what to avoid, rather than to furnish out matter for the evil passions of the mind, or the impertinences of discourse and reproaches of the tongue.

VII. Though it may be proper sometimes to make your observations concerning persons as well as things the subject of your discourse in learned or useful conversations, yet what remarks you make on particular persons, especially to their disadvantage, should for the most part lie hid in your own breast, till some just and apparent occasion, some necessary call of Providence, leads you to speak properly to them.

If the character and conduct which you observe be greatly culpable, it should so much the less be published. You may treasure up such remarks of the follies, indecencies, or vices of your neighbors, as may be a constant guard against your practice of the same, without exposing the reputation of your neighbor on that account. It is a good old rule, that our conversation should rather be laid out on things than on persons; and this rule should generally be observed, unless names be concealed, wheresoever the faults or follies of mankind are our present theme.

Archbishop Tillotson has written a small but excellent discourse on evil speaking, wherein he admirably explains, limits, and applies, that general apostolic precept, " Speak evil of no man."

VIII. Be not too hasty to erect general theories from a few particular observations, appearances, or experiments. This is what the logicians call a false induction. When general observations are drawn from so many particulars as to become certain and indubitable, these are jewels of knowledge, comprehending great treasure in a little room : but they are therefore to be made with the greater care and caution, lest errors become large and diffusive, if we should mistake in these general notions.

A hasty determination of some universal principles, without a due survey of all the particular cases which may be included in them, is the way to lay a trap for our understandings in their pursuit of any subject, and we shall often be taken captive into mistake and falsehood. Niveo in his youth observed, that on three Christmas-days together there fell a good quantity of snow, and now hath writ it down in his almanac, as a part of his wise remarks on the weather, that it will always snow at Christmas. Euron, a young lad, took notice ten times, that there was a sharp frost when the wind was in the north-east; therefore in the middle of last July he almost expected it should freeze, because the weathercocks showed him a north-east wind; and he was still more disappointed, when he found it a very sultry season. It is the same hasty judgment that hath thrown scandal on a whole nation for the sake of some culpable characters belonging to several particular natives of that country; whereas all the Frenchmen are not gay and airy; all the Italians are not jealous and revengeful; nor are all the English overrun with the spleen.

EFFECT OF LEARNING ON THE MANNERS.

Two lines of Ovid are quoted in Lilly's Syntaxe, which deserve the attention of every scholar:

Adde, quod ingenuas didicisse fideliter artes,
Emollit mores, nec sinit esse feros.

There is in most tempers a natural ferocity which wants to be softened; and the study of liberal arts and sciences will generally have this happy effect in polishing the manners. When the mind is daily attentive to useful learning, a man is detached from his passions, and taken as it were out of himself; and the habit of being so abstracted, makes the mind more manageable, because the passions are out of practice. Besides, the arts of learning are the arts of peace, and furnish no encouragements to a hostile disposition.

There is a dreadful mistake too current among young people, and which their own experience is apt to cherish and commend in one another; that a youth is of no consequence, and makes no figure, unless he is quarrelsome, and renders himself a terror to his companions. They call this honor and spirit; but it is false honor, and an evil spirit: it does not command any respect, but begets hatred and aversion; and as it cannot well consist with the purposes of society, it leads a person into a sort of solitude, like that of the wild beast in the desert, who must spend his time by himself, because he is not fit for company.

If any difference arises, it should be conducted with reason and moderation: scholars should contend with wit and argument, which are the weapons proper to their profession. Their science is a science of defence; it is like that of fencing with the foil, which has a guard or button upon the point, that no offence may be given: when the sword is taken up instead of the foil, fencing is no longer an exercise of the school, but of the field. If a gentleman with a foil in his hand appears heated, and in a passion with his adversary, he exposes himself by acting out of character; because this is a trial of art, and not of passion.

The reason why people are soon offended, is only this—that they set too high a value upon themselves. A slight reflection can never be a great offence, but when it is offered to a great person; and if a man is such in his own opinion, he will measure an offence, as he measures himself, far beyond its value.

If we consult our religion upon this subject, it teaches us, that no man is to value himself for any qualifications of mind or body; that he has numberless sins for which he ought to humble himself daily in the sight of God; and that it is his duty to think all others better than himself. If Christ humbled himself to exalt us, true greatness must consist in abasing ourselves, and giving honor to our company. What we call complaisance, gentility, or good breeding, affects to do this; and is the imitation of a most excellent virtue. If we obtain the good opinion of men by the shadow of a virtue, the reality will entitle us to the praise of God, which is the only true and lasting honor.

RULES OF IMPROVEMENT BY CONVERSATION.

I. If we would improve our minds by conversation, it is a great happiness to be acquainted with persons wiser than ourselves. It is a piece of useful advice therefore to get the favor of their conversation frequently, as far as circumstances will allow: and if they happen to be a little re-

served, use all obliging methods to draw out of
them what may increase your own knowledge.

II. Whatsoever company you are in, waste not
the time in trifling and impertinence. If you
spend some hours amongst children, talk with
them according to their capacity; mark the young
buddings of infant reason; observe the different
motions and distinct workings of the animal and
the mind, as far as you can discern them; take
notice by what degrees the little creature grows
up for the use of his reasoning powers, and what
early prejudices beset and endanger his understanding. By this means you will learn how to
address yourself to children for their benefit, and
perhaps you may derive some useful hints and
facts for your own entertainment.

III. If you happen to be in company with a
merchant or a sailor, a farmer or a mechanic, a
milkmaid or a spinster, lead them into a discourse
of the matters of their own peculiar province or
profession; for every one knows, or should know,
his own business best. In this sense a common
mechanic is wiser than the philosopher. By this
means you may gain some improvement in knowledge from every one you meet.

IV. Confine not yourself always to one sort of
company, or to persons of the same party or opinion, either in matters of learning, religion, or civil
life, lest, if you should happen to be nursed up or
educated in early mistake, you should be confirmed and established in the same mistake by conversing only with persons of the same sentiments.
A free and general conversation with men of very
various countries, and of different parties, opinions, and practices, so far as it may be done safely, is of excellent use to undeceive us in many

wrong judgments which we may have framed,
and to lead us into juster thoughts. It is said,
when the king of Siam, near China, first convers-
ed with some European merchants, who sought
the favor of trading on his coast, he inquired of
them some of the common appearances of sum-
mer and winter in their country; and when they
told him of water growing so hard in their rivers,
that men and horses and laden carriages passed
over it, and that rain sometimes fell down as
white and light as feathers, and sometimes almost
as hard as stones, he would not believe a syllable
they said; for ice, snow, and hail, were names
and things utterly unknown to him and to his
subjects, in that hot climate: he renounced all
traffic with such shameful liars, and would not
suffer them to trade with his people. See here the
natural effects of gross ignorance.

Conversation with foreigners on various occasions has a happy influence to enlarge our minds,
and to set them free from many errors and gross
prejudices we are ready to imbibe concerning
them. Domicillus has never travelled five miles
from his mother's chimney, and he imagines all
outlandish men are heathens, and worship nothing but idols. Tityrus, the shepherd, was bred
up all his life in the country, and never saw
Rome; he fancied it to be only a huge village,
and was therefore infinitely surprised to find such
palaces, such streets, such glittering treasures and
gay magnificence, as his first journey to the city
showed him, and with wonder he confesses his
folly and mistake.

So Virgil introduces a poor shepherd:

Urbem quam dicunt Romam, Meliboee, putavi
Stultus ego huic nostræ similem, quo sæpe solemus
Pastores ovium teneros depellere fœtus, &c.

Thus Anglicized :

Fool that I was! I thought imperial Rome
Like market-towns, where once a week we come,
And thither drive our tender lambs from home.

Conversation would have given Tityrus a better
notion of Rome, though he had never happened
to travel thither.

V. In mixed company among acquaintance and
strangers, endeavor to learn something from all.
Be swift to hear ; but be cautious of your tongue,
lest you betray your ignorance, and perhaps offend some of those who are present too. The
scriptures severely censure those who speak evil
of the things they know not. Acquaint yourself
therefore sometimes with persons and parties
which are far distant from your common life and
customs : this is the way whereby you may form
a wiser opinion of men and things. Prove all
things, and hold fast that which is good, is a
divine rule, and it comes from the Father of
light and truth. But young persons should practise it indeed with due limitation, and under the
eye of their elders.

VI. Be not frighted nor provoked at opinions
different from your own. Some persons are so
confident they are in the right, that they will not
come within the hearing of any opinions but their
own ; they canton out to themselves a little province in the intellectual world, where they fancy
the light shines ; and all the rest is in darkness.
They never venture into the ocean of knowledge,
nor survey the riches of other minds, which are
as solid and as useful, and perhaps are finer gold
than what they ever possessed. Let not men imagine there is no certain truth but in the sciences

which they study, and amongst that party in which they were born and educated.

VII. Believe that it is possible to learn something from persons much below yourself. We are all short-sighted creatures; our views are also narrow and limited; we often see but one side of a matter, and do not extend our sight far and wide enough to reach every thing that has a connexion with the thing we talk of: we see but in part, and know but in part; therefore it is no wonder we form incorrect conclusions; because we do not survey the whole of any subject or argument. Even the proudest admirer of his own parts might find it useful to consult with others, though of inferior capacity and penetration. We have a different prospect of the same thing (if I may so speak) according to the different position of our understandings towards it: a weaker man may sometimes light on truths which have escaped a wiser, and which the wiser man might make a happy use of, if he would condescend to take notice of them.

VIII. It is of considerable advantage, when we are pursuing any difficult point of knowledge, to have a society of ingenious friends at hand, to whom we may propose it: for every man has something of a different genius and a various turn of mind, whereby the subject proposed will be shown in all its lights, it will be represented in all its forms, and every side of it be turned to view, that a juster judgment may be framed.

IX. To make conversation more valuable and useful, whether it be in a designed or accidental visit, among persons of the same or of different sexes, after the necessary salutations are finished, and the stream of common talk begins to hesitate, or runs flat and low, let some one person take a book which may be agreeable to the whole company, and by common consent let him read in it ten lines, or a paragraph or two, or a few pages, till some word or sentence gives an occasion for any of the company to offer a thought or two relating to that subject: interruption of the reader should be no blame; for conversation is the busi(ness: whether it be to confirm what the author says, or to improve it, to enlarge upon, or to correct it, to object against it, or to ask any question that is akin to it; and let every one that pleases add his or her opinion and promote the conversation. When the discourse sinks again, or diverts to trifles, let him that reads pursue the page, and read on further paragraphs or pages, till some occasion is given by a word or sentence for a new discourse to be started, and that with the utmost ease and freedom. Such a method as this would prevent the hours of a visit from running all to waste; and by this means, even among scholars, they would seldom find occasion for that too just and bitter reflection, ' I have lost my time in the company of the learned.'

By such a practice as this, young ladies may very honorably and agreeably improve their hours; while one applies herself to reading, the others employ their attention, even among the various artifices of the needle; but let all of them make their occasional remarks or inquiries. This will guard a great deal of that precious time from modish trifling, impertinence, or scandal, which might otherwise afford matter for painful repentance.

Observe this rule in general: whensoever it lies in your power to lead the conversation, let it be

directed to some profitable point of knowledge or
practice, so far as may be done with propriety ; and
let not the discourse and the hours be suffered to
run loose without aim or design : and when a subject is started, pass not hastily to another before
you have brought the present theme of discourse
to some tolerable issue, or a joint consent to
drop it.

X. Attend with sincere diligence while any one
of the company is declaring his sense of the ques
tion proposed ; hear the argument with patience,
though it differ ever so much from your sentiments, for you yourself are very desirous to be
heard with patience by others who differ from you.
Let not your thoughts be active and busy all the
while to find out something to contradict, and by
what means to oppose the speaker, especially in
matters which are not brought to an issue.   This
is a frequent and unhappy temper and practice.
You should rather be intent and solicitous to take
up the mind and meaning of the speaker, zealous
to seize and approve all that is true in his discourse,
nor yet should you want courage to oppose where
it is necessary ; but let your modesty and patience,
and a friendly temper, be as conspicuous as your
zeal.

XI. When a man speaks with much freedom
and ease, and gives his opinion in the plainest
language of common sense, do not presently imagine you shall gain nothing by his company.
Sometimes you will find a person who, in his conversation or his writings, delivers his thoughts in
so plain, so easy, so familiar, and perspicuous a
manner, that you both understand and assent to
every thing he says as fast as you read or hear it :
hereupon some hearers have been ready to con

clude in haste, surely this man says none but common things; I knew as much before, or, I would have said all this myself. This is a frequent mistake. Pellucido was a very great genius; when he spoke in the senate, he was wont to convey his ideas in so simple and happy a manner as to instruct and convince every hearer, and to enforce the conviction through the whole illustrious assembly; and that with so much evidence, that you would have been ready to wonder that every one who spoke had not said the same things; but Pellucido was the only man that could do it; the only speaker who had attained this art and honor. Such is the writer of whom Horace would say,

———————Ut sibi quivis
Speret idem; sudet multum, frustraque laboret
Ausus idem.—*De Art. Poet.*

Smooth be your style, and plain, and natural,
To strike the sons of Wapping or Whitehall.
While others think this easy to attain,
Let them but try, and with their utmost pain
They'll sweat and strive to imitate in vain.

XII. If any thing seem dark in the discourse of your companion, so that you have not a clear idea of what is spoken, endeavor to obtain a clearer conception of it by a decent manner of inquiry. Do not charge the speaker with obscurity, either in his sense or his words, but entreat his favor to relieve your own want of penetration, or to add an enlightening word or two, that you may take up his whole meaning.

If difficulties arise in your mind, and constrain your dissent to the things spoken, represent what objection some persons would be ready to make against the sentiments of the speaker, without telling him you oppose. This manner of address carries something more modest and obliging in it than to appear to raise objections of your own by way of contradiction to him that spoke.

XIII. When you are forced to differ from him who delivers his sense on any point, yet agree as far as you can, and represent how far you agree; and if there be any room for it, explain the words of the speaker in such a sense to which you can in general assent, and so agree with him, or at least by a small addition or alteration of his sentiments show your own sense of things. It is the practice and delight of a candid hearer to make it appear how unwilling he is to differ from him that speaks. Let the speaker know that it is nothing but truth constrains you to oppose him; and let that difference be always expressed in few, and civil, and chosen words, such as may give the least offence.

And be careful always to take Solomon's rule with you, and let your companion fairly finish his speech before you reply; " for he that answereth a matter before he heareth it, it is folly and shame unto him."

A little watchfulness, care, and practice in younger life, will render all these things more easy, familiar, and natural to you, and will grow into habit.

NECESSITY OF HAVING FIXED PRINCIPLES.

THE surest guarantee of success in every great and laudable enterprise, is decision of character; and no one ever attained this enviable characteristic without acquiring the habit of acting upon fixed principles.

In all arts and sciences there are certain fixed principles, which must be known and carefully attended to, if a man wishes to be successful. A mechanic sometimes, by mere dint of habit and knack, becomes very expert; but it is only in some confined instance. Just in that track he proceeds with certainty, but cannot attempt any thing else, nor even aim at improvement in what he does. Nay, if he does not understand the principles on which his operations depend, he must sometimes fail: he is confounded by any new appearance, and knows not how to obviate the least difficulty. But if his knowledge precedes his activity, if he understands why things must so be done, and how the effect is produced, he becomes more adroit in his operations: he can remedy any mistake, can rectify any imperfection, can venture even beyond his accustomed limits, to improvement or new inventions.

Surely then, the art of living honorably, and filling in a respectable manner our station in life, must not be left to hazard, to habit, to custom, to chance, to caprice. He who would be successful and adroit, had need well understand what rules may guide him: else he may weary himself to no purpose, and fail even by excess of exertion.

Does a youth take up the noble resolution, and determine to be a valuable character, good at least, and great if circumstances permit; he has made the first step by such a resolution. Let him carefully examine by what principles he may guide himself, to secure so important an object. Let him be assured, that nothing really valuable will be obtained without care and labor. Chance, as it is called, is indolence in this case, and will certainly produce mischief.

D

A little thinking will show, that men of any character, good or bad, do act thus on a sort of regular plan.

Some general principle, for instance, suffices in many cases. "That honesty is the best policy," has become a proverb; and it has kept many a one from ruin. There are indeed meaner spirits, who cannot form an idea of policy without craft and subtlety; this soon becomes deceit; and when it sinks to this, it is discovered, and defeats its own purpose. Let the youth then exert a little observation, see what general principles conduct to respectability; and let him select such as have been well tried, such as may peculiarly suit his own situation; to guide him in specific difficulties, or to guard him against his peculiar temptations. The very determination to act on principle will lead to his adopting, one after another, such as more appropriately suit his exigencies. How ought I to act? will become a continual inquiry; and the answer will seldom be very difficult to ascertain, when the custom of discrimination is once thoroughly established.

FORMATION OF HABITS.

Success in life depends in a great measure on the early formation of our habits. Whether our grand object be wealth, or fame, or that far nobler one, exalted virtue, we must shape our habits to that object, or we shall fail. What enabled Franklin to attain the highest honors of philosophic fame, to stand, as he expresses it, "before kings," and, what is better, to live in the memory of his

countrymen ?—the early formation of good habits.
The perusal of his autobiography, which no young
man should omit, will show what those habits
were.   What made Girard the richest citizen of
our country, and the benefactor of his race ?—the
formation of early habits of frugality, disinterest-
edness, industry and self-denial.   Such habits are
not formed in a day, nor will they result from a
few faint resolutions.   They are the result of continued effort.

Whatever is of value must in most cases be
sedulously pursued.   Seldom can it be caught in
a moment, like a prize in the lottery, or brought
to perfection like a mushroom in a few hours.
Character most certainly is of slow growth.   No
method can force it, or hasten its ripening ; like
asparagus, so treated it is sickly, and without flavor.   Only by long continuance, and unvaried,
unintermitted care, can this jewel be obtained,
polished, and set ; so as to show itself to the best
advantage. Not by accident, nor by fits and starts,
but by regular, judicious, and permanent habits,
may a youth hope to attain this important qualification, character.

Habit is either an insidious enemy, or a firm
friend. We had need be much on our guard con
cerning its influence ; rather let us enlist it, and
employ it judiciously : it will render us much assistance, in forming a character useful, estimable,
and efficient.

THINKING.

THINKING, not growth, makes manhood. There are some, who, though they have done growing, are still only boys. The constitution may be fixed, when the judgment is immature; the limbs may be strong, while the reasoning is feeble. Many who can run, and jump, and bear any fatigue, cannot observe, cannot examine, cannot reason or judge, contrive, or execute—they do not think.

Accustom yourself then to thinking. Set yourself to understand whatever you see or read. To run through a book is not a difficult task, nor is it a very profitable one. To understand a few pages only, is far better than to read the whole, where mere reading it is all. If the work does not set you to thinking, either you or the author must be very deficient.

Great stores of knowledge are in some cases accumulated, without making the man wise; because, though he has read, and remembers, he has never duly considered. It is most conducive to health to let one meal digest, before we take another: it might be equally beneficial not to take up another book, perhaps not to pass to another page, till we have by reflection securely made that our own which we have just been reading.

To join thinking with reading, is one of the first maxims, and one of the easiest operations. There is something to work upon; the mind has only to shape, to square, to polish it, which may be done with comparative ease.

But he is not to be called a thinking man, who reasons only while he reads; whose mind is vacant, unless some one else fill it. Be not content, therefore, to think merely as some author, or some circumstance, may bid you; but try to think from yourself. Let loose your cogitations, we might say, perhaps with more propriety, watch them, train them, and keep them from running wild and useless. Mind is of necessity ever active : at no waking moment, at least, is it destitute of ideas. The art of thinking, is not always that of creating, but of marshalling the thoughts, which else wander in a desultory, and therefore an ineffective, useless manner. To sit five minutes utterly vacant, is not easy, even to minds the most absent. But to mark the various fancies which flit across the imagination, though a duty, a pleasure of high degree, is what we often neglect. To cure this negligence is the object of this chapter. Be not indolent, be not careless, watch your own thoughts, it will teach you the art of thinking. Accustom yourself to set them each to their proper service.

You will have more work done, and better. Mind can work upon itself, and never to better purpose : all it knows from other sources, will by this means become profitable : it is sowing the grain, not merely grinding it ; and the produce will be accordingly abundant.

It is only by thinking, that a man can know himself. Yet all other knowledge, without this, is splendid ignorance. Not a glance merely, but much close examination will be requisite, for the forming a true opinion of your own powers. Ignorance and self-conceit always tend to make you overrate your personal ability ; as a slight degree of knowledge may make a timid mind pass upon himself too humble a judgment. It is only by thinking, and much impartial observation, that a man can discover his real disposition. A nasty temper only supposes itself properly alive; an indolent indulger imagines he is as active as any one; till by close, and severe examination, each may discover something nearer the truth. So important as such discoveries are, do not grudge the necessary, the appropriate process, on which this self-knowledge depends.

What are your prospects in life? have you any plan, any expectations, any apprehensions? By thinking these over, you may forestall obstacles, and avoid them; may beware of opportunities, and secure them.

Thinking is absolutely necessary to forming an opinion. "For my part, I think so, or so," comes very awkwardly from a youngster, who has not yet begun to think at all. Yet such are most apt to bolt out their opinions. You should be afraid of giving a judgment, on any case which you have not considered. A little thought will give modesty, perhaps hesitation to an opinion, which so circumstanced will pass with much less offensiveness; nay thus it may meet with some friendly mind, to guide it into clearness. It may be much more easy to retract it, if quite absurd, or to mould it, if only mis-shapen. Or it will be more possible, more easy to defend, what has been thus considered, than will the hasty sentiment of the giddy, the obtrusive.

To retain an opinion because once given, however absurdly, is the next step to giving it without consideration. The same fault in the character generates both circumstances. Such retaining a notion once broached, is, however, not firmness, but obstinacy: and if this should be in a case wherein a little thinking would set all to rights, it lets down his character, and shows him to be younger than his years.

A contrary evil in other characters, as often results from the same want of thinking. The opinion given perhaps cannot be defended in itself, at any rate it cannot be defended by one not accustomed to consider; the opinion given is maintained with weakness, or it is given up, in a manner as silly as was its premature broaching.

No reading can make a wise man, without thinking. Scarcely a sentence can be uttered in such a case, which will not subject the youth to contempt; let him take which course he will.

Thinking is indeed the very germ of self-cultivation;—the source from which all vital influence springs. Thinking will do much for an active mind, even in the absence of books, or living instructors. The reasoning faculty grows firm, expands, discerns its own powers, acts with increasing facility, precision, and extent, under all its privations. Where there is no privation, but every help from former thinkers, how much may we not expect from it! Thus great characters rise. While he who thinks little, though much he reads, or much he sees, can hardly call any thing he has his own. He trades with borrowed capital, and is in the high road to literary or mental bankruptcy.

MEMORY.

A READY recollection of our knowledge, at the moment when we have occasion for it, is a talent of the greatest importance. The man possessed of it seldom fails to distinguish himself in whatever sort of business he may be engaged. It is indeed evident that where the power of retention is weak, all attempts at eminence of knowledge must be vain : for memory is the primary and fundamental power, without which there could be no other intellectual operation. Judgment and reasoning suppose something already known, and draw their decisions only from experience. Imagination selects ideas from the treasures of remembrance, and produces novelty only by varied combinations. We do not even form conjectures of distant, or anticipations of future events, but by concluding what is possible from what is past.

MEANS OF IMPROVING THE MEMORY.

Of a faculty so important as memory, many rules have been given for the regulation and improvement; of which the first is, that he who wishes to have a clear and distinct remembrance, should be temperate with respect to eating, drinking, and sleeping. The memory depends very much on the state of the brain, and therefore whatever is hurtful to the latter, must be prejudicial to the former. Too much sleep clouds the brain, and too little overheats it; therefore either of these extremes must of course hurt the memory, and ought carefully to be avoided. Intemperance of all kinds, and excess of passion, have the same ill effects; so that we rarely meet with an intemperate person whose memory is at once clear and tenacious.

The art of memory is little more than the art of attention. What we wish to remember, we should attend to, so as to understand it perfectly, fixing our view particularly upon its impor

fance or singular nature. We should disengage
our minds from all other things, that we may attend more effectually to the object which we wish
to remember. No man can read with much advantage who is not able at pleasure to evacuate
his mind, or who brings not to his author an intellect neither turbid with care, nor agitated with
pleasure. If the repositories of thought are full,
what can they receive? If the mind is employed
on the past or the future, the book will be held
before the eyes in vain.

It is the practice of many readers, to note in
the margin of their books the most important passages, the strongest arguments, or the brightest
sentiments. Thus they load their minds with superfluous attention, repress the vehemence of curiosity by useless deliberation, and by frequent
interruption break the current of narration or the
chain of reason, and at last close the volume and
forget the passages and the marks together. Others
are firmly persuaded, that nothing is certainly remembered but what is transcribed; and they,
therefore, pass weeks and months in transferring
large quotations to a common-place-book. Yet,
why any part of a book, which can be consulted
at pleasure should be copied, we are not able to
discover. The hand has no closer correspondence
with the memory than the eye. The act of writing
itself distracts the thoughts: and what is read
twice, is commonly better remembered than what
is transcribed. This method, therefore, consumes
time, without assisting the memory. But to write
an abridgement of a good book, may sometimes be
a very profitable exercise. In general, when we
would preserve the doctrines, sentiments, or facts,
that occur in reading, it will be prudent to lay the

book aside, and put them in writing in our own words. This practice will give accuracy to our knowledge, accustom us to recollection, improve us in the use of language, and enable us so thoroughly to comprehend the thoughts of other men, as to make them in some measure our own.

Our thoughts have for the most part a connexion; so that the thought which is just now in the mind, depends partly on that which went before, and partly serves to introduce that which follows. Hence we remember best those things of which the parts are methodically arranged, and mutually connected. A regular discourse makes a more lasting impression on the hearer than a parcel of detached sentences, and gives to his rational powers a more salutary exercise: and this may show us the propriety of conducting our studies, and all our affairs, according to a regular plan or method. When this is not done, our thoughts and our business, especially if in any degree complex, soon run into confusion.

As the mind is not at all times equally disposed for the exercise of this faculty, such seasons should be made choice of as are most proper for it. The mind is seldom fit for attention presently after meals; and to call off the spirits at such times from their proper employment in digestion, is apt to cloud the brain and prejudice the health.

Both the mind and body should be easy and undisturbed, when we engage in this exercise, and therefore retirement is most fit for it: and the evening, just before we go to rest, is generally recommended as a very convenient season, both for the stillness of the night, and because the impressions will then have a longer time to settle, before they come to be disturbed by the accession of others proceeding from external objects; and to call over in the morning what has been committed to the memory over-night, must, for the same reason, be very serviceable. For, to review those ideas while they continue fresh upon the mind, and unmixed with any others, must necessarily imprint them more deeply.

But doubtless, the most effectual way to gain a good memory, is by constant and moderate exercise of it; for the memory, like other habits, is strengthened and improved by daily use. It is indeed hardly credible, to what a degree both active and passive remembrance may be improved by long practice. Scaliger reports of himself, that in his youth he could repeat above one hundred verses, having once read them; and Berthicus declares, that he wrote his Comment upon Claudian, without consulting the text. To hope, however, for such degrees of memory as these, would be equally vain as to hope for the strength of Hercules, or the swiftness of Achilles. " But there are clergymen who can get a sermon by heart in two hours, though their memory, when they began to exercise it, was rather weak than strong. And pleaders, with other orators who speak in public, and extempore, often discover, in calling instantly to mind all the knowledge necessary on the present occasion, and every thing of importance that may have been advanced in the course of a long debate, such powers of retention and memory, as, to the man who has never been obliged to exert himself in the same manner, are altogether astonishing. As habits, in order to be strong, must be formed in early life, the memories of children should therefore be constantly exercised : but to oblige them to commit to memory what they do not understand, perverts their faculties, and gives them a dislike to learning." In a word, those who have most occasion for memory, as orators and public speakers, should not suffer it to lie idle ; but constantly employ it in treasuring up, and frequently reviving such things as may be of most importance to them ; for by these means, it will be more at their command, and they may place greater confidence in it upon any emergency.

" Men complain of nothing more frequently than a deficient memory : and indeed, every one finds, that after all his efforts many of the ideas which he desired to retain, have slipped irretrievably away ; that acquisitions of the mind are sometimes equally fugitive with the gifts of fortune ; and that a short intermission of attention more certainly lessens knowledge than it impairs an estate. To assist this weakness of our nature, many methods besides those we have mentioned have been proposed, all of which may be justly suspected of being ineffectual ; for no art of memory, however its effects may have been boasted or admired, has ever been adopted into general use ; nor have those who possessed it, appeared to excel others in readiness of recollection, or multiplicity of attainments."

ON LETTER WRITING.

THE art of epistolary writing, as the late translator of Pliny's Letters has observed, was esteemed by the Romans in the number of liberal and polite accomplishments ; and we find Cicero mentioning with great pleasure, in some of his letters to Atticus, the elegant specimen he had received from his son, of his genius in this way. It seems, in deed, to have formed part of their education ; and, in the opinion of Mr. Locke, it well deserves to have a share in ours. " The writing of letters, (as that judicious author observes,) enters so much into all the occasions of life, that no gentleman can avoid showing himself in compositions of this kind. Occurrences will daily force him to make this use of his pen, which lays open his breeding, his sense, and his abilities, to a severer examination than any oral discourse." It is to be wondered we have so few writers in our own language who deserve to be pointed out as models upon such an occasion. After having named William Cowper, it would perhaps be difficult to add a second. The elegant writer of Cowley's life mentions him as excelling in this uncommon talent; but as that author declares himself of opinion, " That letters which pass between familiar friends, if they are written as they should be, can scarce ever be fit to see the light," the world is deprived of what no doubt would have been well worth its inspection. A late distinguished genius treats the very attempt as ridiculous, and professes himself " a mortal enemy to what they call *a fine letter*." His aversion, however, was not so strong, but he knew to conquer it when he thought proper ; and the letter which closes his correspondence with bishop Atterbury, is, perhaps, the most genteel and manly address that ever was penned to a friend in disgrace. The truth is, a fine letter does not consist in saying fine things, but in expressing ordinary ones in an uncommon manner. It is the *proprie communia dicere*, the art of giving grace and elegance to familiar occurrences, that constitutes the merit of this kind of writing. Mr. Gay's letter, concerning the two lovers who were struck dead by the same

flash of lightning, is a masterpiece of the sort
and the specimen he has there given of his talents
for this species of composition, makes it much to
be regretted we have not more from the same
hand.

Of the style of epistolary composition. Purity in
the choice of words, and justness of construction,
joined with perspicuity, are the chief properties of
this style. Accordingly Cicero says : " In writing
letters, we make use of common words and expressions." And Seneca more fully, " I would
have my letters to be like my discourses, when we
either sit or walk together, unstudied and easy."
And what prudent man, in his common discourse,
aims at bright and strong figures, beautiful turns
of language, or labored periods ? Nor is it always
requisite to attend to exact order and method. He
that is master of what he writes, will naturally
enough express his thoughts without perplexity
and confusion ; and more than this is seldom necessary, especially in familiar letters. Indeed, as
the subjects of epistles are exceedingly various,
they will necessarily require some variety in the
manner of expression. If the subject be something
weighty and momentous, the language should be
strong and solemn ; in things of a lower nature,
more free and easy ; and upon lighter matters,
jocose and pleasant. In exhortations, it ought to
be lively and vigorous ; in consolations, kind and
compassionate ; and in advising, grave and serious.
In narratives, it should be clear and distinct ; in
requests, modest ; in commendations, friendly ; in
prosperity, cheerful, and mournful in adversity.
In a word, the style ought to be accommodated to
the particular nature of the thing about which it
is conversant.

Besides, the different character of the person, to whom the letter is written, requires a like difference in the modes of expression. We do not use the same language to private persons, and those in a public station; to superiors, inferiors, and equals. Nor do we express ourselves alike to old men and young, to the grave and facetious, to courtiers and philosophers, to our friends and strangers. Superiors are to be addressed with respect, inferiors with courtesy, and equals with civility; and every one's character, station, and circumstances in life, with the relation we stand in to him, occasions some variety in this respect. But when friends and acquaintances correspond by letters, it carries them into all the freedom and good humor of conversation; and the nearer it resembles that, the better, since it is designed to supply the room of it. For when friends cannot enjoy each other's company, the next satisfaction is to converse with each other by letters. Indeed, sometimes greater freedom is used in epistles, than the same persons would have taken in discoursing together; because, as Cicero says, " a letter does not blush." But still, nothing ought to be said in a letter, which, considered in itself, would not have been fit to say in discourse; though modesty perhaps, or some other particular reason, might have prevented it. And thus it frequently happens in requests, reproofs, and other circumstances of life. A man can ask that by writing, which he could not do by words, if present; or blame what he thinks amiss in his friend, with greater liberty when absent, than if they were together. From hence it is easy to judge of the fitness of any expression to stand in an epistle, only by considering

whether the same way of speaking would be proper
in talking with the same person. Indeed, this
difference may be allowed, that as persons have
more time to think, when they write, than when
they speak; a greater accuracy of language may
sometimes be expected in one, than the other
However, this makes no odds as to the kind of
style; for every one would choose to speak as cor
rectly as he writes, if he could. And therefore all
such words and expressions, as are unbecoming
in conversation, should be avoided in letters: and
a manly simplicity, free of all affectation, plain,
but decent and agreeable, should run through the
whole. This is the usual style of Cicero's epistles,
in which the plainness and simplicity of his diction is accompanied with something so pleasant
and engaging, that he keeps up the attention of
his reader, without suffering him to tire. On the
other hand, Pliny's style is succinct and witty,
but generally so full of turns and quibbles upon
the sound of words, as apparently render it more
stiff and affected than agrees with conversation,
or than a man of sense would choose in discourse,
were it in his power. You may in some measure
judge of Pliny's manner, by one short letter to his
friend, which runs thus: "How fare you? As I
do in the country? pleasantly? that is, at leisure?
For which reason I do not care to write long letters, but to read them; the one as the effect of
niceness, and the other of idleness. For nothing
is more idle than your nice folks, or curious than
your idle ones. Farewell." Every sentence here
consists of an antithesis, and a jingle of words,
very different from the style of conversation, and
plainly the effect of study. But this was owing

to the age in which he lived, at which time the Roman eloquence was sunk into puns, and an affectation of wit; for he was otherwise a man of fine sense and great learning.

ON LITERARY COMPOSITION.

Composition is not only a difficult task, but is indeed a miserable drudgery, when you have neither rules to direct you, nor matter to work upon; which is the case with many poor boys, who are obliged to squeeze out of their brains an exercise against the time appointed.

To store the mind with good matter, you must accustom yourself to the reading of good authors, such as historians, poets, orators, philosophers, and controversialists; the last are particularly to be studied for the well managing of an argument. The political and theological controversialists are best; but they seldom fall in the way of the younger sort of readers.

When you are to write upon any subject, the best way of entering upon it, is to set down what your own mind furnishes, and say all you can before you descend to consult books, and read upon it: for if you apply to books before you have laid your plan, your own thoughts will be dissipated, and you will dwindle from a composer to a transcriber.

In thinking upon a subject, you are to consider that every proposition is an answer to some question; so that if you can answer all the questions that can be put to you concerning it, you have a thorough understanding of it: and in order to compose, you have nothing to do but to ask your-

self those questions; by which you will raise from
your mind the latent matter, and having once got
it, you may dispose of it, and put it into form
afterwards.

Suppose the discovery of America by Columbus
were proposed, you might put these questions
upon it :—how came he to think of such an expe-
dition ? What evidence had he to proceed upon ?
Did the ancients believe any thing that might
lead him to such a discovery ? What steps did he
take in the affair ? How was his opinion received ?
What happened to him in the attempt ? How did
it succeed ? How was he rewarded afterwards ?
What were the consequences of this discovery to
the old world, and what farther consequences may
still be expected ? When you have given a cir-
cumstantial answer to all these questions, you will
have composed a methodical history of *the discovery of America.*

By this way of asking questions, a subject is
drawn out, so that you may view it in all its parts,
and treat of it with little difficulty, provided you
have acquired a competent knowledge of it by
reading or discoursing about it in time past : if
not, *ex nihilo nil fit;* where no water is in the
well, you may pump for ever without effect.

Subjects are either single or compounded; in
other words, they are either simple or complex. A
single subject consists of one notion or idea, which
is to be pursued in all its branches. A compound
subject is a proposition, in which some one thing
is affirmed of another. These two are to be treated after different methods.

If your subject is simple, you may examine it
under all the following heads, which are called
common-places; as, 1st. Its relation to the senses,

affections, understandings, interests, and expressions of men. 2d. Its several kinds; which are to be described and distinguished. 3d. Its causes or principles. 4th. The effects produced by it, with the ends of good or evil which it does or should aim at. 5th. Its relation to place; which comprehends the state of it in different places, or the places which have been distinguished by it. 6th. Its relation to time; which will include the different state of your subject in different ages.

Thus, for example, suppose the subject to be treated of is *war*. 1st. It is the scourge of God upon the corruptions of mankind; and being so reputed, is never to be undertaken wantonly and unadvisedly : but as things now are, it is, in many cases, unavoidable; so that every nation should be prepared, by having their youth trained to arms, and to all manly exercises, avoiding luxury and effeminacy, by which every nation is weakened, and rendered insufficient for its own defence.

2d. There are several kinds of war : offensive and defensive; a land war and a naval war; an invasion of one's own country by a foreign enemy; but the worst of all is a civil war, in which the people turn their arms against one another, and so make themselves a prey to foreign enemies.

3d. The causes of war are the encroachments and insults of some neighboring kingdom; a want of due authority and subordination at home; the oppression of one part of a nation by another part; improper concessions, which encourage insolence; treaties ill-advised, or not sufficiently explicit, and a want of good faith and honor in observing them.

4th. The end to be obtained by every war is peace, which is often never to be obtained by lighter methods. But too frequently, the ambition of princes tempts them to make war for the vanity of conquest, or to extend their dominions, or to take revenge upon an old enemy that has unfortunately given some advantage.

In some cases, an invasion has the good effect of rousing a nation sunk in pleasure and dissipation; it brings them to their senses, and restores them, by proper exercise, to a military state.

5th. Its relation to place will give occasion to recount the most memorable wars that have been carried on in different parts of the world, and the places that have been rendered famous in history by battles, and sieges, and victories; such as the wars of Cæsar in Gaul; the battles of Cannæ and Pharsalia; the sacking of Rome by Brennus; the victory of the Christians over the Turks at Lepanto; the conquest of Mexico, and the West-Indies, &c.

6th. Its relation to time will bring in the changes that have taken place in the art of war: the different modes of fighting when the Macedonian phalanx and Roman legion were thought impregnable, from the present way of determining a battle by fire-arms and heavy artillery, which have made defensive armor useless. The difference also may be shown, so far as it is understood, between the Roman galleys and an American man-of-war.

Thus you see, that, by pursuing one simple idea under the several common-places above mentioned, we are led through the whole subject, and may soon throw together so many hints, that it would require a folio volume to handle them all distinctly. But here let me admonish you, that it requires more skill, and learning and judgment, to contract a subject, than to expand it; and he is the best composer who knows how to prune away all superfluous matter.

If your subject is compound, or made up of more notions than one, it forms a *proposition*, in which some one thing is predicated (as the logicians speak) of another; as "war is evil; old wine is better than new; old friends are better than new; old music is better than new; old divinity is better than new;" and such like. Here you have a matter *proposed*, which it is your business to *prove* and *illustrate*. In this case your best method is,

1st. To open and explain the sense of your proposition, and distinguish your subjects, if necessary, from other subjects allied to them.

2d. To give a reason or two, to prove the truth of the proposition.

3d. To confirm your reasons by some observation on men and manners, some proverbial sentence, expressing the public judgment of mankind upon the case, or some sentiment from an author of established reputation.

4th. To illustrate your subject with a simile, which is no other than some parallel case in nature; and this you are to apply to the different parts of your subject, if it is so apposite as to admit of such an accommodation.

5th. To add an example either from ancient or modern history, or from your own experience.

6th. Then, lastly, you are to sum up your matter, and show the practical use of it; concluding with some pertinent exhortation.

This is the easiest way of treating a subject, and the most effectual. When we were taught to make a theme at school, we had a model of a theme of this construction composed by Mr. Dryden, which was the pattern we were obliged to follow; and we wish we could give you a copy of it. *Method* is the *light* of a subject, and *expression* is the *life* of it: and, in our judgment, an *immethodical* piece is worse than an *ill-written* one. The art is, to use method, as builders do a scaffold, which is to be taken away when the work is finished: or, as good workmen, who conceal the *joints* in their work, so that it may look smooth and pleasant to the eye, as if it were all made of one piece.

Cicero, in his Orations, speaking generally as a lawyer, pleads for the lawfulness of some fact, or against its unlawfulness. He begins with preparing his hearers for the subject; either winning their attention by a modest approach, or showing them how they are interested in what he has to propose to them.

In the next place, he proceeds to state the case, and lays the facts before them, with all their circumstances; or such at least as make for his purpose. This is called the *narration.*

Then he descends to *reason* upon the case; either justifying his client, or refuting the arguments on the other side. The justification and the refutation generally make two separate articles. If his speech is of the accusatory kind, his method is still the same, *mutatis mutandis.*

After all, he sums up the merit in a conclusion, which is called *peroratio*, because it reviews the several parts of the whole oration, and presses the audience with the force of the evidence, that their judgment may go with his side of the question.

Many sermons in the English language are

some of the finest orations in the world. They are of different sorts; some are *moral*, some *controversial*, and some *expository* : the latter are of more general use, because they take in the two other divisions of moral and controversial, as occasion requires.

Under the first head of a discourse the subject is opened, with some general observations, and distinguished.

Under the second, it is explained and illustrated.

Under the third, the uses are shown, and the inferences deduced, as they follow naturally from the most interesting parts of the exposition.

A sermon written after this, or some like method, will be clearly understood, and easily remembered. Besides, when a thought stands in its right place, it has ten times more force than when it is improperly connected. Compositions are like machines, where one part depends upon another; if any part gets out of place, the motion is disordered, and the whole is of less effect. A rhapsody of miscellaneous thoughts, huddled together in the way of an unconnected essay, with no particular relation to the text, either makes no impression at the time when it is delivered, or leaves no instruction behind it. Not every musician who can make a noise, and show sleight of hand upon an instrument, is fit for a composer of music; neither is every man who can *think* with freedom, able to *write* with good effect.

The three different sorts of composition in prose, are the narration, the epistle, and the speech. Narration should consist of long and clear periods, descriptive of facts, with reflections sparingly intermixed. The epistle is distinguished by short sentences, and an easy unaffected manner. Method is here of no great value. Speeches are different from both, consisting of reasonings, apologies, defences, accusations, refutations, and such like, enforced and ornamented as much as may be with the figures of rhetoric properly introduced; of which I shall endeavor to give you an explanation at some other opportunity

---

REMARKS ON THE STUDY OF ENGLISH GRAMMAR.

THE following curious remarks on the study of grammar, from Cobbett's Advice to a Young Man, are inserted, not from any respect to the writer's political character, but from a conviction of their truth and importance.

The grammar of your own language. Without understanding this, you can never hope to become fit for any thing beyond mere trade or agriculture. It is true, that we do but too often see men have great wealth, high titles, and boundless power heaped upon them, who can hardly write ten lines together correctly; but remember, it is not *merit* that has been the cause of their advancement; the cause has been, in almost every such case, the subserviency of the party to the will of some government, and the baseness of some nation who has quietly submitted to be governed by brazen fools. Do not you imagine, that you will have luck of this sort: do not you hope to be rewarded and honored for that ignorance which shall prove a scourge to your country, and which will earn you the curses of the children yet unborn. Rely you upon your merit, and upon nothing else. Without a knowledge of grammar, it is impossible for you to write correctly, and it is by mere accident if you speak correctly ; and pray bear in mind, that all well-informed persons judge of a man's mind (until they have other means of judging) by his writing or speaking. The labor necessary to acquire this knowledge is, indeed, not trifling : grammar is not, like arithmetic, a science consisting of several distinct departments, some of which may be dispensed with : it is a whole, and the whole must be learned, or no part is learned. The subject is abstruse ; it demands much reflection and much patience : but, when once the task is performed, it is performed *for life*, and in every day of that life it will be found to be, in a greater or less degree, a source of pleasure or of profit, or of both together. And, what is the labor ?   It consists of no bodily exertion ; it exposes the student to no cold, no hunger, no sufferings of any sort. The study need subtract from the hours of no business, nor, indeed, from the hours of necessary exercise : the hours usually spent on the tea and coffee slops, and in the mere gossip which accompany them; those wasted hours of only *one year*, employed in the study of English grammar, would make you a correct speaker and writer for the rest of your life. You want no school, no room to study in, no expenses, and no troublesome circumstances of any sort. I learned grammar when I was a private soldier, on the pay of sixpence a day. The edge of my berth, or that of the guard-bed, was my seat to study in; my knapsack was my book-case; a bit of board, lying on my lap, was my writing-table ; and the task did not demand any thing like a year of my life. I had no money to purchase candles or oil; in winter time, it was rarely that I could get any evening light but that of *the fire*, and only my *turn* even of that. And if I, under such circumstances, and without parent or friend to advise or encourage me, accomplish this undertaking, what excuse can there be for *any youth*, however poor, however pressed with business, or however circumstanced as to room or other conveniences? To buy a pen or a sheet of paper, I was compelled to forego some portion of food, though in a state of half starvation: I had no moment of time that I could call my own; and I had to read and to write amidst the talking, laughing, singing, whistling, and brawling of at least half a score of the most thoughtless of men, and that, too, in the hours of their freedom from all control. Think not lightly of the *farthing* that I had to give, now and then, for ink, pen, or paper! That farthing, was, alas! a *great sum* to me! I was as tall as I am now; I had great health and great exercise. The whole of the money, not expended for us at market, was *two-pence a week* for each man. I remember, and well I may, that, upon one occasion I, after all absolutely necessary expenses, had, on a Friday, made shift to save a half-penny in reserve, which I had destined for the purchase of a *red-herring* in the morning: but when I pulled off my clothes at night, so hungry then as to be hardly able to endure life, I found that I had *lost my half-penny!* I buried my head under the miserable sheet and rug, and cried like a child! And, again I say, if I, under circumstances like these, could encounter and overcome this task, is there, can there be, in the whole world, a youth to find an excuse for the non-performance? What youth, who shall read this, will not be ashamed to say, that he is not able to find time and opportunity for this most essential of all the branches of book-learning?

I press this matter with such earnestness, because a knowledge of grammar is the foundation of all literature; and because without this knowledge opportunities for writing and speaking, are only occasions for men to display their unfitness to write and speak. How many false pretenders to erudition have I exposed to shame, merely by my knowledge of grammar! How many of the insolent and ignorant great and powerful have I pulled down and made little and despicable! And with what ease have I conveyed upon numerous important subjects, information and instruction to millions now alive, and provided a store of both for millions yet unborn! As to the course to be pursued in this great undertaking, it is, first, to read the grammar from the first word to the last, very attentively, several times over; then, to copy the whole of it very correctly and neatly; and then to study the chapters one by one. And what does this reading and writing require as to time? Both together not more than the tea-slops and their gossips for *three months*. There are about three hundred pages in a common English Grammar. Four of those little pages in a day, which is a mere trifle of work, do the thing in *three months*. Two hours a day are quite sufficient for the purpose; and these may, in any *town* that I have ever known, or in any village, be taken from that part of the morning during which the main part of the people are in bed. I do not like the evening candle-light work: it wears the eyes much more than the same sort of light in the morning, because then the faculties are in vigor, and wholly unexhausted. But for this purpose there is sufficient of that daylight which is usually wasted; usually gossipped or lounged away; or spent in some other manner productive of no pleasure, and generally producing pain in the end. It is very becoming in all persons, and particularly in the young, to be civil, and even polite: but it becomes neither young nor old, to have an everlasting simper on their faces, and their bodies sawing in an everlasting bow: and how many youths have I seen, who, if they had spent in the learning of grammar a tenth part of the time that they have consumed in earning merited contempt for their affected gentility, would have laid the foundation of sincere respect towards them for the whole of their lives !

Perseverance is a prime quality in every pursuit, and particularly in this. Yours is, too, the time of life to acquire this inestimable habit. Men fail much oftener from want of perseverance, than from want of talent and of good disposition: as the race was not to the hare, but to the tortoise, so the meed of success in study is to him who is not in haste, but to him who proceeds with a steady and even step. It is not to a want of taste, or of desire, or of disposition to learn, that we have to ascribe the rareness of good scholars, so much as to the want of patient perseverance. Grammar is a branch of knowledge: like all other things of high value, it is of difficult acquirement; the study is dry; the subject is intricate; it engages not the passions; and, if the *great end* be not kept constantly in view; if you lose, for a moment, sight of the *ample reward*, indifference begins, that is followed by weariness, and disgust and despair close the book. To guard against this result, be not in *haste;* keep *steadily on;* and, when you find weariness approaching, rouse yourself, and remember, that if you give up, all that you have done has been done in vain. This is a matter of great moment; for out of every ten, who undertake this task, there are, perhaps, nine who abandon it in despair; and this, too, merely for the want of resolution to overcome the first approaches of weariness. The most effectual means of security against this mortifying result is to lay down a rule to write or to read a certain fixed quantity *every day*, Sunday excepted. Our minds are not always in the same state; they have not, at all times, the same elasticity; to-day we are full of hope on the very same grounds, which, to-morrow, afford us no hope at all; every human being is liable to those flows and ebbs of the mind; but, if reason interfere, and bid you overcome the fits of lassitude, and almost mechanically to go on without the stimulus of hope, the buoyant fit speedily returns; you congratulate yourself that you did not yield to the temptation to abandon your pursuit, and you proceed with more vigor than ever. Five or six triumphs over temptation to indolence or despair lay the foundation of certain success; and, what is of still more importance, fix in you the *habit of perseverance.*

ADVANTAGE OF A VARIETY OF STUDIES.

It has been truly said, that "a man of well-improved faculties has the command of another's knowledge; a man without them, has not the command of his own." This is the business of education.—Of all these faculties, (says Hopkinson,) we would assign the first place to the judgment. It is this which regulates the opinions and conduct of the individual on every occasion on which he is called upon to decide and to act. The memory, the reasoning power, the imagination, should all contribute to inform and enlighten the judgment; and the judgment should be capable of deciding justly, truly, and wisely, on the whole case. To do this it must possess experience, exactness, and vigor. It is abundantly clear, and the remark was made by a very acute observer of human nature, that a man who has been trained to think upon one subject, or for one subject only, will never be a good judge even in that one. The excellence of this faculty is formed by comparison, discrimination, and a quick and certain perception of difference in things apparently alike to a careless observer. To make such comparisons, to acquire this power of perception and discrimination, we must have a full and various stock of ideas. If we have seen and thought of but one subject, and the few simple ideas that belong to it; if the mind has travelled every day in the same narrow circle of observation and reflection, how can the faculty of judgment be exercised, enlarged, or strengthened? What opportunity is afforded to it for comparison, for discrimination, for deciding between one thing and another? It must become palsied by disuse and blinded by darkness. The simple and unvaried process of an occupation which, in its daily exercise, is but the repetition of the same or similar details, must finally extinguish the perception and destroy the vigor of the judgment. To give it health and strength, it should be employed on various subjects; its own force should be put in constant requisition; its own efforts exerted; its resources brought into action. Let no one be the exclusive slave of any profession, nor trammel or benumb his faculties by a sole and undivided attention to one business, but let him spread his mental power over every department of human knowledge and genius. His excellence in his particular business will be thus promoted, and his resources enlarged and enriched. He will acquire the habit of seeing things clearly; of comparing without confounding them; of separating their various attributes, and discriminating their qualities. He will be enabled to dive into motives and interests, thus fixing the true character and estimate of human actions; and, judging of them with exactness, he will not be deceived.

The field for such exercises is found not only in the graver walks of philosophy, but throughout the department of general literature; history and poetry; in works of imagination as well as on the pages of historical truth. Human actions, real or fictitious, are pourtrayed with a master pencil; motives and interests are developed with a deep and searching spirit; principles explained and exemplified—all the springs and workings of passion, folly, and selfishness, are put in motion, and traced from their sources to their termination; from the commencement of their career to its fortunate or fatal conclusion. Who can study, for such books should be read as studies, and not as amusing pastimes, the volumes of Shakspeare, of Milton, Addison, Johnson, Goldsmith, without rising from them with an immense accumulation of new and useful ideas; without seizing important and interesting views of this " state of man;" of the human character and condition, and drawing sublime and penetrating lessons and examples

of every virtue and every vice? Who that takes
these things seriously to heart will not become a
better and a wiser man? What heart, not dead-
ened and torpid as frozen clay, does not throb with
unspeakable sensibility, at the scenes which pass
before it? whose soul does not swell and expand
with the consciousness of the power and dignity
of the genius of man? and whose thoughts are
not thus elevated to contemplate *himself* as a being intended for higher and purer pleasures than
sensuality can bestow? *Go to your lesson*—if ambition is gnawing at your heart. See how the lust
of power has transformed others into demons of
blood and destruction; and be content to be loved
and respected, rather than to be hated and feared.
The creations of fancy do not move me more than
the vivid and strong representations of history.—
Who can peruse the volumes of Hume and Gib-
bon, without being filled with the mighty subjects
of their pens? I speak of the political facts and
transactions they narrate.—What a thirst for
something more oppresses the heart! How all the
elements of the soul effervesce! How every faculty is strained, and labors to understand every action, every motive and interest of the great actors
in the scene; to discriminate and decide between
them, to approve or condemn!—It is when we are
worked up to this state of excitement by contem-
plating the deeds of man, we feel and know that
man must be immortal; for the deeds themselves,
and the spirit that records them, bespeak a being
whose powers extend beyond this world. Such
minds were not made, such capacity was not given
to deck the life of an ephemeron; nor to be exhausted for the amusement or use of creatures
whose being will terminate after a short and fret-

ful existence. Let the man who presumes, on some shallow sophism, to *doubt* on this subject, for *disbelieve* he cannot, look well to it.—Let him answer me, if his reason, in which he confides so much, can be satisfied with the belief, that a being with such miraculous gifts and faculties can perish like the worm he treads on?

But my purpose, from which I have wandered for a moment, is to impress upon you the necessity of exercising your judgment on various subjects of inquiry, in order to improve it in your particular business, whatever it may be; and to eradicate a false and dangerous error, that a man engaged in one occupation need not extend his knowledge beyond it. Judgment, in its most extended sense, has been defined, by Montaigne, to be "a master principle of business, literature and talent, which gives a person strength on any subject he chooses to grapple with, and enables him to seize the strong point of it."—How unusual then are its application and use! How infinite its importance to every man in every situation!—It is the great teacher of our opinions; the guide of our conduct; the arbiter of what is fit or unfit, prudent or imprudent, safe or dangerous, profitable or injurious. When then should we begin to acquire and make perfect this "master principle?" When should that education commence its work, which is to give to the mind that quickness of sight, that vigor of action, and exactness of comparison, which constitute judgment? It must be done in early life, or it never will be well done. Except in a few extraordinary cases, the education of a youth is so far completed before the age of twenty years, as to have fixed his leading principles, fashioned his habits, and given a direction to

F

his faculties, at least in a sufficient degree to affect, if not decide, his character and standing in life. Every portion of this eventful period has some influence on his ultimate destiny. Day by day he forms opinions; he adopts tastes; he establishes maxims; he surrenders himself to theories; he accumulates prejudices, all of which, if not furnished and governed by a sound and enlightened instruction, by wise teachers and just models, will lead him into a thousand errors, perhaps into incurable vices, to be the bane of his life; the destruction of his happiness, character and usefulness. It is to your libraries you must look for these excellent and approved teachers and models

CHOICE OF BOOKS.

IT is always to be regarded as a fortunate circumstance where a young person has early acquired a taste for reading. So much may our usefulness and happiness be increased by the results of well-directed reading, that a fondness for it may justly be considered as affording the best augury of a respectable and virtuous character. Books are the guides of youth, the pastime of manhood, the solace of old age. They furnish the materials of conversation and reflection, the embellishment of refined society; they enlighten and perpetuate the liberal arts; and pour the balm of Christian hope on the latest moments of existence.

It is a good sign in the present times, that a taste for reading is becoming nearly universal. The exertions made by the enlightened friends of education in this country, have gone far towards making us a reading nation; and the increasing

demand for books of science and literature, as well
as for those of mere entertainment, inspires the
brightest hopes of the philanthropist.

To all our young friends, and especially to the
young man just entering on the stage of life, we
would say—" *Read.* If you have not already acquired a taste for this most delightful of all occupations, begin with the most interesting book you
can find—a book of amusement, if you cannot
relish any thing better ; then try something more
solid, and so proceed until you can relish the most
abstruse reasonings, or the most scientific disquisitions. Be assured that any sacrifice of inclination you may make at first will be amply repaid
in solid enjoyment at last."

Great caution, however, is required in the choice
of books, for if they produce no effect on the
mind, the time spent in reading them is wasted ;
if a bad effect, it is worse than wasted : every
book should be read, therefore, with a distinct
view to some good effect on the mind, or to some
definite object in the business of life.

The choice of books is important in every
point of view; and where a judicious and well-
read friend can be found, his advice should be
constantly sought in this matter. For those who
may not have the opportunity of constantly re-
ferring to such an one, we will take the liberty to
offer a few hints towards the selection of a young
man's library.

In the first place, a considerable portion of
every one's leisure for reading should be devoted
to that all-important subject in which every rational being has an equal interest; we mean, of
course, the subject of Religion.

The Bible, with such works as the present ad-

vanced state of biblical literature furnishes for elu-
cidating the sacred text, should form the basis of
every library, however small.

The most convenient and elegant edition of the
Scriptures, for reference, is that which is popularly
called the Polyglott Bible, which, we are happy to
observe, has been recently published in Philadelphia. The copious marginal references, and the
superior correctness of the text, render this edition
invaluable to the private Christian as well as the
theological student.

A careful examination of the Evidences of
Christianity is the duty of every Christian, so far
as his means will allow; and there are very few
who cannot easily find time for this examination,
when we recollect that it is a very proper study
for that day which is set apart for religious improvement. The best and most popular treatises
on the Evidences, viz. those of Watson, Jenyns,
Leslie, and Paley, with an introductory discourse
by the Rev. Dr. Alexander of Princeton, have recently been published in Philadelphia, in a pocket
volume, and the trifling amount demanded for
this invaluable collection, places it in the power
of the humblest individual to furnish himself with
a complete panoply of Christian argument and defence. These treatises are all masterly compositions. Watson, who was one of the leading
minds of his age, often rises to sublimity. Paley
is almost unrivalled for sound sense and practical
wisdom, and Jenyns for cogent reasoning. Indeed,
there is scarcely any excellence of style of which
specimens may not be found within the compass
of this small volume; when this secondary recommendation is superadded to the vital importance
of the subject treated, we can scarcely excuse our

young friends from placing this book by the side of the Bible when they commence the formation of a library for their own reading.

Paley's Natural Theology is not only an admirable specimen of conclusive reasoning, but one of the most entertaining books ever written. It contains a selection of curious and striking facts, as the basis of his arguments, conveyed, not in technical and philosophical, but in plain and popular language. His work on Moral and Political Philosophy is written in the same delightful style. Whitaker's popular edition of this treatise is sold at a surprisingly low rate, considering the amount of matter.

In extending your collection of books on serious subjects, you will naturally have recourse to the standard productions. of the early English divines. Jeremy Taylor's writings are not less remarkable for their devotional spirit, than the richness and beauty of the style. His Holy Living and Holy Dying are in the hands of almost all serious people. A Life of Christ from his pen has recently been published in a separate form, and bids fair to become equally popular. The all-pervading interest of the subject gives this small volume a strong claim to your notice.

The writings of Doctor South and Doctor Barrow are scarcely less celebrated than those of Doctor Taylor. The reputation of all these writers is richly deserved. We can never spend an hour in the perusal of their writings without feeling that we have been conversing with great minds, and catching something of that fervor which eloquence in any form is sure to commu nicate. Among the more recent English divines, the Reverend Sidney Smith is one of the most distinguished. The brilliancy and power displayed in his style are only surpassed by his admirable good sense and genuine piety. We are surprised that no American edition of his sermons has appeared. If once made known here, they would soon pass into general use.

Dr. Chalmers is well known to the American public—so well as to render any commendation of ours superfluous. Whatever opinion may be entertained by different portions of the Christian community respecting his particular theological opinions, all unite in commending his fervor, eloquence, and disinterested devotion to the good of mankind.

We could go to an indefinite extent in commending excellent works on practical religion to your notice, but we must hasten to the other departments of your library, with only this concluding admonition concerning serious reading, viz. read for the heart more than for the head; and strive to imbibe the spirit of the great divines, (or rather the spirit of true religion) more than to become thoroughly versed in their speculative notions and theories.

So wide a field of literature and science is now opened to the general reader, that we are almost at a loss where to begin our choice of books. History certainly claims early attention, not only as supplying materials for conversation, but as furnishing subjects for profitable reflection and study. One should commence this branch of reading with some local history, because it is more interesting, and because the inductive is generally the proper method of study, not only in natural but in civil history. Dr. Ramsay's History of the Revolution, the translation of Botta's History of the War of Independence, Marshall's Life of Washington, or

Wirt's Life of Patrick Henry, may serve to commence with. Robertson's History of the Discovery and Settlement of America, and of Charles the Fifth, and Washington Irving's histories, are among the most fascinating of all historical compositions.

Sir Walter Scott is a delightful author. His novels and historical tales abound with moral truth and just views of life; but his Life of Napoleon is any thing but a sound work of History. His History of Scotland is undoubtedly more to be relied on, and is truly a most delightful and instructive composition.

Novels, in general, however, are very unprofitable reading. When exclusively read, they enfeeble the mind and unfit it for serious exertion; just as a continual round of amusement destroys the virtuous energies of our nature. Novels, therefore, should only be resorted to occasionally, as a recreation or relaxation from more profitable and severer study.

Most of Scott's novels, and all the works of Miss Edgeworth and Mrs. Opie, may safely be recommended for occasional reading, when one chooses to spend an idle hour on a work of fiction. Miss Edgeworth never loses sight of utility, and if this were made the standard of value, hers would claim the brightest place among writings of this class. Mrs. Opie is a very fascinating writer, always directing her efforts to the advancement of genuine morality and virtue.

To return to the subject of history. The following works may be taken up in any order which your inclination may prompt: Rollin's Ancient History, Ferguson's Roman Republic, Gillies's Greece, Frost's History of Greece, Hume's England continued by Smollett and others, Mackintosh's England, and Russell's Modern Europe.

The following translations from the Greek and Roman historians are of course ancient authorities: Beloe's Herodotus, Langhorne's Plutarch, Baker's Livy, Murphy's Tacitus, Whiston's Josephus. In the study of ancient history Lempriere's Classical Dictionary will prove an invaluable auxiliary; and the Encyclopædia Americana may be referred to with equal advantage on this, as well as on innumerable other topics of useful knowledge.

The histories of England, France, and the Netherlands, you will find treated by deservedly popular writers in the Cabinet Cyclopædia; and you can obtain any of these histories separately.

When you have carefully perused the histories of several different countries, it would by all means be advisable to take up some general history of the world, in order to see how the different periods, events, and countries stand related to each other; and to take a sort of bird's eye view of the whole. For this purpose a recent publication, entitled, "The Outlines of Universal History," may be recommended with the utmost confidence. It is written with great ability and impartiality; and comprises more information in a moderate sized duodecimo, than we have ever seen condensed within the same narrow compass. It is a sort of grammar of history, which, used as a book of reference, will serve as a guide through your whole course of historical reading, and will furnish a retrospective review at the end.

Natural history, and a view of the manners and customs of nations, will claim some of your attention. Buffon's Natural History is a work of deservedly popular character from its fascinating style, and its numerous embellishments. Dr. Godman's Natural History possesses an additional interest from the circumstance that the materials are drawn from original sources in our own country.

You will require some standard work on the subject of Natural Philosophy, to refresh your recollection of what you may have learned at school, or to serve as a guide while you are attending a course of lectures. Arnott's Physics will answer this purpose admirably, as it accomplishes the difficult problem of treating a scientific subject in a popular style.

Chemistry will claim some attention, as every well-informed person is expected to know something of this science, which is not less pleasing as a subject of study than useful in the ordinary pursuits of life. Conversations on Chemistry is an excellent popular treatise on this subject, especially for beginners; as it anticipates the usual objections, and removes the difficulties which naturally present themselves to the mind of the learner.

You will think that it is high time for us to recommend some works of poetry and eloquence. But we have thought proper to place the useful before the fanciful—the scientific before the imaginative. Cowper is certainly the poet whose works we should first place in the hands of a young man; then Milton, Scott, Wordsworth, Southey, Coleridge, Campbell, Rogers, Montgomery, Beattie, and Thomson; Mrs. Hemans, Kirk White, and Joanna Baillie. Scott's poetry you will read, we think, with unmingled pleasure, and Cowper's with continual improvement in all that warms and ennobles the heart. The others are all deservedly illustrious poets, whose works you cannot peruse without intellectual and moral improvement.

Should you deem it worth while to take a cursory survey of the great masterpieces of poetry in our language, you will find the elegant collection, entitled Aikin's British Poets, a work well suited to your purpose. This, you will understand, is not one of those pieces of patch-work, entitled " Beauties :"—it contains no disjointed fragments —but entire poems selected from the works of the standard writers.

Specimens of eloquence are worthy of your occasional attention; especially of that species of eloquence in which great and momentous questions are debated, as in the discussion of national measures, and in state trials. These unite the dignity of history with the vividness and fancy of poetry. Webster's Speeches, which have recently been collected and published, will claim your attention; and the debates of our own congress and state legislatures are worth reading, as they present themselves in the journals.

The Speeches of the Irish Orators, Phillips, Curran, Grattan, and Emmett, which have recently been published in a single volume, are interesting to the American; as these orators, like the noblest of our own country, are always found advocating the great cause of civil and religious liberty.

We subjoin the titles of a few favorite writers, to aid you in the difficult task of selection : Mason on Self-Knowledge, Wirt's British Spy, Wirt's Old Bachelor, Franklin's Life, Franklin's Works, The Federalist, (written by Jay, Hamilton, and Madison, in explanation and defence of the Fed-

eral Constitution), Irving's Sketch Book, Brace-
bridge Hall, Tales of a Traveller, Knickerbocker's
New-York, Johnson's Works, Boswell's Life of
Johnson, The Spectator, Locke's Essay on the
Human Understanding, Goldsmith's Works, and
last, not least, the incomparable Shakspeare.

We have casually mentioned Lardner's Cabinet
Cyclopædia. This is a series of distinct works on
subjects of practical importance, composed by
some of the most able authors of the age. The
finest writers in the department of polite literature, Scott, Moore, Grattan, and Mackintosh, for
example, furnish the history and biography ; and
the leading men of science in England, such as
Herschel, Lardner, and Kater, the articles on natural philosophy, astronomy, and mathematics.
Each work may be purchased by itself, but the
whole should be admitted into the library of every
young man who has the means and inclination for
liberal study. Harper's Family Library is of a
lighter and more popular character, but that also
comprises works from some of the first writers of
the age.

It would be an easy matter to increase this
short catalogue of books to an indefinite extent,
but the careful perusal of all these works, and the
attentive study of some of them, will be of more
service to you than superficially skimming over a
whole college library. (What is really worth reading once, is worth reading twice. For this reason
a small and well selected library is really more
conducive to mental improvement than a large
and very miscellaneous one.)

It was well observed by a late writer, that an
author is a silent tutor ; one of the cheapest, most
important, convenient, and efficient, in the grand

work of instruction. Persons who do not read, may pick up much by observation, but their knowledge must be comparatively scanty. An author is one who has picked up much by observation too; and if you read fifty authors, you have the advantage of fifty times the observation which can possibly come under your own eye. Nay, though a mere observer, who does not read, may gain ideas, yet on such terms, seldom is judgment attained. The ideas picked up are rather kept huddled together, than sorted, arranged, and displayed in their proper beauty. The bag may be soon filled on the sea-shore with glittering pieces; much, however, which may catch the eye is not worth preserving; what has in it beauty or value, ought to be understood, and placed in an orderly manner in the cabinet.

It is seldom that intelligent persons are disinclined to reading. Mind finds so excellent a feast in a well written book, that it is always rather voracious, as far as opportunity and ability go; and when, through some mistake in education, persons of good abilities grow up careless of books, giving them little of their time or their affection, they betray themselves on every occasion; their range of knowledge is very confined; their actual acquaintance with science, history, or any thing which requires thought, is extremely shallow. They cannot but be conscious of their deficiency in these respects, and either take no part in the conversation, or labor to turn it into some channel less deep, where their little knowledge may suffice, or their knack of observation give them opportunity to shine. It is reading, says lord Bacon, makes a full man. If persons of good natural talents feel the want of reading, how much more

will those whose powers are more allied to mediocrity? Such have not in themselves great effi-
ciency for observation; they had need borrow the
experience of others; they are not apt at the
striking out new ideas from any hint which conversation may furnish; they had need, by reading,
attain the knowledge of what has been done to
their hand. Unless your talents are very considerable, reading is absolutely necessary for you;
even with the greatest powers, reading will be
extremely advantageous. We shall judge more
favorably of your intellect, if we perceive it in-
clines you to read, with due attention and selection; the desire to improve is already a good proficiency.

We have many instances of deep and effective
knowledge being obtained from books, by those
whose unfortunate situation in life prevented access to any other mode of instruction. An old
book, bought at a stall for a few pence, has been
the foundation of much science. The mind, set
thus a-going, will proceed; and when it is covetous of books, books will be had. If the number
attainable shall be few, those few will be the more
often read, and the better understood and digested.
The poorest need not despair, even of proficiency,
if only a trifling sum can now and then be spared
for a book; while the richer are often half-starved,
as to mentality, in the midst of a large library,
untouched or slightly scanned over.

You have some books brought from school,
some presented to you, perhaps, on that occasion;
regard them as a treasure; add to them as opportunity offers; you will prize them the more as
your stock increases, and especially as your acquaintance with their contents becomes more

familiar, as your amusements and satisfactions are interwoven with your intimacy with them. Should you be evidently studious, you will easily find some friend who, having similar feelings, will be pleased with yours, and will be ready to foster them, by lending you from his own stores; with the additional advantage of his more ripened judgment, in selecting what is suitable for your use, with hints and observations, guiding you to a proper understanding of the author, to a necessary caution in regard to some of his sentiments, or a peculiar recommendation of principles found to be important.

Adopt reading, therefore, as one staple means of mental improvement; and give it that sort of attention which its importance deserves. Many young persons will read a book, and are even fond of it, when they happen on one which greatly excites curiosity; when this fit is over, then for weeks, or months possibly, they never con over a single page. Such a desultory mode can seldom effect any thing of value. The mind accustomed to such fits and starts of exertion will never be healthy : like the body, it is kept up in best condition by regular, constant, and sufficient exercise; without this it will be feeble, liable to nervous irritability, and its actions will be unsatisfactory, because, although laborious, they are inefficient. Indeed, where the excitement of curiosity is the sole or principal motive for reading, the sort of book chosen will often be not that which is likely to yield the best instruction. That curiosity must already be under good regulation which conducts to works of worth and eminence. The time given to frivolous volumes is but lost, as to self-cultivation; and although amusement may claim a share of attention, with the young especially, yet ought such a principle to be well watched, lest the share taken be exorbitant; lest it swallow up more im portant concerns.

To attain the love of reading, and obtain the benefit it is calculated to afford, bring it into a habit. Do not be content to read whenever you meet with an alluring author, but adopt it as a rule, *always to have a book in reading.* This will not require you to be always reading that book : will not oblige you to give more than its proper share of time and attention to this departmen of your duty ; but rather, having determined tha this is your duty, having ascertained what sort of attention you may with propriety give it, this method will enable you to cultivate your mind ef ficiently, and make the most of such opportunities as you may lawfully devote thereto.

Could we, after each day, take a just retrospect of the time past, and its various modes of occupa- tion, it would be found that there were several, perhaps small portions of it, which passed away unheeded and unimproved. Nothing immediately claimed our attention, and nothing was therefore actually attended to. Now, a book at hand would have filled up those lesser blanks of time to good purpose ; five minutes now, and ten minutes then, would, in a comparatively short time, get through a volume. Some morsel of instruction, like the specks of gold obtained from the sand, would in time become a valuable store. It would not be wise in those who sift the rivers, to say such little bits are not worth regarding ; see how the heap rises ; nor let the youth give up the habit of read- ing, because it is only a few minutes at a time which he can lawfully devote to it.

When there is a book at hand, the excitement of the mind is kept up ; it can seek its gratification readily, and it gains, although by slow degrees. Should the book not be determined on, or not be near, the opportunity might be lost in procuring it, or given up, in hope of some season occurring which should be more favorable. This, it might be safely predicted of such minds, they will never find. He who has his author at his elbow, will get through many a volume, before the other will find his opportunity of selecting a work upon which to begin.

Whatever habit we allow, and especially whatever habit we deliberately form, had need be very carefully adjusted, watched, and pursued. The resolution to read, should be accompanied with a resolution to select the author, subject, and rotation, with the utmost care. A friend at hand, as has been already suggested, may be of incalculable benefit. It is needful to add, this friend should not be one young, ignorant, and prejudiced : what advice can such a one give, better than what your own unformed judgment might suggest? The case of a youth must be rather peculiar, who has not at hand, or at least within reach, one whose years and knowledge may help to guide him, if he be truly desirous of such assistance. His first care should be to gain a judgment riper than his own. Any sacrifice of self-conceit, or pertinacity, will be well bestowed, if by such means the desired guidance may be more easily obtained.

That much depends upon the choice of authors, will appear, from considering that many men of admirable knowledge have not the knack of instructing ; that many of exquisite talents are destitute of principle ; that science is elucidated every day, and although one cannot say that the newest treatise is the best, yet certainly many older works are greatly set aside by new discoveries. A young student may arrive with much greater ease and certainty at his object, if he is aware which statement in any case is most just, most lucid, or most full upon the point. How much hard study might have been saved to many a scientific man, if, at his first setting out he had bought the right author. Much has the unfortunate wight to unlearn who has been led astray, if it be but by one erroneous principle, or even by the indistinct statement of a true one.

The books decidedly the most important are those which relate to your specific profession. There can scarcely be any situation or occupation which has not something to be learnt from authors. Those persons who, in your present stage of life, undertake to instruct you, must be very ignorant themselves, if they cannot point out to you the specific treatises most suitable, and in the order best adapted to your progress. Put so much confidence in their judgment, as to study well what they may recommend. It may be possible, that the book so placed before you, may not be alluring by graces of style, or even by cheerfulness of matter; but be careful how you call that dull, heavy, or uninter- esting, which comes recommended as appropriate to your opening prospects in life. Should it even be so in all fair estimate, yet its being suitable, ought to overcome reluctance : its being necessary should, if you feel rightly, stimulate to exertion. Action will take off *ennui ;* victory will reward the most plodding toil.

Supposing it is scarcely needful to urge you to studies so powerfully recommended, we proceed to

state, that, however important specific knowledge
may be, there is a sort of general information in its
own nature extremely useful, and in the intercourse
of life almost necessary ; and, as an intermixture
with more serious studies, highly beneficial. However the being a lawyer, a farmer, a landlord, &c.
may form the distinguishing character of any one,
yet the general character of man, of intellectual,
should not be forgotten : this cannot be merged
in the former, without some considerable loss, both
of respectability and of enjoyment. The reasoning
powers, if wholly confined to technical subjects,
will become cramped, perhaps distorted, as fre
quently the limbs of a mechanic, by some con-
strained position, or awkward exertion : free, open
exercise is most conducive to health in all cases.
Give full play to the faculties, at least in some degree ; it will enable you to return to your stated
labors, freshened and alert.

Whatever, therefore, may enlarge your mental
powers, will be worth your while to study. One
small volume may open to you many views which
you could no otherwise obtain ; to have had only
a glimpse of them, is to be many degrees above
absolute ignorance. To know that some things
exist, is to keep ourselves from many a foolish
speech, from many a false judgment, from many
a ruinous deception. A new science attained, is
almost as a new soul given ; it is, at least, as a
new sense obtained. Where couching may cause
the blind to see, it is a pity the man should continue in darkness ; or be shut out of society by
deafness, if any operation may give him hearing.
Regard your mind as having many powers and
faculties, every one of which deserves to be brought
into action ; esteem yourself but half a man, while

destitute of knowledge—any honorable knowledge which comes within your reach.

The works of nature are multifarious, ever new, ever leaving much more to be known. Do not shrink from the contemplation, because the subjects are endless, but determine rather, out of so many, to seize hold on a few. A walk in the country will be made far more interesting, by even a slight acquaintance with natural history. The flower, which many pass as a weed, will become a prize, if a little skill in botany enable you to discern its qualities, its beauties, or its scarcity. To have so fair, so large a book as that of nature, presented to us, and we not able to read it, is a state of ignorance, which the energetic mind ought not patiently to bear. Whatever page is open to you, con it well; but to do this, it will be requisite that you borrow the assistance of some able authors.

There is a knowledge of man too, highly important for every one to obtain. He will be liable to much deception, who is ignorant of the common principles by which human nature is actuated. He will expect more than he ought, and will be disappointed; he will address himself to principles which have generally but feeble influence, and will wonder he does not succeed. Read authors who have seen life, and display it. Travellers show the species in many varieties; history marks the grander movements of the multitude: biography shows you more minutely some single individual. You will from each, and especially from all, gain an insight into the true nature of the world you live in, and the beings whom you must encounter, either in a friendly, or in an adverse manner. To know your company is of great importance to your own proper behavior, to your comfort, and your safety.

As the mind of man is his prime excellence, emanations of mind are peculiarly valuable. General literature has peculiar charms, and dull must our eye-sight be, if we are not more or less fascinated by them. The mind should not only be cultivated, but dressed into neatness; let the rose-bush find a place, as well as the apple-tree; both must be pruned, and guided, to display themselves in the most elegant, or most productive manner. Facts are the solid treasures of the mind; reasoning assorts, and shapes them into their most useful forms. With a few of them, or with only their mere semblances, will taste, and fancy, and literature, as by magic, conjure up visions delightful, ennobling, highly stimulative to mental energy; which not merely amuse as speculations, but instruct, by bringing into view possibilities, which plain facts have never realized, but which sometimes start into being by the mere circumstance of having had such visionary existence.

ADVANTAGES OF FEMALE SOCIETY.

The title of this chapter may surprise some; it may seem needless to introduce it, in a work that affects the formation of the manly character: to the author, this chapter appears of peculiar importance. The influence of the female sex on a young man must be something, may be much; it had need, therefore, be regulated, nay, it is worthy of being cultivated, with the greatest care.

One of the first symptoms of manliness is to

rail at the whole sex. The boy begins sparring
with his sisters, learns the common-place jokes
which aim to lower their talents, their importance
in society, and their general estimation; not aware
that hereby he exposes his own ignorance, his
want of discernment, and of manners.

That any one should aim to defile the fountain
at which he drinks every day, would be esteemed
strange; a mark rather of folly than of wisdom.
Yet what is it better, when a lad who owes every
thing worthy the name of comfort to female assiduity, knowledge, or kindness, is ungrateful
enough to spurn at the hand which proffers so
many enjoyments; to return sarcasm for affection,
and treat with contumely, daily care?

That youth is ignorant of many things must be
owned; but ignorance, in this case, can scarcely
be pleaded; for the facts arise every day, and
force themselves upon his observation; where the
principle is not more base, we must impute it to a
silly affectation of manliness, which fancies it is
raised above whatever it can seem to despise; forgetting that the very character of dependence
proves the contrary.

We have already treated of relative duties, and
do not intend to repeat what has there been stated.
My purpose now is rather to show how great is
the operation of female influence in forming the
young man's character; and how important it is
that he does not set out with spurning at that,
which might yield him so much assistance.

It is well for the child that his mother, and his
sisters, if older, or perhaps even if younger than
himself, had the formation of his infancy. Gently
were his ideas expanded under such fostering care;
sweetly were his feelings trained to sensibility

and honor, and his limbs to activity. **Is the time come for despising their assistance?**—No! says common sense, nor will it ever. Our connexion with that fairer, feebler, more refined part of our nature, is too intimate, too constant, too efficient, ever to be disregarded with propriety.

When, therefore, any one of your young companions affects the wit, and would sharpen his leaden sarcasms against the female character, as a fair butt; set it down as a mark of a weak head or a base heart: it cannot be sense, or gratitude, or justice, or honorable feeling of any kind. There are, indeed, nations where a boy, as soon as he puts off the dress of a child, goes that same day and beats his mother, to show his manhood. These people live in the savage realms of Africa, and there let them be; to imitate them in any degree is to affect barbarism, and return to the savage state. If any of your elder associates thus defame the sex, suspect him of having cause, which implies in him a vile taste as to the parties whose intimacy he has sought; he is exposing himself and his own base conduct while he rails. He may, perhaps, never have found an excellent character among them; but the fault lies in his not looking where they were.

Seeing that we must of necessity associate much with females, it is wisdom to make what fair advantage of it we can, and this is by no means a difficult business; we have only to be true to ourselves, to our natures, and to the opportunities afforded by their intimacy. That much injury may be done a young man by improper associations of this kind, is allowed; and why? because their influence is natural, insinuating, powerfully coercive. Surely such reasons must weigh much to prove that well-intended similar influence must be of admirable use.

The very presence of a respectable female will often restrain those from evil, whose hearts are nevertheless full of it. It is not easy to talk, or to look obscenely, or even to behave with rudeness and ill manners under such restraint. The frequent, the customary company of one whom the youth respects, must have a happy influence, in teaching him to love honorable conduct; we may fairly hope, at least, in accustoming him to restrain his less honorable feelings. Frequent restraint tends to give the actual mastery; every approach towards this must be of value. There is a delicacy too in female society which serves well to check the boisterous, to tame the brutal, and to embolden the timid. Whatever be the innate character of a youth, it may be polished, perhaps essentially fostered and exalted, by approbation so alluring, so gratifying.

He must have obtained great obduracy who can come from some shameful excess, or in a state of inebriety, into the presence of ladies. At your age, we will not suppose such a case possible; yet we state it to show that the general known character of female society is inimical to, and tends to repress immorality and every species of indecorum. An influence very suitable to that age, when powers grow faster than does that reason which should direct their operations.

A young man, whose connexions afford him no female society, must be the worse for this privation, upon these principles; he has not had that to repress him which his over-active spirits required, nor that to shape him which his uncouth manners needed. Stiff, awkward sheepish, or else indeli-

cate, boorish, and gross is he likely to be, when
occasionally he comes into a lady's presence. He
takes shelter against his own feelings by an ob-
streperous mirth, or retires, to hide himself from
observation which he cannot endure. He feels
conscious of his deficiencies, and perhaps avoids,
for that reason, the very society which might tend
to cure them. Should he, in his awkwardness,
unfortunately commit himself, so as to excite a tit-
ter, his feelings toward the sex will possibly sink to
disgust or hatred; his character will thus suffer a
deterioration of great extent.

Many a diffident youth has been taken under
the protection, if it may be so called, of some considerate and respectable woman. A respectable
woman, especially with a few years' advantage,
can do this without in the least injuring her character, or stepping a hair's breadth beyond the
bounds which should surround her sex. Favored
is he who enjoys a fostering care so important :
he may learn the value of the sex; learn to esteem them, to discriminate among them, to become
proud of such approbation, and in time to deserve
it. It is easy to see that the favor of silly, flirting
girls (and there are some such), is not what we
recommend as thus of value.

Where, then, the character of such society is
pure, is eminent; where sense, cultivation, intellect, modesty, and superior age mark the parties,
it is no small honor to a young man to be in favor.
Should he be conscious that epithets of a different,
of a contrary quality, belong, his being in favor is
no honor. He must be like them in some degree,
or they would not approve.

When, for your own improvement, you are advised to seek female intercourse, it is proper you

should begin where nature began with you. We
have already said, respect your mother; we will
go further, and say, aim to make her your friend;
her inclinations are strong towards such a scheme.
If on your side there seems to be any difficulty in
it, it shows considerable error, most likely in your
own conduct towards her. Are you indeed in a
state of estrangement from your nearest, first, and
most affectionate guide? Endeavor to restore familiar connexion with her. Whatever judgment
your father may have, and far be it from me to
undervalue it, yet your mother's opinion is not
only another help to your own, but, as a woman's,
it has its peculiar character, and may have its appropriate value. Women sometimes see at a
glance what a man must go round through a train
of argumentation to discover. Their *tact* is delicate, and therefore quicker in operation. Sometimes, it is true, their judgment will be not only
prompt, but hasty and not well formed. Your
own judgment must assist you here. Do not,
however, proudly despise hers, but examine it; it
will generally well repay the trouble: and the
habit of deferring to her opinion will generate in
you much consideration, much self-command,
much propriety of conduct.

Well do we remember many words of gentle,
but sound advice given, as occasions offered, by
an affectionate mother. The tender warning, the
pious wish, the prophetic hope, came from the
heart, and may well be allowed to reach equally ·
deep, if a son's mind be rightly disposed. If she
be a woman of sense, why should you not profit
by her long exercised intelligence? Nay, should
she even be deficient in cultivation, or in native
talent, yet her experience is something, and her

love for you will well sharpen all her faculties in
your behalf. It cannot be worthiness to despise, or
wisdom to neglect, your mother's opinion.

Have you a sister ?—What, several? then you
are favorably situated; especially if one at least
is older than yourself. She has done playing with
dolls, and you with bats and balls. She is more
womanly; her carriage becomes dignified: do not
oblige her, by your boyish behavior, to keep you
at a distance. Try to deserve the character of
her friend. She will sometimes look to you for
little services, which require strength and agility ;
let her look up to you for judgment, steadiness,
counsel also. You may be mutually beneficial.
Your affection, and your intertwining interest in
each other's welfare, will hereby be much increased.

A sister usually present, is that sort of second
conscience, which, like the fairy ring in an old
story, pinches the wearer whenever he is doing
any thing amiss. Without occasioning so much
awe as your mother, or so much necessary reserve
as a stranger, her sex, her affection, and the familiarity between you, will form a compound of
no small value in itself, of no small influence, if
duly regarded, upon your growing character. Do
not think *that* a good joke at which a sister blushes,
or turns pale, or even looks anxious. If you do
not at first perceive what is amiss in it, it will be
highly worth your while to examine all over
again. Perhaps a single glance of her eye will
explain your inconsiderateness ; let it put you on
your guard, as you value consistency and propriety
of conduct.

There is a sort of gallantry due to the sex,
which is best attained by practising at home.

Your mother may frequently require your atten
tion—your sisters much more often. Do not want
calling, or teazing, or even persuading, to gain
from you such attentions as their safety, or their
comfort, or their respectability may require. What
a *hobbe-de-hoy* is that, who can exclaim with disgust, "Now shall I have to conduct my sisters
home. I wish they would not go out. I hate to
dance after them of all persons." To gallant a
sister, in such a case, is her due. You are paying respect to yourself, when you suppose you are
capable of, and suitable for such a service. She
could, perhaps, come home very well by herself;
but it would be a sad reflection on you were she
to do so. She knows your honor and interest better. Accustom yourself then to wait upon her,
if you are able; it will teach you how to wait on
others by and by, and, meanwhile, it will give a
graceful set to your character.

It will be well for you, if your sisters have young
friends, whose acquaintance with them may bring
them sometimes into your society. The familiarity
allowable with your sisters, though it may well
prepare you to show suitable attention to other ladies, yet has its disadvantages. You had need
sometimes have those present, who may keep you
still more upon your guard. Your attentions to
them will have a more respectful manner. Your
endeavors to appear, that is to be, all right, will become more exact, more systematic.

Do not then try to get out of the way of female
intercourse. We have known young men avoid
what they ought to have rejoiced in, and thus lose
its beneficial influence. They were, indeed, sensible of not being quite suitable company for any
thing delicate or genteel and they sunk, rather

than rose to the occasion. This was not to their improvement, but quite the contrary. We have known some who had not a female cousin, or an acquaintance, whose company might refresh, or polish, or improve them in the least; the consequence must be a degree of rusticity, of awkwardness. What, perhaps, is worse still, this privation made them ready to attach themselves to the first female with whom they afterwards came in contact. Having no conception of the different shades of character among the sex, they were ready to suppose all excellent who appeared fair, all good who seemed gentle. Total privation has its dangers, as well as too great intimacy.

We say too great intimacy; for nothing here advanced is intended to make you a fribble, or sink the dignity of your own sex in the delicacy of theirs. Though you should be attentive to every female, because of her sex, yet there is a sort of attention some men pay them, extremely degrading to themselves, and to the objects of their idolatry. No woman of sense can be pleased with it. No man of sense can endeavour to please by it.

As the object of these remarks is to guide you in the formation of your own character, it is but fair to guard you against this error. You will sink, not rise, if you assimilate to their employments, fears, or frivolity. Should you mingle with females of sense and intelligence, their will be little danger; but all women are not either sensible, or well brought up. Girls especially, whose character, like your own, is as yet unformed, are but silly themselves; and can hardly suffice to give strength, direction, or even polish, to yours. We have, therefore, hoped that your sister was older than yourself: and advise, that you frame your

notions of propriety, from those whose conduct has
the probability of being most proper in itself.

If the selection of companions of your own sex
be important, it is not less so in the case under
consideration.   For the influence to be good, it is
needful that the power which yields it should be
good also. There are some even of that sex, which
ought to be all purity, simplicity, and kindness;
there are some whom every principle would teach
you to avoid, although received in what is called
respectable society. The general idea of what a woman ought to be, is usually sufficient to guide you,
with a little care, in the application.   Such as are
forward, soon get marked; the character is what
no man of taste can bear. Some are even anglers,
aiming to catch gudgeons, by every look ; placing
themselves in attitudes to allure the vagrant eye.
There is scarcely any need to warn you; they
give you sufficient notice themselves, unless you
are younger than your years. The trifler can
scarcely amuse you for an evening ; dull must be
the company of one who has nothing to say but
what is common-place, whose inactive mind never
stumbles upon an idea of its own.   You can learn
nothing from her, unless it be the folly of a vacant
mind.   Come away, lest you also catch the same
disorder. Of a contrary description are the artful,
the manœuvring; such will at a glance penetrate
your inmost mind, and will become any thing
which they perceive will be agreeable to you; the
assimilation is very flattering. You might learn
by her what to think of yourself, if you had half
her skill.

Prize your privilege, however, should you meet
with a few intelligent, agreeable, and respectable
of the sex, to whose society you can have frequent

access. It must be your own fault if you do not reap much advantage. But should your lot be cast near any who, with good natural abilities, have a judicious education, who may approximate to what is called an elegant mind, we think we need not urge you highly to esteem your opportunity. When wit flies quick and sharp as an arrow, but without any barbed point; when gentleness smooth as ivory, as fair too, and as firm, appears in all the conduct; when literature ornaments and stores; when rectitude of sentiment gives sterling value to the mind, and piety crowns the whole; the near access to such a woman exalts the character. Her genial influence is always on the side of goodness and propriety. Her loveliness of mind will give an agreeableness to her person; it is something "than beauty fairer," and recommends to the heart every sentiment, justifies every opinion, gives weight to arguments in their own nature solid, and soothes to recollection and recovery, such as, if reproved by any other voice, might have risen into resistance, or sunk into despair. The caution in such a case need be, take heed of idolatry. Keep yourself clear from fascination, and call in the aid of your severest judgment, to keep your own mind true to principle, which else is in danger of being good, only as a matter of taste, feeling, and blind approbation.

As this is advice to young men, perhaps in their *teens*, it will be supposed that what is now to be said must refer to the latter end of that term. We scruple not to say, keep matrimony in view. Should parents, guardians, and elder sisters cry *hear! hear!* we repeat it distinctly, as our advice to every young man, keep matrimony in view. Never conceive yourself complete, without the

other half of yourself. The fashion among young
men of the present day, is to make up their minds
to do without it; an unnatural, and therefore an
unwise system. Much of our character, and most
of our comfort and happiness, depend upon it.
Many have found this out when too late, when
age and fixed habits have rendered matrimony
hazardous. The effect, however, of matrimony in
future life, comes hardly within the present address; unless it be to hold it up by honorable testimony, and thereby resist the tendency to despise
it, which is, perhaps, even now beginning to operate.

Our business is with your growing character.
All that has been said of female influence, bears
upon this point, and then will its utmost efficacy
be tried, when your mind shall fancy it worth
while to deserve the approbation of some *one*,
whose attractions come upon you with peculiar,
and increasing energy. According to her character will your own be, in a considerable degree.
Should a mere face fascinate you to a little doll,
you will not need much mental energy to please
her; and the necessity of exertion on this account
being small, your own self will sink, or at least
not rise, as it else might do.

Suppose the contrary. Let us imagine that your
secret palpitations veered incessantly towards one
whose dignity of carriage repressed all improper
familiarity, whose refined sentiment, whose literary accomplishments, make it evident that mind
must be her object; that answering, nay superior
cultivation, can alone impress her with a favorable opinion : ask your own heart, if every feeling
would not be drawn out to deserve, even if there
were little hope of obtaining, her regards. The

story of Cymon and Iphigenia intimates the power
of beauty, mere beauty, to rouse latent abilities,
and urge a man of reputed stupidity, to actions
which might obtain favorable notice. If, however,
the mere external charms can operate to so high
and beneficial a degree, what may we not expect
when mind, attractive, impulsive mind, operates
on a congenial mind, well calculated to receive the
impression, and vibrate in harmony with every
elegant, honorable, and exalted sensation.

However false in fact the romances of old days
may be, they must be true to nature, or they could
not interest. If, therefore, some young knight,
smitten with the loveliness of the chieftain's daughter, and urged thereby to deeds of chivalry, should
purposely attack a giant, or slay a dragon; let us
smile, if we please, at the falsehood of the tale;
but, let us ask, if many a time the story has not
been actually true; not in its literal, but its meta-
phorical import. Giant difficulties have been overcome; the dragon's destruction has been at all
hazards achieved, by those who have had it as
the impelling principle of action, to deserve one,
whose character placed her above hope, on any
other terms.

Were we acquainted with you personally, and
perceived some honorable attachment thus taking
possession of you, we should regard it as a happy
circumstance if rightly directed, if managed with
prudence, honor, and good sense. Some of the
younger part of the company may hail this advice, may prize it above their mother's, and resolve to be in love, and that presently. Do; but
remember, to think yourself in love, and to be in
love, are very different things. Again, to be in
love, and to play the fool or the knave, under that

pretence, are not necessarily joined. However,
try. Be deeply smitten, for a week—nay, for a
month, if you please. There is not much fear of
a longer duration to such a fancy. The hope of
one attachment driving out another, in such a case,
is no mean consolation. If you can be kept in
tolerable order the while, it were better you were
thus honorably, though sillily, set to form plans
and hopes, than that you should grow up in the
habit of railing at the sex, and at the state, till you
almost believed your own rhapsodies.

Couple with this advice the very necessary caution, that, with all your fancies, you must not permit yourself to intimate in any manner to the fair
object of them, the silly things which are passing
in your mind. If she have sense, she will laugh
at, and avoid you; if she have not, then will engagements take place, of the most pernicious tendency, if kept, or of the most unhappy influence,
if afterwards broken. You bring yourself into
very uncomfortable bonds. If your sentiments
and character are honorable, you oblige yourself,
perhaps, to do violence, by snapping injudicious
promises, or to ruin your own peace, and the happiness of your partner, by fulfilling vows which
time and better experience show ought never to
have been made. The liberty to fall in love, does
not include a permission to go a courting. That
is quite another thing.

In the Life and Letters of the Rev. J. Newton,
a circumstance is recorded greatly corroborative
of the present advice. He formed a strong attachment in very early life, at a time when he could
not mention it to the fair object, which was well
for both parties; but, in future scenes of sorrow,
suffering, and temptation, the recollection of her

image soothed him, and the hope of one day obtaining her, kept him from perpetrating many dishonorable actions. " The bare possibility of seeing
ner again was the only present and obvious means
of restraining me from the most horrid designs
against myself and others."

It will not be quite in vain to you, if your imagination should be haunted with any favorite image,
especially if her character be respectable, to say
now and then, what would she think, were she
now to see me? It might help to show you the
true character of your employment; might assist
in breaking the force of fascinating temptations,
and stimulate you to exertions honorable, and, thus
made, successful.

Even the activity needful to your success in
business, may be thus excited and maintained.
The wish to marry, if it be prudently indulged,
will always be connected with the attaining such
an income, as may fairly be proposed to the party
and her friends. He who determines to live a single life, perhaps contracts his endeavors to his sole
wants; or squanders without proper calculation,
on the idea that he can always procure enough for
himself. A bad system, this, in every view. That
hope which aims at a partner beloved, a family, a
fire-side, will become active beyond expectation;
will elicit talents, and urge them to their full energy; will court the powerful assistance of economy; and thus eventually will be attained an object,
which had, at one time, appeared to be at an inaccessible distance. Little Cupid redeems his character now and then, as well he had need. It is
only, however, when he calls in the assistance of
prudence, that he is likely to do good.

No doubt but this advice is liable to abuse. But

it may be fairly asked, what is there which is free from such liability? The counsel may be just, may be important, nevertheless. Let those who disapprove of it give better. If they wholly neglect female influence, that influence will yet be operative. Is it not better to make adequate use of principles so strong, abounding everywhere, and capable of easy application?

There is nothing better calculated to preserve you from the contamination of low pleasures and pursuits than frequent intercourse with the more intelligent and virtuous portion of the other sex. The society of well-educated ladies is sure to add dignity and refinement to the character of a young man. Without such society his manners can never acquire the true polish of a gentleman, nor his mind and heart the truest and noblest sentiments of a man.

Make it an object, therefore, as we have already said, to spend some portion of your leisure time in the company of intelligent and virtuous ladies. Few young men in our happy and free country are so situated as not to have access to such society; but if you should be so unfortunate as not to be able to number among your acquaintance any ladies who answer this description, do not solace yourself with the society of the ignorant and vulgar; but wait patiently till your own industry and good conduct shall give you admission to the most respectable domestic circles; and in the mean time cultivate your mind, so that when admitted to them you may be able to contribute your share to the social and intellectual pleasures which are there to be found.

When you are in the company of ladies, beware of the folly of treating them as mere play-

things, or children. Nothing is more sure to offend them, unless it be to offer coarse flattery.
Nor on the other hand must you assume the pedant, and lecture them on technical and abstruse
subjects. They are very ready to perceive the
ridiculousness of a man's making a parade of
such attainments. Neither is it good manners
or good policy to talk much of one's self before
the ladies. They, at once, see and despise the
vanity which is at the bottom of this kind of ostentation.

A young man will profit most from the society
of the ladies, who enters it in a modest and respectful spirit; seeks to conciliate their good will
at first by very quiet and unostentatious attentions; discovers more willingness to draw out and
appropriate their stock of information than to display his own; and finally, appears, in all his intercourse, to consider a most chivalrous disregard
of his own comfort and convenience, when it
comes in competition with theirs, as a matter of
course.

You should go into the society of ladies, not to
trifle away an idle hour in talking nonsense, but
to interchange ideas, learn their modes of thinking, study their characters, as displayed in the in
nocent sprightliness of social intercourse. You
should endeavor to acquire that refined spirit and
that elevated tone of moral sentiment which per-
vade every well-regulated domestic circle, and to
attain that ease and polish, which can only be
received in societies where female influence is
paramount.

You should observe and reverence the purity
and ignorance of evil, which is the characteristic
of well-educated young ladies, and which, while

we are near them, raises us above the sordid and sensual considerations which hold such sway over men in their intercourse with each other. You should treat them as spirits of a purer sphere, and try to be as innocent, if not as ignorant of evil as they are; and in assimilating yourself to their purity and refinement, you are most assuredly raising yourself in the scale of intellectual and moral beings.

To whatever degree of intimacy you may arrive, you should never forget those little acts of courtesy and kindness, and that peculiar sort of respect, which lend their charm to every kind of polite intercourse; and which are particularly appropriate where ladies are present.

Where it can be done without the appearance of ostentation, it is best to give the conversation such a turn as will lead to mutual improvement. Sensible ladies always appreciate the compliment which is paid to their understanding, by the discussion of dignified and improving subjects; or by handling any trifling subject which may present itself, in such a style and with such allusions as evidently suppose them to be well acquainted with the current literature of the day; and it frequently happens that their remarks present the subject in such a light, as could only be shed upon it by the sprightliness and delicacy of female fancy. When you happen to be attending to the same study, or pursuing the same course of reading with any of your female acquaintance, it serves to enliven your intercourse with them in a very agreeable manner, by furnishing a topic of conversation and an opportunity of mutual assistance.

To grow up without attachment to the sex is hardly possible. Wherever it occurs, it includes

a loss of some of the sweetest sensations which
can swell the bosom. To let such attachments be
irregular, is to debase those sensations, to the ruin
of character and of internal worth. To regulate
them is the only chance for good; and if early
trained to the support of proper feeling and honorable conduct, a great advantage is gained, a power
like the fulcrum for which Archimedes longed,
when he talked of moving the whole globe.

IMPORTANCE OF EARLY RISING.

EARLY rising is a habit so easily acquired, so
necessary for business, so advantageous to health,
and so important to devotion, that, except in cases
of necessity, it ought not to be dispensed with by
any prudent or diligent person. The lying late in
bed is one of the ills of the aged and the sick, but
ought not to be an enjoyment to persons in perfect health.

If any, therefore, have been so unfortunate as to
have acquired this idle habit, let them get rid of it
as soon as they can. Nothing is easier; a habit
is only the repetition of single acts, and may be
broken, as it was formed, by degrees: it is a succession of short steps which conveys us from the
foot to the top of a mountain. Let a person accustomed to sleep till eight in the morning, rise
the first week in April a quarter before eight; the
second week at half past seven; the third at a
quarter after seven; and the fourth at seven: let
him go on in this way to the end of July, and he
will accomplish a work which might at first ap-

pear difficult, and render a month equal to five weeks of his former indolent life.

Lying late in bed is an intemperance of the most pernicious kind; it impairs the health, is the cause of many diseases, and in the end destroys the lives of multitudes: it makes the blood forget its way, and creep lazily along the veins: it relaxes the fibres, unstrings the nerves, evaporates the animal spirits, saddens the soul, dulls the fancy, and subdues and stupifies man to such a degree that he dislikes labor, yawns for want of thought, trembles at the sight of a spider, or at the fancies of his own imagination.

He who rises early is met by the domestic animals with peculiar pleasure; one winds and purs about him, another frisks and capers, and does every thing but speak. The stern mastiff, the plodding ox, the noble horse, the harmless sheep, the prating poultry, the dronish ass, each in its own way expresses joy when he first appears. Then how incomparably fine is the dawning of the day, when the soft light comes stealing on, at first glimmers with the stars, but gradually outshines them all! How beautiful are the folding and parting of the gray clouds, drawn back like a curtain, to give us a sight of the most magnificent of all appearances, the rising of the sun! How rich is the dew, decking every spire of grass with colored spangles of endless variety, and of inexpressible beauty! Birds mount and fill the air with a cheap and perfect music, and every tree, every steeple, and every hovel emits a cooing or a twittering—a warbling or a chirping—a hailing of the return of day. The solemn stillness of the morning is fit and friendly to the cool and undisturbed recollection of a man just risen from his bed, fully refreshed and in perfect health. Let him compare his condition with that of half the world, and let him feel an indisposition to admire and adore his Protector if he can. How many great events have come to pass in these six hours while I have been asleep! The heavenly bodies have moved on; the great wheels of nature have none of them stood still; vegetation is advanced; the season is come forward; fleets have continued sailing; councils have been held; and, on the opposite side of the world, in broad noon-day, business and pleasure, amusements, battles, and revolutions have taken place without my concurrence, consent, or knowledge.

DIVERSIONS.

It is laid down as a principle of action by most young people of fortune, that there is no enjoyment of life without diversion: and this is now carried to such excess, that pleasure seems to be the great object which has taken place of every other. The mistake is very unhappy, as we intend to show, by taking the other side of the question, and proving that there is no enjoyment of life without work.

The words commonly used to signify play, are these four—relaxation, diversion, amusement, and recreation. The idea of relaxation is taken from a bow, which must be unbent when it is not wanted, to keep up its spring: diversion signifies a turning aside from the main purpose of a journey, to see something that is curious and out of the way: amusement means an occasional for

saking of the Muses, when a student lays aside
his books: recreation is the refreshing of the spirits when they are exhausted with labor, so that
they may be ready in due time to resume it again.
From these considerations, it follows, that the idle
man, who has no work, can have no play; for
how can he be relaxed who is never bent? how
can he turn out of the road, who is never in it?
how can he leave the Muses, who is never with
them? how can play refresh him, who is never
exhausted with business?

When diversion becomes the business of life, its
nature is changed. All rest presupposes labor;
and the bed is refreshing to a weary man: but
when a man is confined to his bed, he is miserable,
and wishes himself out of it. He that has no variety can have no enjoyment; he is surfeited with
pleasure, and, in the better hours of reflection,
would find a refuge in labor itself. And, indeed,
we apprehend there is not a more miserable, as
well as a more worthless being, than a young man
of fortune who has nothing to do but to find some
new way of doing nothing. A sentence is passed
upon all poor men, that if they do not work they
shall not eat; and it takes effect, in part, against
the rich, who, if they are not useful, in some respect, to the public, are pretty sure to become bur-
thensome to themselves. This blessing goes along
with every useful employment; it keeps a man
upon good terms with himself, and consequently
in good spirits, and in a capacity of pleasing and
being pleased with every innocent gratification.
As labor is necessary to procure an appetite to the
body, there must also be some previous exercise
of the mind to prepare it for enjoyment; indulgence on any other terms is false in itself, and

ruinous in its consequences; mirth degenerates into senseless riot, and gratification soon terminates in corruption.

If we compare the different lots of mankind, we shall find that happiness is much more equally distributed than we are apt to think, when we judge by outward appearance. The industrious poor have, in many respects, more enjoyment of life than the idler sort of gentry, who, by their abuse of liberty and wealth, fall into temptations and snares; and in the immoderate pursuit of imaginary pleasures, find nothing in the end but real bitterness. The remedy of all is in this short sentence: "to be useful, is to be happy." If Eugenio had followed the profession for which his father intended him, he might now have been alive, and a happy member of society : but his father dying when he was young, he used his liberty (as he called it), and threw himself upon the world as a man of leisure with a small fortune. His idleness exposed him to bad company, who were idle like himself; they led him into extravagance; extravagance led him to gambling, as a last resort for the repairing of his fortune; but it had a contrary effect, and completed his ruin : his disappointments made him quarrelsome, and a quarrel brought on a duel, in which he lost his life at five-and-twenty. In this short account of Eugenio you have the history of many young men of this age, who are bewitched with the ideas of liberty and pleasure; but with this difference— that some are destroyed by others, and some destroy themselves.

The progress is much the same with a nation as with an individual : when they rise from poverty, activity, and industry, to improvement, ease and elegance, they sink into indolence and luxury, which bring on a fever and delirium; till having quarrelled among themselves, and turned their swords against one another, they fall by a sort of political suicide, or become a prey to some foreign enemy.

DEBT AND CREDIT.

The following remarks are from the same work of Cobbett which we have already had occasion to quote.

Men ought to take care of their means, ought to use them prudently and sparingly, and to keep their expenses always within the bounds of their income, be it what it may. One of the effectual means of doing this, is, to purchase with ready money. St. Paul says, " Owe no man any thing :" and of his numerous precepts this is by no means the least worthy of our attention. There is a trade in London, called the " Tally-trade," by which, household goods, coals, clothing, all sorts of things, are sold upon credit, the seller keeping *a tally*, and receiving payment for the goods, little by little ; so that the income and the earnings of the buyers are always anticipated; are always gone, in fact, before they come in or are earned; the sellers receiving, of course, a great deal more than the proper profit.

Without supposing you to descend to so low a grade as this, and even supposing you to be lawyer, doctor, parson, or merchant; it is still the same thing, if you purchase on credit, and not, perhaps, in a much less degree of disadvantage. Besides the higher price that you pay, there is the

temptation to have what you really do not want.
The cost seems a trifle, when you have not to pay
the money until a future time. It has been observed, and very truly observed, that men used to
lay out a one dollar note when they would not lay out
a dollar in silver; a consciousness of the intrinsic
value of the things produces a retentiveness in the
latter case more than in the former: the sight and the
touch assist the mind in forming its conclusions,
and the one dollar note was parted with when the
silver dollar would have been kept. Far greater
is the difference between credit and ready money.
Innumerable things are not bought at all with
ready money, which would be bought in case of
trust: it is so much easier to *order* a thing than to
pay for it. A future day; a day of payment must
come, to be sure, but that is little thought of at the
time; but if the money were to be drawn out, the
moment the thing was received or offered, this
question would arise, " Can I do without it?" Is
this thing indispensable; am I compelled to have
it, or, suffer a loss or injury greater in amount
than the cost of the thing? If this question were
put every time we make a purchase, bankruptcies
would be less frequent.

I am aware, that it will be said, and very truly
said, that the concerns of merchants, that the
purchasing of great estates, and various other
great transactions, cannot be carried on in this
manner; but these are rare exceptions to the rule:
even in these cases there might be much less of
bills and bonds, and all the sources of litigation;
but in the every-day business of life, in transactions
with the butcher, the baker, the tailor, the shoemaker, what excuse can there be for pleading the
example of the merchant, who carries on his work

by ships and exchanges? I was delighted, some time ago, by being told of a young man, who, upon being advised to keep a little account of all he received and expended, answered, " that his business was not to keep account-books; that he was sure not to make a mistake as to his income; and, that as to his expenditure, the little bag that held his dollars would be an infallible guide, as he never bought any thing that he did not immediately pay for."

I believe that nobody will deny, that, generally speaking, you pay for the same article a fourth part more in the case of trust than you do in the case of ready money. Suppose, then, the baker, butcher, tailor, and shoemaker, receive from you only one hundred dollars a-year. Put that together; that is to say, multiply twenty-five by twenty, and you will find, that, at the end of twenty years, you have $500, besides the accumulating and growing interest. The fathers of the Church (I mean the ancient ones), and also the canons of the Church, forbade selling on trust at a higher price than for ready money, which was in effect, to forbid *trust;* and this, doubtless, was one of the great objects which those wise and pious men had in view; for they were fathers in legislation and morals as well as in religion. But the doctrine of these fathers and canons no longer prevails; they are set at naught by the present age, even in the countries that adhere to their religion. The fashion of running in debt has prevailed over the fathers and the canons; and men not only make a difference in the price regulated by the difference in the mode of payment; but it would be absurd to expect them to do otherwise. They must not only charge something for the want of the *use* of the money; but they must charge something additional for the *risk* of its loss, which may frequently arise, and most frequently does arise, from the misfortunes of those to whom they have assigned their goods on trust. The man, therefore, who purchases on trust, not only pays for the trust, but he also pays his due share of what the tradesman loses by trust; and, after all, he is not so good a customer as the man who purchases cheaply with ready money; for there is his name indeed in the tradesman's book; but with that name the tradesman cannot go to market to get a fresh supply.

Infinite are the ways in which gentlemen lose by this sort of dealing. Servants go and order, sometimes, things not wanted at all; at other times, more than is wanted; at others, things of a higher quality; and all this would be obviated by purchasing with ready money; for, whether through the hands of the party himself, or through those of an inferior, there would always be an actual counting out of the money; somebody would *see* the thing bought and see the money paid; and as the master would give the house-keeper or steward a bag of money at the time, he would *see* the money too, would set a proper value upon it, and would just desire to know upon what it had been expended.

How is it that farmers are so exact, and show such a disposition to retrench in the article of labor, when they seem to think little, or nothing, about the sums which they pay in taxes upon malt, wine, sugar, tea, soap, candles, tobacco, and various others things? You find the utmost difficulty in making them understand, that they are affected by these. The reason is, that they *see* the money which they give to the laborer on each succeeding

Saturday night; but they do not see that which they give in taxes on the articles before mentioned.

Just thus would it be with every man that never purchased but with ready money : he would make the amount as low as possible in proportion tc his means : this care and frugality would make an addition to his means, and, therefore, in the end, at the end of his life, he would have had a great deal more to spend, and still be as rich as if he had gone on trust; while he would have lived in tranquillity all the while; and would have avoided all the endless papers and writings and receipts and bills and disputes and law-suits inseparable from a system of credit. This is by no means a lesson of *stinginess ;* by no means tends to inculcate a heaping up of money; for, the purchasing with ready money really gives you more money to purchase with; you can afford to have a greater quantity and variety of things ; and I will engage, that, if horses or servants be your taste, the saving in this way gives you an additional horse or an additional servant, if you be in any profession or engaged in any considerable trade. In towns, it tends to accelerate your pace along the streets; for, the temptation of the windows is answered in a moment by clapping your hand upon your thigh; and the question, " Do I really want that ?" is sure to occur to you immediately; because the touch of the money is sure to put that thought in your mind.

Now, supposing you to have a plenty, to have a fortune beyond your wants, would not the money which you would save in this way, be very well applied in acts of real benevolence ? Can you walk many yards in the streets ; can you ride a mile in the country; can you go to half a dozen cottages;

can you, in short, open your eyes, without seeing some human being, some one born in the same country with yourself, and who, on that account alone, has some claim upon your good wishes and your charity; can you open your eyes without seeing some person to whom even a small portion of your annual savings would convey gladness of heart? Your own heart will suggest the answer; and if there were no motive but this, what need I say more in the advice which I have here tendered to you.

Another great evil arising from this desire to be thought rich, or rather from the desire not to be thought poor, is the destructive thing which has been honored with the name of " *speculation ;*" but which ought to be called gambling. It is a purchasing of something which you do not want, either in your family or in the way of ordinary trade: a something to be sold again with a great profit; and on the sale of which there is a considerable hazard. When purchases of this sort are made with ready money, they are not so offensive to reason, and not attended with such risk; but when they are made with money *borrowed* for the purpose, they are neither more nor less than gambling transactions; and they have been, in this country, a source of ruin, misery, and suicide, admitting of no adequate description. I grant that this gambling has arisen from the facility of obtaining the fictitious means of making the purchases; and I grant that that facility has been created by the system, under the baneful influence of which we live. But it is not the less necessary that I beseech you not to practise such gambling; that I beseech you, if you be engaged in it, to disentangle yourself from it as soon as you can. Your

life, while you are thus engaged, is the life of a
gamester; a life of constant anxiety; constant desire to overreach; constant apprehension; general
gloom, enlivened, now and then, by a gleam of hope
or of success. Even that success is sure to lead
to further adventures; and, at last, a thousand to
one, that your fate is that of the pitcher to the
well.

The great temptation to this gambling is, as is
the case in other gambling, the *success of the few*.
As young men, who crowd to the army, in search
of rank and renown, never look into the ditch that
holds their slaughtered companions; but have their
eye constantly fixed on the general-in-chief; and
as each of them belongs to the *same profession*, and
is sure to be conscious that he has equal merit,
every one deems himself the suitable successor of
him who is surrounded with *aides-de-camp*, and
who moves battalions and columns by his nod; so
with the rising generation of " speculators :" they
see the great estates that have succeeded the pen-
cil-box and the orange-basket; they see those whom
nature and good laws made to black shoes, sweep
chimneys or the streets, rolling in carriages; and
they can see no earthly reason why they should
not all do the same; forgetting the thousands and
thousands, who, in making the attempt, have reduced themselves to that beggary which, before
their attempt, they would have regarded as a thing
wholly impossible.

In all situations of life, avoid the *trammels of
the law*. Man's nature must be changed before
law-suits will cease; and, perhaps, it would be
next to impossible to make them less frequent than
they are in the present state of this country; but
though no man who has any property at all, can

I

say that he will have nothing to do with law-suits, it is in the power of most men to avoid them, in a considerable degree. One good rule is, to have as little as possible to do with any man who is fond of law-suits; and who, upon every slight occasion, talks of an appeal to the law. Such persons, from their frequent litigations, contract a habit of using the technical terms of the courts, in which they take a pride, and are, therefore, companions peculiarly disgusting to men of sense. To such men a law-suit is a luxury, instead of being, as it is to men of ordinary minds, a source of anxiety and a real and substantial scourge. Such men are always of a quarrelsome disposition, and avail themselves of every opportunity to indulge in that which is mischievous to their neighbors. In thousands of instances men go to law for the indulgence of mere anger.

Before you go to law, consider well the *cost;* for if you win your suit and are poorer than you were before, what do you accomplish? You only imbibe a little additional anger against your opponent; you injure him, but do harm to yourself. Better to put up with the loss of one dollar than of two, to which latter is to be added all the loss of time; all the trouble, and all the mortification and anxiety attending a law-suit. To set an attorney to work to worry and torment another man is a very base act; to alarm his family as well as himself, while you are sitting quietly at home. If a man owes you money which he cannot pay, why add to his distress without the chance of benefit to yourself? Thousands of men have injured themselves by resorting to the law; while very few ever bettered themselves by it, except such resort were unavoidable.

Nothing is much more discreditable than what is called *hard dealing*. They say of the Turks, that they know nothing of *two prices* for the same article : and that to ask an abatement of the lowest shopkeeper is to insult him. It would be well if Christians imitated Mahometans in this respect. To ask one price and take another, or to offer one price and give another, besides the loss of time that it occasions, is highly dishonorable to the parties, and especially when pushed to the extent of solemn protestations. It is, in fact, a species of lying ; and it answers no one advantageous purpose to either buyer or seller. I hope that every young man, who reads this, will start in life with a resolution never to higgle and lie in dealings.

PRINCIPLES NECESSARY TO BE OBSERVED BY THOSE YOUNG MEN WHO ARE NOT YET IN BUSINESS FOR THEMSELVES.

Every young man should remember that the character which he is to sustain, and which is to *sustain him*, when he shall be in business for himself, is to be formed while he is yet in a subordinate station. This observation holds true, not only with respect to the reputation which he is to possess among men, but also with regard to his real characteristics. The habits, principles, and manners of the *youth* will be essentially those of the *man ;* and as it is our object to place these on a solid basis, and form them in a manner suited to the real exigencies of life, we shall express ourselves plainly, going directly to the point ; and calling the vices and virtues by their right names. We begin by pointing out some practices which are to be avoided: and as the foundation of all that is beautiful in character is ingenuousness, we shall first bear our testimony against

LYING.

To lie to the prejudice of others, argues malice and villany: to lie in excuse of ourselves, guilt and cowardice; both ways, a design to delude with false representations of things, and advantage ourselves by the deceit. Now, however artificially we may carry on this infamous practice for a while, in the end it is always discovered; and it is hardly to be imagined what infinite contempt is the consequence. Nay, the more plausibly we have conducted our fallacies before, the more severely shall we be censured afterwards. From that moment, we lose all trust, all credit, all society; for all men avoid a liar as a common enemy; truth itself in his mouth loses its dignity, being always suspected, and often disbelieved.

If, therefore, you should ever unwarily fall into an offence, never seek to cover it over with a lie: for the last fault doubles the former, and each makes the other more inexcusable; whereas, what is modestly acknowledged is easily forgiven, and the very confession of a small trespass establishes an opinion that we are innocent of a greater.

DISHONESTY.

But truth in speech must likewise be accompanied by integrity in all your dealings; for it is as impossible for a dishonest person to be a good agent, as it is for a madman, or an idiot, to govern himself or others by the laws of common sense. Dare not, therefore, allow yourself even to wish to convert the property of another to your own use, more especially where it is committed to your charge; for breach of trust is as heinous an aggravation of theft, as pretended friendship is of murder. If, therefore, you should be lucky in your frauds, and escape without being punished or detected, you will nevertheless stand self-condemned, be ashamed to trust yourself with your own thoughts, and wear in your very countenance both the consciousness of guilt and dread of a discovery; whereas innocence looks always upwards, meets the most inquisitive and suspicious eye, and stands undaunted before God and man. On the other hand, if ever your knaveries come to light (to say nothing of the penalties of the law), with what shame and confusion of face must you appear before those you have wronged! and with what grief of heart must your relations and friends be made eye or ear witnesses of your disgrace? Nor is this all; for, even supposing you should be convinced of your folly, and sincerely abhor it for the future, you must nevertheless be always liable to suspicion, and others will have the boldness to pilfer, on the presumption that you will be understood to be the thief.

CONNIVANCE.

But it is incumbent on you, not only to be honest yourself, but disdain to connive at the dishonesty of others. He that winks at an injury he might prevent, shares in it; and it is as scandalous to fear blame or reproach for doing your duty, as to deserve reproof for the neglect of it. Should there be, therefore, a general confederacy among those in his service to abuse the confidence or credulity of your employer, divulge it the very moment you perceive it, for fear your very silence should be thought to participate in their guilt.

FIDELITY.

There is still another sort of fidelity, which may be called that of affection, as the other is of action, being almost of as much consequence, too, and what never fails to endear you to those in whose favor it is employed; we mean, that of defending their reputations, not only negatively, by avoiding all reproachful, indecent, or even familiar terms in speaking of them, but positively, by endeavoring at all times to vindicate them from the open aspersions and base insinuations of others.

TEMPERANCE.

But, that your integrity may be permanent, it must be founded on the rock of temperance. First, therefore, banish sloth, and an inordinate love of ease; active minds only being fit for employments, and none but the industrious either deserving, or having a possibility to thrive; which gave occasion to Solomon to exclaim, "The sluggard shall be clothed with rags; because he cries, Yet a little more sleep, a little more slumber!" But the folly of sleeping away one's days, is obvious to the dullest capacity, it being so much time abated from our lives, and either returning us into a like condition with what we were in before our births, or anticipating that which we may expect in the grave. In short, sleep is but a refreshment, not an employment; and, while we give way to the pleasing lethargy, we sacrifice both the duties and enjoyments of our being.

PLEASURE.

Neither is it enough to avoid sloth; you must likewise fly the excesses of that enchantress, pleasure. Pleasure, when it becomes our business, makes business a torment; and it is as impossible to pursue both, as to serve God and Mammon. You may perhaps think this lesson hard to learn; but it is nevertheless the reverse of the prophet's roll; and, if bitter in the mouth, is sweet in the belly.

To explain ourselves more fully on this head; Do not imagine we mean by this, that, though you must live by the sweat of your brow, you must not reap the harvest of your own labors. No man exacts it of you, nor would nature submit to the ungrateful dictate, if he did We speak only of pernicious or unlawful pleasures, such as are commonly ranged under the word intemperance, such as prey on the body and purse, and in the end destroy both.

EXCESS.

Excess is a deceitful evil, that smiles and seduces, enchants and destroys. Fly her very first appearance, then: it is not safe to be within the glance of her eye, or sound of her voice; and if you once become familiar with her, you are undone. Let us further add, that she wears a variety of shapes, and all pleasing; all accommodated to flatter our appetite and inflame our desires.

To the epicure she presents delicious banquets;

to the bacchanal, store of exquisite wines ; to the
sensualist, his seraglio of mistresses ; to each, the
allurement he is most prone to ; and to all, a pleasing poison, that not only impairs the body, but stupifies the mind, and makes us bankrupts of our
lives, as well as our credits and estates.

EATING.

Above all things, then, be temperate. And first,
then, in eating. One expensive mouth will wear
out six pair of hands ; and a dime will appease the
wants of nature more effectually, as well as more
innocently, than a dollar. This caution deserves
your attention so much the more, when you recollect that excessive eating is unfavorable to efficient
exertion of the body or the mind ; that it is the inevitable precursor of disease in some form or other ;
and, finally, that even while a man is compliment-
ed as a *bon vivant,* he is despised as a glutton

DRINKING.

But, however injurious this species of excess
may be to the body, or the purse, it is not so criminal, in many respects, as that of living only to be
a thoroughfare for wine and strong drink. For he
that places his supreme delight in strong drink, and
is uneasy till he has drank away his senses, renders
himself soon unfit for every thing else : frolic at
night is followed by pains and sickness in the
morning ; and then, what was before the poison,
is administered as a cure ; so that a whole life is
often wasted in this expensive frenzy ; poverty
itself only cutting off the means, not the inclination ; and a merry night being still esteemed worth

living for, though fortune, friends, and even health itself, have deserted us; nay, though we are never mentioned but with contempt and disgrace, and to warn others from the vices that have been our undoing. When you are most inclined to stay another bottle, be sure to go. That is the most certain indication which can be given, that you have drunk enough. The moment after, your reason, like a false friend, will desert you, when you most need its assistance; you will be ripe for every mischief, and more apt to resent, than follow any good counsel that might preserve you from it. The only effectual security against intemperance in drink, is to fly temptation, taste not, handle not the cup which leads to intoxication; for when once its moderate use becomes habitual, in vain our best resolves against intemperance.

DRESS.

There is likewise an intemperance in dress, which, though not so blamable and dangerous as either of the others, is nevertheless worth your care to avoid. Dress is, at best, but a female privilege; and, in men, argues both levity of mind, and effeminacy of manners. But, in a man of business, an affectation of this kind is never to be pardoned: in him it is a vice as well as a folly, as opening a door to extravagance, which never fails to be attended with ruin; and the prudent never care to deal with a man who must injure either them or himself. Wherever there is a woman in the family, there is a natural issue for all the expense that can be spared on that article; and that poor wretch must have a miserable head, who would inflame his wife's follies by his own. In short,

to lay out money in fine clothes, may be justified
in fortune-hunters, because it is their stock in
trade, but in nobody else; the wall in the street
or some little deference where you are not known,
being all the advantages attending it; and, when
you are, absurd finery is no more regarded, than a
poor player on the stage, in the robes of a prince.
The fop who came into the presence of Henry
VIII. with an hundred tenements upon his back,
would have had twice as many hats off, if he had
annually put the rents into his pocket. It is therefore wisdom to wear such apparel as suits your
condition; not sordid and beggarly, or foppish and
conceited; agreeable to what the poet puts in the
father's mouth, speaking to his son of his habit,
which he advised to be " rich, not gaudy, or expressed in fancy."

GOVERNMENT OF THE TONGUE.

The art or virtue of holding your tongue, is the
next topic we shall lay before you; both a rare
and an excellent quality, and what contributes
greatly to our ease and prosperity. In general,
therefore, remember it is as dangerous to fall in
love with one's own voice, as one's own face.
Those that talk much cannot always talk well, and
may much oftener incur censure than praise; few
people care to be eclipsed; and a superiority of
sense is as ill brooked as a superiority of beauty
or fortune. If you are wise, therefore, talk little
but hear much; what you are to learn from yourself, must be by thinking; and from others, by
speech; let them find tongue, then, and you ear:
by which means such as are pleased with themselves, which are the gross of mankind, will like-

wise be pleased with you, and you will be doubly paid for your attention, both in affection and knowledge.

TALKING OF ONE'S SELF.

When people talk of themselves, lend both your ears: it is the surest way to learn mankind; for, let men be ever so much upon their guard, it is odds if some such escape is not made, as is a sufficient clue to the whole character. We need not observe to you, that, for the very same reason, you are never to make yourself the subject of your own conversation: though, we hope, you will have no vices to conceal, all men have infirmities; and it is as unnecessary as impolitic to expose them.

ILL-NATURED JESTS.

If it is dangerous to speak of ourselves, it is much more so to take freedoms with other people. A jest may tickle many; but, if it hurts one, the resentment that follows it may do you more injury than the reputation service.

FAMILY SECRETS.

But, over and above all these general cautions for the government of the tongue, you must, in a more particular manner, be careful of the secrets of the family where you live; from whence hardly the most indifferent circumstance must be divulged: for he that will drop any thing indiscreetly, may very justly be thought to retain nothing; and those who are on the watch for information, will, from a very remote hint, conjecture all the rest.

SECRETS REPOSED IN YOU.

We do not advise you to seek the confidence of others; for, if the secret intrusted should happen to take air, though you are innocent of the discovery, it is odds but it is imputed to your infidelity. But, if any such trust is reposed in you, suffer the torture, rather than disclose it; for, beside the mischief it may occasion to him who confided in you, it must argue an extreme levity of mind, to leak out to one man what was communicated to you by another; which last must likewise, in his heart, despise you for your incontinence, and secretly resolve never to trust his affairs to the custody of such a sieve.

ONE'S OWN SECRETS.

Hence we are naturally led to caution you not to be talkative of such designs as you have in your head, of bargains to buy, or business to do. For by this means, you give others an opportunity to forestall you, if they think it worth their while; and such, whose interest interferes with yours, will take the alarm, and endeavor to disappoint you, to their own advantage; beside all which, it is no bad policy to take such as we mean to deal with unprepared. In brief, never talk of your designs, till they have taken place; and even then you had better continue silent, lest it should prejudice your future dealings.

It must, however, be owned a very difficult task, as self is always uppermost in the mind, not to give vent sometimes to the joy of having acted with notable shrewdness and address. But that man has not half enough of either, who cannot prevail on nimself to stifle all pretensions to both. To proclaim one's skill, is to beat an alarm to those we deal with; as he that draws his sword puts every body else on his guard; and whoever is persuaded he is overmatched by you, will never negotiate with you again, at least in commodities that fluctuate in their value, according to the demand at market.

EXPECTATIONS.

Neither is it prudent to talk of our expectations, or of our dependences on the promises of others; for, if we meet with disappointments instead of services, we sink as much in our reputations, as if they were owing to our own bad conduct; and it is well we are not derided for our credulity, into the bargain. For some people are disingenuous enough to make use of all advantages to gratify their malignity; and it must be our business to give them as few opportunities as possible.

OTHER PEOPLE'S QUARRELS.

Be likewise warily silent in all concerns that are in matter of dispute between others; for he that blows the coals in quarrels he has nothing to do with, has no right to complain if the sparks fly in his face; it being extremely difficult to interfere so happily, as not to give offence to either one party or the other; almost all men having their eyes immovably fixed on their own interest, and continuing obstinately blind to the demands of their antagonist; and therefore you must either side with each by turns, and thereby deceive both, or expose yourself to the disgust and ani mosity of the loser, who will judge of your conduct, not according to truth, but his own selfish prejudices.

TALE-BEARING.

But nothing can be more scandalously odious, than officiously to carry inflaming tales between persons at variance, and thereby keep up that rancor which, for want of fresh provocations, might otherwise expire. Beside, it is as dangerous an office, as holding a wolf by the ears. You can neither safely proceed nor leave off; and, if ever they come to an accommodation, the incendiary is sure to be the first sacrifice.

ONE'S OWN QUARRELS.

In all such cases, therefore, let your tongue be dipped in oil, never in vinegar; and rather endeavor to mollify than irritate the wound; and even where you yourself may become a principal, avoid anger as much as possible, that you may avoid giving the provocations almost inseparable from it. If injured, the less passion you betray, the better you will be able to state your case, and obtain justice; and, if you are the aggressor, rudeness, reproach, disdain, and contempt, but render your adversary more implacable; whereas by mildness and good manners, the most untractable may be qualified, and the most exasperated appeased.

We have insensibly strayed from the government of the tongue to that of the heart; and therefore it will not be impertinent to inform you, that quarrels are easier avoided than made up; for which reason, do not let it be in the power of every trifle to ruffle you. A weathercock, that is the sport of

every wind, has more repose than a choleric man;
sometimes exposed to the scorn, sometimes to the
resentments, and always to the abhorrence, of all
who know him. Rather wink at small injuries,
than be too forward to avenge them. He that, to
destroy a single bee, should throw down the hive,
instead of one enemy, would make a thousand.

It is abundantly better to study the good will
of all, than excite the resentment of any; of all,
we mean, but those whose friendship is not to be
gained but by sharing in their crimes. For there
is not a creature so contemptible, which may not
be somewhat beneficial, and whose enmity may
not be as detrimental. The mouse in one fable,
spared by the lion, afterwards, in gratitude, set the
same lion free from the toils he was entangled in,
by gnawing them to pieces; and, in another, the
gnat is represented challenging the lion, and having the best of the combat.

AFFABILITY.

Make a trial, therefore, and you will always
find the force of affability; daily experience showing us, that we make only those brutes our play-
fellows which are mild and gentle, and keep those
at a distance, and in chains, which we take to be
our enemies.

FRUGALITY.

What we shall next recommend to you, is frugality; the practice of which is expedient for all,
but especially for those who are, like the silk-worm,
to spin their riches out of their own bosoms.

Be anxiously solicitous to preserve your credit
even from suspicion; for, next to losing it, is the

doubt of its being endangered. In order to do which most effectually, be frugal: credit, bought at the expense of money, belongs only to persons of estate, or such as have already made their fortunes; in every body beside, thrift approaches nearest to virtue, and will be esteemed accordingly.

By thrift we would have you to understand, not only the avoiding profusion, or the limiting your expenses to pounds and shillings, but even to pence and farthings. The neglect of trifles, as they are called, is suffering a moth to eat holes in your purse, and let out all the profits of your industry. Nothing is more true than the old proverb, " That a penny saved is two pence got." When, therefore, you wrangle for a farthing in a bargain, or refuse to throw it away in sport, do not let fools laugh you out of your economy; but leave them their jest, and keep you your money.

Remember, the most magnificent edifice was raised by laying first one single stone, and every access, how little soever, helps to raise the heap. Let a man once begin to save, and he will soon be convinced that it is the straight road to wealth. To hope it may be gained from nothing, is to build castles in the air; but no trifle is so small, that will not serve for a foundation. He that hath one shilling may with more ease increase it to five, than he procure a penny who is not master of a farthing. It was on this principle the poor drover scraped together enough to purchase a calf, and from that contemptible beginning went gradually on, till he became master of many thousands a-year. He that is not a good husband in small matters, does not deserve to be trusted with great.

EMPLOYER'S CASH.

But this you are sacredly to observe: if you should be intrusted with the custody of your employer's cash, look on it as a plague-sore, that, but touched, would be your utter ruin. Remember, the day of account must come, when the most minute trespass cannot be concealed, and when scarcely an oversight will be forgiven. In cases of property, men alter their very natures, are ever suspicious of wrongs, and, if any are proved, incline rather to punish than forgive. Do not be seduced, then, into a fault of this nature, on any consideration whatever. Though you are taught to be frugal of your own money, you are forbid to covet another's; and, while you are a subordinate agent, your employer is entitled to the benefit of all your virtues.

INDUSTRY.

But to be frugal is not sufficient, you must be industrious too. What is saved by thrift must be improved by diligence; for the last doubles the first, as the earth by reflection renders the sunbeams hot, which would otherwise seem but warm. What cannot be done by one stroke, is effected by many; and application and perseverance have often succeeded, even where all other means have failed; it having been often observed, that a small vessel, which makes quick and frequent returns, brings more gain to her owners, than the large hulk, which makes but few voyages, though she holds much, and is always full. "Go to the ant, thou sluggard," says Solomon, "and learn her ways, and be wise!" as if in her the power of

K

dustry was most happily and clearly illustrated.
Nothing can be more ridiculous, than that, because
our means will not suit with our ends, we will not
suit our ends to our means; or because we cannot
do what we will, we will not do what we may;
depriving ourselves of what is in our power, because we cannot attain things beyond it; whereas
the way to enlarge our ability is to double our
industry; for, by many repeated efforts, we may
compass in the end what in the beginning we
despaired of.

The fool that promises himself success without
endeavors, or despairs at the sight of difficulties, is
always disappointed; but, on the contrary, he that
is indefatigable, succeeds even beyond his expectations.   There is not a more certain sign of a cra-
ven spirit, than to have the edge of one's activity
soon turned by opposition; as, on the contrary,
there is no disputing his fortitude, who contends
with obstacles, and never gives over the pursuit,
till he has reached the end he aimed at.   Indeed,
to tempers of this last kind, few things are impossible; and the historian, speaking of Cosmo the
first Duke of Tuscany, concludes with this strong
remark, "that the Duke, by patience and industry,
surmounted all those difficulties which had otherwise been invincible."

To say the truth, it argues a weak pusillanimous
spirit, to sink beneath perplexities and calamities,
and rather lament one's sufferings, than attempt to
remove them.   If ever, therefore, you apprehend
yourself to be in a manner overwhelmed with ad-
versities, bear up boldly against them all: it will
be the longer before you sink at least, and may
perhaps give time and opportunity for some friendly
hand to interpose for your preservation.   It was a

sensible device that a man made use of by way of sign : a pair of compasses, with this motto, " By constancy and labor;" one foot being fixed, the other in motion. Make this a rule, and you will be very little in fortune's power ; there being, humanly speaking, as certain roads to wealth, if men resolve to keep within the proper bounds, as from one city to another.

You must, moreover, make industry a part of your character as early as possible. Be officiously serviceable to your employer on all occasions : if possible, prevent his commands ; understand a nod, a look ; and do rather more than is required of you, than less than your duty. He merits little that performs but just what would be exacted ; but we learn to love him who takes a pleasure in his business, and seems obliged by our commands. If you should even be enjoined to do those offices which are called mean, or which you may think beneath your station, undertake them cheerfully, nor betray the least disgust at the imposition. To dispute a master's will is both undutiful and unmannerly ; and to obey him with reluctance, or resentment, argues you obey only through fear ; whereby you have both the pain of the service, and lose the merit of it too.

VALUE OF TIME.

Above all things, learn to put a due value on time, and husband every moment as if it were to be your last. In time is comprehended all we possess, enjoy, or wish for ; and in losing that, we lose them all. This is a lesson that can never be too often or too earnestly inculcated, especially to young people ; for they are apt to flatter them selves, they have a large stock upon their hands, and that, though days, months, and years are wantonly wasted, they are still rich in the remainder. But, alas! no mistake can be greater, or more fatal. The moments thus prodigally confounded are the most valuable that time distils from his alembic; they partake of the highest flavor, and breathe out the richest odor; and as, on one hand, they are irretrievable, so neither, on the other, can all the artifice of more experienced life compensate the loss.

COMPANY.

But we have already premised, that the bow of life must not be kept continually bent: to relax sometimes, is both allowable, and even necessary; and as, in those hours of recreation, you will be most in danger, it will behove you to be then most vigilantly on your guard. Companions will then be called in to share with you in your pleasures; and, according to your choice of them, both your character and disposition will receive a tincture; as water, passing through minerals, partakes of their taste and efficacy. This is a truth so universally received, that to know a man by his company is become proverbial; in the natural as well as the moral world, like associating with like, and laboring continually to throw off whatever is heterogeneous. Hence we see, that discordant mixtures produce nothing but broils and fermentations, till one becomes victorious; and as what God has joined, he will have none to put asunder, so what he has thus put asunder, he forbids to be joined. We have said thus much, only to convince you how impossible it will be for you to be thought a person of integrity, while you converse with the abandoned and licentious : and, by herding with such, you will not only lose your character, but your virtue too; for, whatever they find you, or whatever fallacious distinctions you may make between the men and their vices, in the end the first qualify the last, and you will assimilate or grow like each other; that is to say, by becoming familiar with evil courses, you will cease to regard them as evil; and, by ceasing to hate them, you will soon learn both to love and to practise them And this may be concluded without breach of charity; for it is extremely difficult for frail human nature to recover its lost innocence, but as facile for it to precipitate itself into all the excesses of vanity and vice.

Nor does the danger of bad company affect the mind only. Say that you preserve your integrity, which is as bold a supposition as can be made, by countenancing them with your presence, though not equally guilty, you may be liable to equal danger. In cases of riots and murders, all are principals, and you may be undone for another person's crime. Nay, in cases of treason, even silence is capital; and, in such unhappy dilemmas, you must either betray your friend's life, or forfeit your own. Thus, the infamous assassin, who attempted the murder of one of the princes of Orange, not only brought destruction on himself, but on his confidant also, who, though he abhorred the fact, yet kept the counsel of the contriver; and the discovery of the last was made merely by observation, that he was often seen in company with the former.

Fly therefore the society of sensual or designing men; or expect to forego your innocence, feel

your industry, from a pleasure, become a burden,
your frugality give place to extravagance, and your
sobriety to beastly intemperance. These mischiefs
follow in a train : and, when you are linked to bad
habits, it is as hard to think of parting with them,
as to plunge into a cold bath, to get rid of an ague.
Neither does the malignity of the contagion appear all at once ; the frolic first appears harmless,
and, when tasted, leaves a longing relish behind
it : one appointment makes way for another, one
expense leads on to a second ; some invite openly,
some insinuate craftily, and all soon grow too im-
portunate to be denied. Some pangs of remorse
you will feel on your first degeneracy, and some
faint resolutions you would take to be seduced no
more ; which will no sooner be discovered by these
panders and factors to destruction, but all arts will
be used to allure you back to bear them company,
in the broad beaten path to ruin. Of all which,
none is more to be dreaded than raillery. And
this you must expect to have exercised upon you
with its full force : business, and the cares of life,
will be rendered pleasantly ridiculous ; looseness
and prodigality, and drunkenness, will be called
living like a gentleman ; and you will be upbraid-
ed with meanness and want of spirit, if you dare
to persist in the ways of economy, of sobriety, and
of virtue. Here, then, is a fair opportunity to show
your steadiness, courage, and good sense ; encounter wit with wit, raillery with raillery, and appear
above being hurt by banter ill-founded, and jests
without a sting. There is as much true fortitude
in standing such a charge as this, and being
staunch to your integrity, as in facing an enemy
in the day of battle, or rolling undismayed in a
tempest, when winds and seas seem to conspire

your destruction. Many men, who could stand both the last shocks, have relented in the first, and through stark impotence of mind have been undone.

We could enforce all these arguments to induce you to avoid ill company, with examples without number: but these will every day occur to your own observation. And as we have already pointed out to you whom to avoid, we shall next direct you whom to choose, viz. persons as carefully educated, and as honestly disposed as yourself; such as have property to preserve, and characters to endanger; such as are known and esteemed; whose pursuits are laudable, whose lives are temperate, and whose expenses are moderate. With such companions as these, you can neither contract discredit, nor degenerate into excesses; you would be a mutual check to each other; and your reputation would be so established, that it would be the ambition of others to be admitted members of your society.

Such should be your company in general; for particulars, as a life of trade is almost incompatible with study and contemplation, and as conversation is the most natural and easy path to knowledge, select those to be your intimates, who, by being excellent in some art, science, or accomplishment, may, in the course of your acquaintance, make your very hours of amusement contribute to your improvement. For the most part, they are open and communicative; and take as much pleasure in being heard, as you to be informed: whence you will attain, at your ease, what they achieved with great expense of time and study. And the knowledge thus procured is easier digested, and becomes more our own, than what we make ourselves masters of in a more formal and contemplative way; facts, doctrines, opinions, and arguments, being thoroughly winnowed from their chaff, by the wind of controversy, and nothing but the golden grain remaining. Thus it is observed of Francis I. of France, that, though he came to the crown young and unlearned, yet, by associating himself with men of genius and accomplishments, he so improved himself, as to surpass in knowledge the most learned princes of his time. And we knew a young gentleman, who was taken from school to sit in a legislature, and had never much leisure to return to his books; and yet, so well did he choose his companions, and make so good a use of their conversation, that nobody spoke better on almost all points, or was better heard; it being immediately expected from the characters of those he choose to be familiar with, that he was either already wise, or soon would be so; whence his youth and inexperience were so far from exposing him to contempt, that they greatly contributed to establish a universal prejudice in his favor.

MEN OF SENSE.

Yet farther: with men of capacity, you may not only improve in your understanding by conversing, but may have the benefit of their whole judgment and experience, whenever any difficulty occurs that puzzles your own. Men of superior sense and candor, exercise a ready and flowing indulgence towards those who entreat their favour, and are never more pleased than when they have an opportunity to make their talents more serviceable to mankind. Prudence, address, decorum, correctness of speech, elevation of mind, and delicacy of manners, are learned in this noble school; and, without affecting the vanity of the name, you imperceptibly become a finished gentleman.

THE VULGAR.

Whereas, low, sordid, ignorant, vulgar spirits would debase you to their own level, would unlearn you all the decencies of life, and make you abhor the good qualities you could not attain. To preside among a herd of brutes, would be no compliment to a man; and yet this ridiculous pre-eminence would be all the advantage you could expect from such boorish companions; which likewise, if not purchased, would not be allowed; for those who pay an equal share of the reckoning, allow no precedency, and our countrymen are too proud to make any concessions, unless they are paid for them.

SOTS.

In advising you to shun excess of wine yourself, it must be understood we have already advised you to shun such as are mighty in strong drink. Bears and lions ought not to be more dreadful to the sober, than men made beasts by inflaming liquors. Danger is ever in their company; and reason, on your side, is no match for the frenzy on theirs. In short, he that is drunk, is possessed; and though in other cases, we are to resist the devil, that he may fly from us; in this, to fly from the devil, is an easier task than to make him fly from us.

FALSE COMPLAISANCE.

We shall add but one word more on this topic: beware of a false complaisance, or a too easy ductility in being swayed by another person's humor. If business calls, or you dislike the conversation, or you incline to go home, or whatever the call is, if it is reasonable, obey it. A man ought to be able to say, No, as well as a woman. And not to have a will of one's own, renders one ridiculous, even to the very persons who govern us. Take leave then resolutely, but civilly; and you will find a very few instances of steadiness on such occasions, will secure you from future importunities.

FRIENDSHIP.

Though we have said much under the head of companions, it is still necessary to add something concerning friends. Friend and companion are terms often used as meaning the same thing; but no mistake can be greater. Many persons have variety of companions; but how few, through their whole lives, ever meet with a friend! Old stories, indeed, talk of friends who mutually contended which should die for the other; and talkative Greece has not been sparing to trumpet out their praises. But, even by the manner of celebrating these heroes of friendship, it is very evident such examples are extremely rare. Our records, at least, show none such. The love of interest seems to be the reigning spirit in our bosoms: and wherever this pure and delicate union is to be expected, *meum* and *tuum* must be words utterly unknown. Friendship, therefore, is confined within very narrow bounds.

CHOICE OF FRIENDS

You cannot be too wary in the choice of him you would call your friend; nor suffer your affections to be so far engaged, as to be wholly at his devotion. It is dangerous trusting one's happiness in another person's keeping, or to be without a power to refuse what may be your ruin to grant. But, if ever the appearance of wisdom, integrity, and every other virtue, should lead you to cultivate a more than ordinary friendship, never profess more than you design to make good; and, when you oblige, let it be freely, gallantly, and without the mercenary view of a rigid equivalent. Neither put your friend to the pain of soliciting a good office, but spare his modesty, and make it appear, that you are happy in an opportunity of doing him service; but in this, as in all other things, be guided by discretion. As you would never apply to another for what would endanger his fortune, and of course ruin his family, so, never be induced, on any consideration, to run the like risk yourself. What interest you can make, what time you can devote, what ready money you can spare, for the advantage of your friend, is nobly disposed of; and never upbraid him, even should he prove ungrateful.

BONDS AND SECURITIES.

But bonds, notes, or securities, which it is possible neither he nor you may be able to make good, never engage in. It is not only mortgaging your whole credit and fortune, but peace of mind; you will never think of your obligation without terror, and the nearer the day of payment approaches, the more exquisite will be your pangs. In a word, almost as many men are dragged into ruin by these fatal encumbrances, as by a life of riot and debauchery. Consider, therefore, that it is a breach of friendship for any man to ask so unreasonable a kindness; and, from that moment, be upon your guard; it being but a poor consolation to be pitied under calamities undeserved; or have it said of you, "He was a good-natured man, and nobody's enemy but his own."

In fine, as to what concerns yourself, live in such a manner, as may challenge friendship and favor from all men; but defend yourself, with the utmost vigilance, from ever standing in need of assistance from any. Though it is a glorious thing to bestow, it is a wretched thing to apply; and, over and above the tyranny, the capriciousness, ingratitude and insensibility you will expose yourself to, when reduced to such expedients, you will then see human nature in such a light, as will put you out of humor with society.

ADVICE ON ENTERING UPON BUSINESS.

PROPER PERSONS TO DEAL WITH.

Deal with those of the fairest characters, and best established circumstances; for they can both afford to sell better bargains, and afford longer credit, and have too much depending on their conduct to be easily induced to do or connive at a fraudulent action. Nevertheless, to be secure, you must put yourself in no man's power; for, if you neglect your own interest, how can you complain of infidelity in others? Besides, though we should allow there are numbers of men so unfeignedly honest, that no consideration could prevail with them to do an immoral thing, however covered from observation: yet, experience will teach you, there are many others who are only the counterfeits of these, who make use of virtue as stock in trade, and are ready to bring it to market the moment there is an opportunity to dispose of it for as much as they think it worth.

FAIR PROFESSIONS.

But, above all, be most cautious of those who profess the most; especially if their advances are sudden, extraordinary, or without a plausible foundation. Depend upon it, all the commerce of mankind is founded upon mutual interest; and, if it is not apparent by what means you could deserve all these blandishments, conclude they are artificial, and keep yourself out of danger. For the gilding the pill is not peculiar to apothecaries; the same craft prevails through every scene of life; and more mischief has been done under the mask of friendship, than by the most avowed and inveterate enmity. In such cases, men are upon their guard, and, generally speaking, very effectually provide for their own security; but, where the heart is open, it is assailable, and you are undone, before you suspected you were in harm's way.

SUSPICION.

But, though you are to beware of credulity on one hand, you are to beware as much of betraying your suspicions on the other; for that sets fire to the train at once, and, of a doubtful friend, you make a certain enemy. Besides, the circumstances that justify your fears may make but a very poor figure in evidence; and, though you may be perfectly in the right in being upon your guard, you will appear as much in the wrong in making out a charge only from your own apprehensions.

RASH RESENTMENTS.

Neither is it safe or prudent to declare open war upon every trifling injury. It is impossible to live without suffering; and, if we give way to our resentments on all such occasions, quarrels will be, in a manner, the business of our lives. On the other hand, if ever, through accident, or human infirmity, you should be the aggressor, let it be your glory to acknowledge your fault, and make instant retribution. Next to the merit of doing right, is the atoning for what is done wrong; and, in spite of the vulgar notion that it is mean to submit, or acknowledge a trespass, do you esteem it the height of moral gallantry. And, if the conquest of one's self is the most difficult of all achievements, you will think it the noblest of all triumphs. Nor let the poverty or impotence of your adversary induce you to overlook or despise him; for, the weaker he is, the less courage was required to oppose him, and the more tyranny appears in oppressing him, merely because the odds

of strength were on your side.   Besides, the most
abject of men may be able to ruin the proudest
and, in the Turkish history, you will find a story
of a prime vizier killed in the divan by the hand
of a common soldier whom he had aggrieved. Remember, on all occasions, that anger is an impertinent passion: if it intrudes while you complain
of or seek redress for injuries received, truth will
be hurt by the medium through which it is seen;
and that will be esteemed prejudice or spleen,
which is in fact both truth and evidence.   On the
other side, if it breaks out when you are yourself
accused, it argues a sore place is touched, and your
very sensibility proclaims your guilt.

COMPLACENCY.

Instead, therefore, of seeking quarrels, or husbanding debates, endeavor to make friends, if possible, of all you have concerns with. And this can
be done by no means so effectually, as by an affable and courteous behavior.   We have known a
bow, a smile, or an obliging expression, people a
shop with customers.   In short, no rhetoric has
more force than a sweet and gentle deportment:
it will win favor and maintain it; enforce what is
right, and excuse what is wrong.

Let this be the rule of your conduct in general;
and, in particular, when induced to bestow a favor, do it as before hinted, with a frankness that
shall give it a tenfold value: or, if applied to for
what you are obliged to refuse, let it be manifest
you are governed by necessity, not choice, and
that you share with him you so refuse in the pain
of the disappointment.

But there are some persons that neither affabil-

ity nor even obligations can win; and those are
the covetous and the proud : both of which are
ungrateful soils, that yield no returns ; one thinking all but his due, and the other either laughing
in his sleeve at your foolish generosity, or fancy-
ing it is only meant as a snare to render him your
bubble.

TEMPERS OF MEN TO BE STUDIED.

To study the tempers and dispositions of men,
will therefore be of signal use in your commerce
with the world, both to carry your own points, and
secure you from the designs of others.   In the
first of which cases, be sure never to solicit a man
against his ruling passion : for, to induce a miser
to act liberally, a coward bravely, or a selfish man
disinterestedly, exceeds all power of persuasion ;
and you may as well hope to reduce all faces to
the same similitude, as work them to such ends as
contradict their own.   But, nevertheless, all may
be made serviceable, if managed with dexterity
and address : and the miser, in particular, to secure his purse from importunities, will give you
such of his time or industry as you please.
He is willing to be on good terms with his fellow-
creatures, and will purchase their friendship on
any terms, but that of parting with his money.
However sordid, therefore, his principles or practice, it is not amiss to have such a character among
the number of your acquaintance ; and, especially
in arbitrations, nobody more deserves your confidence.   He will there stickle for your interest as
if it was his own, and wrangle obstinately for
trifles that you would be ashamed to mention ;
whence it is odds but he procures you better terms

than you either expected, or could have attained
by your own endeavors.

FACES OF MEN TO BE STUDIED.

But, to be able to turn all the different inclinations effectually to your own advantage, we would
have you (however whimsical or romantic it may
at first appear) to study the expression which the
hand of nature has written in every face. Men
may disguise their actions, but not their inclinations; and though it is not easy to guess, by the
muscles of the countenance, what a man will do,
it is hardly to be concealed what he wishes to have
done. Judge, therefore, of characters, by what
they are constitutionally, and what habitually;
that is to say, in other words, what they would be
thought, and what they really are, but principally
the last; for however diligently a man may keep
guard on his passions, they will sally out sometimes in spite of him; and those escapes are a
never-failing clue to wind the whole labyrinth of
his life.

We say again, therefore, take your first impressions of men from their faces; and, though it is
exceedingly difficult to lay down rules to inform
your judgment, or assist your conjectures, on
this occasion, you have nothing to do but to make
the study familiar to you, and you will very rarely
be mistaken. Observation and experience presently unveil the mystery; and even hypocrisy can
hardly preserve itself from the rigor of your scrutiny. Not that we would advise you to be too pe-
remptory in your decisions, neither; but compare
men's faces with their actions, and their actions
with their faces, till, by the light mutually reflect-

L.

ed from each other, you are able to ascertain the truth. Nor is this custom alone serviceable in judging of a man in the gross; it will likewise help you to determine of every extempore impulse, that, for the time being, governs the heart. Thus, while you barter, purchase, solicit, or any other way confer, the uncontrollable emotions of the countenance will more infallibly indicate the purpose of him you treat with, than any thing he utters, and give you earlier notice to be on your guard. But, in order to do this effectually, your own eye must warily watch every motion of his, especially when you are delivering what you think will affect him most; you must likewise weigh every hasty syllable he lets fall; for these are generally the imbecilities of human nature, as well as the involuntary symptoms in the face; and what deliberate speeches and cool reasonings conceal, these flash out at once, without warning, and beyond recall. But, however curiously you examine the eye or heart of another, it will be to little purpose, unless you have art enough to conceal your own.

ARTIFICIAL INSENSIBILITY.

Now, the best and nearest way to attain this self-continence, is to cultivate an artificial insensibility of fear, anger, sorrow, and concern of any sort whatever. He that actually feels either pain or pleasure, cannot help expressing it some way or other; and whoever makes the discovery has the springs of the affections at his command, and may wind them up or let them down at pleasure; whereas, he that witnesses no sensation of the mind, betrays no weakness, and is wholly inaccessible. Labor then indefatigably to subdue your resentments; for, as you are to bustle through the busy world, the more exquisite your sensations are, the more frequent and more severe will be your pangs. The passions are, like the elements, excellent servants, but dreadful masters; and whoever is under their dominion, will have little leisure to do any thing but obey their dictates.

DISSIMULATION OF INJURIES.

In the particular of injuries, it is above all things necessary, sometimes, not only not to resent them, but even to dissemble the very feeling of them. Whoever complains, declares he would punish if he had the power; and from that moment your adversary both thinks his animosity justifiable, and will do you all the mischief possible, by way of self-defence; whereas, if you seem ignorant of the ill turn he has done you, he concludes himself safe from your expostulations and reproaches, and will believe it his interest to behave so as to avoid an explanation. Again, in wrestling with those that have more strength and power than yourself, though equity is on your side, it is ten to one but you are hurt more by contending for redress, than you suffered by the very grievance itself. Remember, then, the fable of the brazen and earthen pots, and keep as far as you can from the dangerous encounter. Again, we have known many a man interpret the most innocent action or expression into an affront, and, in the foolish pursuit of what he called justice, has lost the best friend he had in the world: and therefore those forward tongues, or peevish tempers, which rather choose to vent their present

spleen than make it give place to their future convenience, not only keep themselves in perpetual
troubles, but also shut the door against those opportunities which otherwise might have presented
to their advantage.

IRRESOLUTION AND INDOLENCE.

But, though you must not let your actions be
governed by every sudden gust of appetite or passion that rises, you are not, on the other hand, to
deliberate so lazily on every proposal, that you lose
the occasion, while you are pausing whether you
shall use it. Some fall into this aguish disease,
through doubt, irresolution, and timidity; and
others through downright indolence, flattering
themselves, that if wind and tide court them to-day,
they will do the same to-morrow. But nothing is
more dangerously fallacious; one moment sometimes offers what whole ages might be wasted in
soliciting in vain. If, therefore, such a nice and
delicate crisis as this should court your acceptance,
be bold! be vigilant! be resolute! and never sleep
till you have made the most of it. There is more
reason to use economy in the husbanding time
than money, since it is infinitely more valuable;
and he that does not make this the ruling maxim
of his life, may be said, very pertinently, to shorten
his days.

CHOICE OF OPPORTUNITIES.

We would further advise you, when you have
any point to carry which depends on the will of
another, to choose the minute of application, with
all the sagacity you are master of; for there is no

man living, whose temper is so even, as not to be sometimes more liable to impression than at others. Even contingencies govern us; we are more inclined to generosity, when a prosperous gale has breathed upon us; and more prone to peevishness and obstinacy, when ruffled by perplexities or misfortune. Some men are even so irritated by hunger, that, till they are appeased by a hearty dinner, they are inaccessible; and others so reserved and sullen, that, till a bottle or two has thawed their frozen humors, they have neither eyes, ears, or understanding. Such as these, therefore, are not to be esteemed the same men in one mood as they are in another; and, if you happen to mistake the moment, do not immediately give out in despair, but renew the attack, till you find the soul open, and apt to receive what direction you please to give it.

BEHAVIOR TO THE CHOLERIC.

At all adventures, never take fire from an angry man, and oppose fury to fury; but give the frenzy way, and it will melt into a tameness that you yourself will wonder at. From being fiery and intractable, he will become pliant and gentle; and, fearful that, during his transport, he has broken the rules of decency and decorum, he will make a thousand concessions to re-establish himself in your good opinion, the least of which he would not have borne the mention of before; whereas, if, on the first provocation, you had flung away with resentment, you had not only lost your point, but your interest in the man for ever.

SAFEST TO DEAL WITH THOSE ON ONE'S OWN LEVEL.

It is best, however, to confine your dealings, if possible, to such as are pretty near on your own level; where dependence may be mutual, and no great consequence to be feared from the overbearing humor of a would-be lion, without teeth or claws. But where such a temper happens to meet with large power, carefully avoid coming within the reach of it; such tyrants delighting in making a prey of their fellow-creatures, pleading their humor as a sufficient excuse for all manner of mischief, and making use of their odds of strength to cut off every mean of reparation. In the days of Queen Mary of England, Philip King of Spain, her husband, demanded the guardianship of her heir, if she should have one, with certain places of strength, to confirm his authority; offering at the same time his bond to deliver up his trust, in case the child died immediately. But when the House, out of a false complaisance to the throne, was on the point of conceding, an unlucky question of Lord Paget's, "Who should put the King's bond in suit, in case he trespassed on the conditions?" turned the tide at once, and the proposal was rejected. Public transactions may sometimes be applied to private: never enter into articles, therefore, but where there is a reasonable prospect of recovering the penalty.

IMPORTANT AFFAIRS TO BE MANAGED IN PERSON.

It is another wholesome rule for your conduct, to manage all your important affairs in person, if possible. More deference is generally paid to the

principal than to any delegate whatever; nor can
any other person be either so well instructed in
your views, or so capable to improve every advantage that may arise, as yourself. But, if want of
health, or any other equal incapacity, should prevent your attendance, rather negotiate by letter
than by the mouth of another : your meaning may
be ill understood, and worse delivered; offence
may be taken at omissions, or additions, of which
you are wholly innocent; your very apologies may
be so misrepresented, as to inflame instead of appease ; and you may be defeated in your designs,
by a series of blunders, more deserving laughter
than serious and passionate expostulation. But if
ever you should happen to be entangled in such a
ridiculous labyrinth, take it immediately upon
yourself to wind your way out. A few minutes'
conversation will clear up the misunderstandings
of a year, if there is no rancor at the bottom ; for
which reason, never conclude, either to your
friend's disadvantage or your own, till you have
had the satisfaction of canvassing the affair face
to face.

RUMORS AND TALES.

For the same reason, do not suffer yourself to
be misled by idle rumors and gossipping tales.
Expressions, harmless when first let fall, receive
their venom from the channel through which they
are conveyed; and, by concluding at second-hand,
you are governed, not by the fact itself, but the
apprehensions, humors, passions, follies, and even
wantonnesses of other people. If then you will
give these officious tale-bearers the pleasure of
listening to them, let it be with a guard upon your

heart, not to suffer it to be seduced by what perhaps is a downright forgery, or at least the grossest
misrepresentation. But weigh well the character
of him that speaks against his spoken of; the
circumstances, views, and interests of both; and
whatever else may help you to come at the truth,
clear of prejudice or disingenuity.

LETTERS.

Having advised you to treat by letters, rather
than message, when hindered by inconveniences
from attending in person, we must take a step
back, to caution you to write with the utmost deliberation, seldom without taking copies, and never
without reading what you have written twice or
thrice over. Letters are generally preserved, and
thence are always at hand as a sort of evidence
against you. You cannot, therefore, write too
cautiously; we will not say ambiguously, according to the maxim of Tiberius, who sometimes
wrote in that manner to the senate, by design, to
answer his own corrupt purposes. In a word,
write so as not to deceive others, or expose yourself; with all the subtlety of the serpent, but the
innocence of the dove.

CAUTION IN SETTING UP.

When the period of your minority has expired,
and you grow ambitious of appearing your own
master, consider it as an affair that is to influence
your whole future life. Many, by their haste and
precipitation in this particular, have only hastened
their own undoing; and, to get rid of a gentle
subjection, have rendered themselves the perpetual

slaves of want and wretchedness. To set up, and miscarry, is like the blast to the blossom; if it does not absolutely kill, it leaves it diseased, and the fruit is both worthless and despised. Hold the rein, then, tight on your impatience, and examine the ground over and over again, before you start for the prize. It has been observed, that few or none thrive, who set up the moment they are out of the leading-strings, as it were: hope has too great an ascendency at that time of life, and the stripling is sanguine enough to begin where his old master left off. But the ship that sets out with all sail, and no ballast, is sure to turn bottom upwards; and, as we have before more at large laid down, curiosity, pleasure and expense have so strong an influence upon the inexperienced mind, that solicitude and application, though the best friends a tradesman has, are dismissed without a hearing.

Would you, therefore, be prevailed on to tread in the same steps that have carried many through life with credit to themselves, enter for a year or two into the service of the shrewdest and most experienced person of your profession. You will learn more dexterity and address in the procuring and dispatch of business during that interval, than in the whole seven years you had served already. It will, besides, give you leisure to look round for a proper place to settle in, where there is a vacancy in trade, that you may hope to fill with success; as likewise to select those dealers who are likeliest to serve you best on one hand, and to court those customers who are the surest pay, and give the largest orders, on the other. Or, if you are too weary of servitude and dependence, to endure it any longer, enter into partnership with such a one

as is above described; and, though you may expect he will manage so, that the contract shall
rather incline to his advantage, you will be a gainer
upon the whole; thenceforward his experience, his
address, and his sagacity, will be yours; and, for
the sake of his own interest and character, he will
be equally vigilant of yours.

GREAT RENTS.

But, if no such opportunity offers, and you prepare to set out wholly on your own bottom, do not
encumber yourself with a house of a greater rent
than the current profits of your business will
easily pay. Many young beginners have half undone themselves by want of foresight in this one
article. Quarter days are clamorous visitants, and
their dues must be sliced off from the capital
stock, if their product does not swell in proportion
to the demand. Before, therefore, you attempt the
dangerous experiment, make the exactest estimate
possible of the expenses you may incur, and the
prospects you have to make the balance even; and
rather trade within your compass than beyond it :
it is easy to enlarge your risk, but not to contract
it; and, once out of your depth, it is great hazard
if ever you recover your footing any more.

It is a plain but sensible rustic saying, " Eat
your brown bread first;" nor is there a better rule
for a young man's outset in the world. While
you continue single, you may live within as narrow
bounds as you please; and it is then you must begin to save, in order to be provided for the more
enlarged expense of your future family. Besides,
a plain frugal life is then supported most cheerfully; it is your own choice; it is to be justified

on the best and honestest principles of the world;
and you have nobody's pride to struggle with, or
appetites to master, but your own. As you advance in life and success, it will be expected you
should give yourself greater indulgence; and you
may then be allowed to do it both reasonably and
safely.

FINE SHOPS.

Beware likewise of an ostentatious beginning ,
a huge, unwieldy, tawdry sign, and of laying out
as much to adorn a shop as to fill it.   There is,
here and there, a street in all large towns, where
the shops are set out with looking-glasses, carvings,
gildings, columns, and all the ornaments of architecture; where both masters and men are
beaux in their way, and make it a science to in-
veigle customers by their civilities, as well as their
outside finery; and yet more young men of good
fortunes are here wrecked by these prodigal strata-
gems, than in half the town beside; and all for
want of proper forethought in estimating the certain issues and uncertain gains, with proper al-
lowance for unavoidable losses, by some customers
who cannot pay, and others who will not, some
who are above the reach of the law, and others
beneath it.   And truly, from their wretched examples, we have often been induced to conclude, that
young sparks, who set up with a large and affluent
fortune, are not in so sure a road to thrive as those
who are limited to a more scanty pattern : for the
first think they may command fortune, and therefore launch into expenses without fear or wit, nor
believe they can be undone, till it is too late to
prevent it; whereas the last, by being ever in fear

of ruin, make use of all their wit, application, and industry, to be above the danger, and hence get into such a habit of temperance, solicitude, and frugality, as no prosperity can get the better of; whence, in process of time, every dollar becomes a hundred, every hundred a thousand, and the labor of one life enriches a whole family for ages.

SERVANTS.

What next occurs to me, is on the head of servants, who are of much more importance both to your quiet and welfare than you may at first imagine. And, by the way, let me premise to you in general, that they are but too frequently domestic enemies, whose views, designs, and inclinations, are opposite to yours; hating your authority, despising your person, and watching every opportunity to injure you, even to gratify their malice, in defect of other more interesting motives. Such they are in general; and you will find all their little cunning and dexterity will be employed to cheat and impose upon you; for which, in spite of your utmost caution, opportunities will not be wanting, nor will they fail to improve them. Some there are, however, among them, who retain their integrity, who consider their master's interest as their own, and who labor as indefatigably to serve it. And these indeed are diamonds of the first water; nor can their endeavors be too cordially accepted, or too punctually rewarded. Yet even these are not to be trusted too much with the secret of their own strength; importance of any kind being what human frailty is least able to bear. We do not advise you to place an unlimited confidence in any, even the most promising: but,

above all, beware of him who fawns and flatters to
insinuate into your favor: for they are such whom
nature has gifted to deceive, and they study to
make the most of that dangerous talent. We never
knew any of this class who had any thing else in
view; and they have generally such consummate
impudence, that they practise their rogueries,
while they stare you in the face, and ever mean
the most mischief, when they pretend the most
service.

FAMILIARITY WITH THEM.

Though we would have you trust your servants
as your fellow-creatures, however humble their
lot, you should avoid all approaches to an indecent
familiarity with them; for, to a proverb, it is accompanied with contempt, and contempt never
fails to break the neck of obedience; those servants
that are not kept under a proper subjection, being
apter to dispute than obey; which, if you would
preserve your authority, you are not to permit
even in the best.

TRUSTING THEM WITH SECRETS.

Few friends are to be trusted with secrets—servants never, if it is possible to be avoided; for,
once at their mercy, they grow insolent, and make
no difficulty to withhold their service, when they
know you dare not exact it. And what a lamentable figure must that family make, where subordination is reversed, and the master, instead of com-
manding, is forced to obey!

You are farther to observe, that servants are
commonly a barren soil in point of gratitude, and

however lavishly you scatter your favors, seldom think themselves obliged to make any return. Like wild beasts, you may bribe them, for a while, into something like a relenting softness; but upon the first distaste, they return to their natural fierceness, and forget they ever had any reason to be thankful. Besides, they ever interpret your favors as their due, and, though they loudly repine when they are withheld, never make acknowledgments when they are bestowed. In which conceit, the more liberality appears on your side, the more sufficiency breaks out on theirs; and, immediately, on being ruffled, bid you provide yourself.

But, rather than be in a servant's debt, never keep one at all; for if, by way of convenience to yourself, you should run into arrear with them, without making them an instant requital, they will take care to do it for you; and assure yourself, it is no good husbandry to suffer them, in any thing, to be their own carvers.

SERVANTS NOT TO BE OPPRESSED.

Having proceeded thus far to secure you from being injured by them, we shall now drop a hint or two on the other side of the question, to dissuade you from being the aggressor. In order to which, behave to them with mildness and affability, not passionately abusing them, or peevishly cavilling with them, to gratify your own splenetic humor, but giving orders with decency, and reprehending faults with temper, that conviction may wait on the one, and respect on the other. For nothing more impairs authority, than a too frequent or indiscreet exertion of it. If thunder itself was to be continual, it would excite no more terror than the noise of a mill, and we should sleep in tranquillity when it roared the loudest. If ever then you give way to the transports of anger, let it be extremely rare, and never but upon the highest provocation.

SERVANTS TO BE USED WITH LENITY.

If your domestics fall sick in your service, remember you are their patron, as well as their master; and let your humanity flow freely for their preservation; not only remit their labors, but let them have all the assistance of food and physic which the malady requires.

Again, never let your ear be too curious in listening to their conversation. Passages will sometimes occur amongst the best servants, that will argue much levity and little respect; yet are void of rancor; and, as not expected to be overheard, are not fit for your notice or resentment.

In one word, rather exceed your contract with them, than make the least abatement; what is a trifle to you, is of importance to them; and nothing is more reasonable, than to let them be gainers, in proportion to the time they have spent in your service. As we would advise you to keep them close to their business, so we recommend it to you likewise to indulge them, now and then, in certain hours of recreation. Their lives, as well as ours, ought to have their intervals of sunshine; it keeps them in temper, health, and spirits; and is really their due in equity, though you may, politically, bestow it as an act of grace. To conclude on this head, if they have any peculiar whims in their devotions, leave their consciences free; you may take what care you please of their moral conduct; but, in their opinions, they are accountable to none but God themselves.

CHOICE OF A WIFE.

First, with regard to marriage itself. If you incline to venture on this critical state, we charge you to look upon it as a point on which your whole happiness and prosperity depend, and make your choice with a becoming gravity and concern. We charge you, likewise, with equal earnestness, if, by ill fortune or ill conduct, your affairs should be in ruins, not to make marriage an expedient to repair them. We do not know a worse kind of hypocrisy than to draw in the innocent and unsuspecting, by false appearances, to make but one step from ease and affluence, to all the disappointment, shame, and misery of a broken fortune. If, therefore, you must sink, sink alone; nor load yourself with the intolerable reflection, that you have undone a woman who trusted you, and entailed misery on your offspring, who may have reason to look on you with abhorrence, for having cursed them with being.

Till, therefore, you are not only in a thriving way yourself, but have a fair prospect that wedlock will, at least, be no encumbrance to your fortune, never suffer yourself to think of it at all. The portions received with wives, pay so large an interest, by the increase of family expenses, that, in the end, the husband can hardly be said to be a gainer. Do not be deceived, therefore, with that bait; but build on your own bottom; and calculate your charge, as if there was no such thing as a fortune to be depended upon at all.

Which done, proceed in your choice on the following rational principles

Let her be of a family not vain of their name,
or wealth, or connexions; those additions on her
side, being certain matter of insult to defects on
yours; but remarkable for their simplicity of manners, and integrity of life. Let her own character
be clear and spotless, and all her pride be founded
on her innocence.

BEAUTY.

Let her also be alike free from deformity and
hereditary diseases; the one being always, and the
other often entailed on the breed, and witnessing
the father's indiscretion from generation to generation. Neither fix your eyes on a celebrated
beauty: it is a property hard to possess, and
harder to secure. To such a one a husband is but
an appendix: she will not only rule, but tyrannize;
and the least demur to the most capricious of her
humors, will be attended with the keenest upbraid-
ings and invectives, the most cordial repentance
that she threw herself away on one so insensible
of the honor he had received, and the most sincere
resolutions to make herself amends by the first op
portunity.

But do not, for these reasons, wholly despise
harmony of shape, or elegance of features. Women
are called the fair sex, and, therefore, some degree
of beauty is supposed almost indispensable. No
doubt, it is the first object of desire, and what
greatly contributes to continue it fresh and unde-
caying. It is, likewise, often seen to be derived
from the mother to the child; and, therefore, as an
accomplishment universally admired and coveted,
to be esteemed worthy the caresses of the wise, as
well as the pursuit of the libertine for a prey.

M

GOOD NATURE.

What we call good nature, is another ingredient of such importance in a matrimonial state, that, without it, the concord can never be complete, or the enjoyment sincere. On which account, it is both allowable, and even expedient, to make some experiments beforehand, on the temper that is to blend or ferment for life with your own. If you find it fickle and wavering, she will sometimes storm like March, and sometimes weep like April, not only with cause, but for want of it; if sluggish and insensible, her whole life will be a dead calm of insipidity, without joy for your prosperity, concern for your misfortunes, or spirit to assist in preventing the one, or forwarding the other; if testy and quarrelsome, you will cherish a hornet in your bosom, and feel its sting every other moment in your heart; or, if morose and sullen, your dwelling will be melancholy as a charnel-house; and you will be impatient for a funeral, though almost indifferent whether hers or your own. But you must not be too scrupulously exact in this scrutiny; there are none of these jewels without flaws, and the very best method of enduring their faults, is to remove your own.

A GOOD MANAGER.

This, however, bear always in mind, that, if she is not frugal, if she is not what is called a good manager, if she does not pique herself on her knowledge of family affairs, and laying out money to the best advantage, let her be ever so sweetly tempered, gracefully made, or elegantly accomplished, she is no wife for a man of business; and all those otherwise amiable talents, will but open just as many ways to ruin.   We remember, on the wedding night of an acquaintance, where we were guests, a motion was made, to pass an hour at an old game called Pictures and Mottoes; the manner of which, is for every person in turn, as he is called, to furnish out a device for the painter, with a short sentence, by way of explanation.   The bride began it, and addressed herself first to her husband; who readily gave for his conceit, " A yoke of oxen," and for his motto, " Let us draw equally."   This is the only true condition of matrimony; and nothing is more reasonable than that, as one has the whole burden of getting money, the other should make economy her principal study, in order to preserve it.

PORTION.

In the affair of portion, as, on the one hand, your conduct ought to be provident and wary; so, on the other, it ought to be genteel and noble.   Nothing can be more sordid, than to bargain for a wife, as you would for a horse, and advance or demur in your suit, as interest rose or fell; and if she you solicit should betray too strong an attachment to the like mercenary motives, be assured she is too selfish to make either a fast friend, a decent wife, or a tender parent.   Fly from such, therefore, the moment the bargaining spirit displays itself.   But do not fly to one who has nothing but beauty, or, if you please, affection, to recommend her! A fair wife with empty pockets, is like a noble house without furniture, showy, but useless; as an odious one with abundance, resembles fat land in the midst of fens, rich, but uninhabitable. Let an agreeable person, then, first invite your affections, good qualities fix them, and mutual interest tie the indissoluble knot.

Of the two, though, as reasonable happiness is the end of life, if your circumstances will bear it, rather please your fancy in one you like, than sacrifice your domestic peace to the possession of wealth you will never be able to enjoy. But, if the narrowness of your fortune will not allow you such an indulgence, tremble to think of the unavoidable consequences! for if happiness does not consist in abundance, be assured it flies from necessity! and, though the protestations of unextinguishable passion make a very good figure in poetry, they have very little relation to common sense. Besides, though many have flattered themselves, that, by taking a wife out of the arms of affliction, the condescension, the obligation, would warrant a suitable return of gratitude and affection, we have known such as have been miserably disappointed. Few minds are strong enough to bear prosperity: is it a wonder, therefore, that it should turn a weak woman's brain, and that she should make her demands in point of figure, prodigality, and expense, not according to her own birth, fortune, or expectations, but yours?

POOR RELATIONS.

However, if all this is not sufficient to deter you from such a choice, at least take care that she is not surrounded with hungry relations; for, if she is, they will throng about you like horse-leeches; and, by the connivance, artifice, or importunity of your wife, either beg, borrow, or steal your substance, till they have plucked you as bare as the jay in the fable.

But take this along with you: there is not a perfection, either of body or mind, to be met with in low life, which is not to be as easily attained in high; and this is certain, that a great fortune gives no adamantine quality to the heart; and, if opportunity favors, she who has that advantage, and almost every other, may be won by address and assiduity, in as little time, as she who is void of all.

COURTSHIP.

In the affair of courtship nature is the best tutor, and the eloquence of unfeigned passion more persuasive than the most artful strokes of the most accomplished orators.

There is not, however, any thing more necessary, than so to regulate the progress of this insinuating impulse, as to have it thoroughly at your command; for, if you give it too large a scope, instead of being master of it, it will be the master of you; and you will thenceforward lay your weakness so open, and appear so manifestly in the power of your mistress, that the pleasure of tyrannizing will be irresistible, and she will exert her sovereignty to the utmost.

WEDDING-DAY.

Do not distinguish your wedding-day too ostentatiously, or suffer it to pass away without proper marks of acknowledgment. Let it wear a sober smile, such as would become your bride and you for life; not be convulsed with riotous laughter, that leaves tears in the eyes, and heaviness at the heart, as soon as the fit is over.

COMPLAISANCE AFTER MARRIAGE.

Suffer us likewise to remind you, that, though most men marry, few live happily; which manifestly proves, that there is more art necessary to keep the affection alive, than to procure its gratification. But, as this is a point of the highest importance, let us advise you to study it as the science of life. In order to which, do not permit yourself to think cheaply of your wife, or neglect her, because you are secure in possession. It is impossible but a woman must be grievously shocked to see the servile lover transformed at once into the tyrant husband. Assure yourself, there are but very few steps between indifference, neglect, contempt, and aversion. And, therefore, if you have any respect for your own repose, let your first transports be moderate; and, when over, do not so much as with a look betray either satiety or repentance; but let the same cheerfulness appear on your brow, the same tenderness in your eyes, the same obliging turn in your behavior, and give her daily and hourly proof, if possible, that she is as dear to you as ever. Above all things, never let her imagine it is a penance to you to stay at home, or that you prefer any company whatever to hers; but, on the contrary, let her share with you in all your pleasures, and find frequent opportunities to induce her to think it will be her own fault if she is not the happiest woman in the world. By these means she will not only dread to lose your favor, but, from inclination and gratitude, endeavor to preserve it. Those husbands are fools who think to terrify their wives into subjection; for, whatever is yielded through compulsion will be resumed as soon as ever occasion offers; and those that restrain the unwilling, experience as much trouble to keep them in obedience, as pleasure in being obeyed.

But, if ever this delightful calm should be ruffled by any little escape of peevishness or anger, do not widen the breach with bitter expressions, or give way to a dogged sullenness, that may prolong resentment till it becomes unappeasable. Where frailty is mutual, offences will be the same; and so should forbearance and forgiveness too: Love, like charity, should cover a multitude of sins; and there is no room for malice in the heart which harbors that amiable guest. Interpret favorably, then, every incident that provokes your disgust: if obliged to complain, do it gently and dispassionately, and gladly receive the first acknowledgment as a very sufficient atonement. Nor vainly and obstinately insist on her submitting first. Depend upon it, the most obstinate of the two is the most foolish; and it will be for your credit, that the odds of wisdom should be on your side. To say the truth, no woman would marry if she expected to be a slave, and there can be no freedom where there is no will: in all trifling matters, then, leave her to her own discretion; it will be of advantage to you on more important occasions, and she will cheerfully forbear interfering in your province, if she finds herself undisturbed in her own.

As to what remains, have but one table, one purse, and one bed; either separate, will be attended with separate interests; and there cannot be too many ties to strengthen a union, which.

though calculated to last for life, is of such a cob
web kind, as often to wear out before the honey
moon.

We conclude on these domestic articles, with
advising you to be modest in the furniture of your
house, and not over-curious in your bills of fare.
Let there be always such plenty, that, if any accidental guest drop in, you need not blush, or apolo-
gize for his entertainment; but no superfluity at
your own board, or waste at your servants'. Even
when you entertain, which should be as seldom as
possible, do not swell out the pride of a day to such
an exorbitant size, as to make a reduction of your
expenses necessary for a month to come; but remember your whole life ought to be of a piece:
and that, though you were to entertain a sovereign,
a private man must defray the charge. Neither
think it beneath you to be your own caterer: it
will save you many a dollar at the year's end, and
your kitchen will be much better supplied into the
bargain.

A maxim of the same prudent nature, is to go
to market always with ready money; for, whoever
runs in debt for provisions had better borrow at
ten per cent., and will find it easier to balance his
accounts.

To which may be added, that such idle profusion only excites envy in your inferiors, hatred in
your equals, and indignation in your superiors;
who are, moreover, apt to think every extraordinary item in your banquet is made an article in
their bill; and therefore will incline, with a certain
wit, to *deal* with one who scarce affords himself
necessaries, and *dine* with you.

EDUCATION OF CHILDREN.

As to what concerns the education of your children, recollect your own; recollect the precepts we here present you with for the conduct of your future life, and you cannot be at a loss to render them wise, honest, and thriving men. First, take care of their health; then, their morals; and, finally, of their making their way successfully through the world. Under which last head, we recommend it to you, in the most earnest manner, not only to make them scholars, or even gentlemen, in case your fortune will afford the means, but men of business too. It is the surest way to preserve an estate when got, amass together money enough to purchase one, or keep the wolf of poverty from the door in case of misfortunes. How many descendants of eminent citizens have we seen undone, through a neglect of this rule! who, set up early in polite life, have been even ashamed of their origin, and would, if possible, have disowned their fathers, to whose indulgence and application they owed the very means of living idly and prodigally; the only title they had to be ranked among the gentry!

ADVICE WITH RESPECT TO MANNERS AND BEHAVIOR.

GOOD BREEDING.

Vorn of good breeding, every other qualification will be imperfect, unadorned, and, to a certain degree, unavailing

Good breeding being the result of good sense and good nature, is it not wonderful that people possessed of the one should be deficient in the other? The modes of it, varying according to persons, places, and circumstances, cannot indeed be acquired otherwise than by time and observation; but the substance is everywhere and always the same.

What good morals are to society in general, good manners are to particular ones; their band and security. Of all actions, next to that of performing a good one, the consciousness of rendering a civility is the most grateful.

We seldom see a person, let him be ever so illbred, wanting in respect to those whom he acknowledges to be his superiors; the manner of showing this respect, then, is all we contend for. The well-bred man expresses it naturally and easily, while he who is unused to good company expresses it awkwardly. Study, then, to show that respect, which every one wishes to show, in an easy and graceful way: but this must be learnt by observation.

In company with your equals, or in mixed companies, a greater latitude may be taken in your behavior: yet it should never exceed the bounds of decency; for, though no one, in this case, can claim any distinguished marks of respect, every one is entitled to civility and good manners. A man need not, for example, fear to put his hands in his pockets, sit, stand, or occasionally walk about the room; but it would be highly unbecoming to whistle, wear his hat, loosen his garters, or throw himself across the chairs. Such liberties are offensive to our equals and insulting to our inferiors. Easiness of carriage by no means implies inattention and carelessness. No one is at liberty to act, in all respects, as he pleases; but is bound, by the laws of good manners, to behave with decorum.

Let a man talk to you ever so stupidly or frivolously, not to pay some attention to what he says is savageness to the greatest degree. Nay, if he even force his conversation to you, it is worse than rudeness not to listen to him; for your inattention, in this case, tells him, in express terms, that you think him a blockhead, and not worth the hearing. Besides, you never can conciliate a person's affections more than by listening to him. Now, if such behavior is rude to men, it is much more so to women, who, be their rank what it will, have, on account of their sex, a claim to officious attention from the men. Their little wants and whims, their likes and dislikes, and even their impertinences, are particularly attended to and flattered, and their very thoughts and wishes guessed at, and instantly gratified, by every well-bred man.

In promiscuous companies, you should vary your address, agreeably to the different ages of the persons you speak to. It would be rude and absurd to talk of your amusements, or your pleasures, to men of certain dignity and gravity, to clergymen, or men in years; but still you should be as easy with them as with others, your manner only should be varied; you should, if possible, double your respect and attention to them; and were you to insinuate, occasionally, that by their observation and experience you wish to profit, you would insensibly win their esteem; for flattery, if not fulsome and gross, is agreeable to all.

When invited to dinner or supper, be there always in time: never usurp to yourself the best places, the best dishes, &c.; but always decline them, and offer them to others, except, indeed, you are offered any thing by a superior, when it would be a rudeness, if you liked it, not to accept it immediately, without the least apology. Thus, for example, was a superior, the master of the table, to offer you a thing of which there was but one, to pass it to the person next you would be indirectly charging him that offered it to you with a want of good manners and proper respect to his company; or, if you were the only stranger present, it would be a rudeness if you made a feint of refusing it, with the customary apology, "I can not think of taking it from you, sir;" or, "I am sorry to deprive you of it;" as it is supposed he is conscious of his own rank, and, if he chose not to give it, would not have offered it; your apology, therefore, in this case, is putting him upon an equality with yourself. In like manner, it is rudeness to draw back, when requested by a superior to pass a door first, or to step into a carriage before him. In short, it would be endless to particularize all the instances in which a well-bred man shows his politeness in good company, such as not yawning, singing, whistling, lounging, putting his legs upon the chairs, and the like familiarities, which every man's good sense must condemn, and good breeding abhor.

But good breeding consists in more than merely not being ill-bred. To return a bow, speak when you are spoken to, and say nothing rude, are such negative acts of good breeding, that they are little more than not being a brute. Would it not be a very poor commendation of any man's cleanliness, to say, that he was not offensive? If we wish for the good will and esteem of our acquaintance, our good breeding must be active, cheerful, officious, and seducing.

For example, should you invite any one to dine or sup with you, recollect whether ever you had observed them to prefer one thing to another, and endeavor to procure that thing ; when at table, say, "At such a time, I think you seemed to give this dish a preference, I therefore ordered it. This is the wine I observed you best like, I have therefore been at some pains to procure it." Trifling as these things may appear, they prove an attention to the person they are said to ; and as attention in trifles is the test of respect, the compliment will not be lost.

We need only refer you to your own breast. How have these little attentions, when shown to you by others, flattered that self-love which no man is free from ? They incline and attach us to that person, and prejudice us afterwards to all that he says or does. The declarations of the women in a great degree stamp a man's reputation of being either ill or well bred ; you must then, in a manner, over- whelm them with these attentions ; they are used to them, and naturally expect them ; and, to do them justice, they are seldom lost upon them. You must be sedulous to wait upon them, pick up with alacrity any thing they drop, and be very officious in procuring their carriages or their chairs in pub- lic places ; be blind to what you should not see, and deaf to what you should not hear. Opportuni- ties of showing these attentions are continually presenting themselves ; but in case they should not, you must study to create them.

If ever you would be esteemed by the women, your conversation to them should be always re- spectful and lively. Every thing you say or do

should tend to show a regard to their beauty or
good sense: even men are not without their vani-
ties of one kind or other, and flattering that vanity,
by words and looks of approbation, is one of the
principal characters of good breeding.   In female
conversation be as pleasant as possible: the very
name of an argument frightens a woman, who is
commonly sooner convinced by a happy turn, or
witty expression, than by any demonstration, or by
all the rules of logic.   You must converse with
them, as a man would with those from whom he
might have expectations, but without making requests.   The great secret, with them, is to be amiable without design; and, whenever you commend,
add your reasons for so doing.   It is this which
distinguishes the approbation of a man of sense
from the admiration of fools and the flattery of
sycophants.

Address and manners, with weak persons, who
are actually three-fourths of the world, are every
thing; and even people of the best understanding
are taken in with them.   Where the heart is not
won, nor the eye pleased, the mind will be seldom
on our side.

In short, learning and erudition, without good
breeding, are tiresome and pedantic: and an ill-
bred man is as unfit for good company as he will
be unwelcome in it.   Nay, he is full as unfit for
business as for company.   Make, then, good breeding the great object of your thoughts and actions.
Be particularly observant of, and endeavor to imitate, the behavior and manners of such as are distinguished by their politeness; and be persuaded,
that good breeding is to all worldly qualifications
what charity is to all Christian virtues: it adorns
merit, and often covers the want of it.

GENTEEL CARRIAGE.

Next to good breeding is a genteel manner and
carriage, wholly free from those ill habits, and
awkward actions, which many very worthy persons are addicted to.

A genteel manner of behavior, how trifling
soever it may seem, is of the utmost consequence
in private life. Men of very inferior parts have
been esteemed, merely for their genteel carriage
and good breeding, while sensible men have given
disgust for want of it. There is something or other
that prepossesses us, at first sight, in favor of a
well-bred man, and makes us wish to like him.

When an awkward fellow, says a witty author,
first comes into a room, he attempts to bow, and
his sword, if he wears one, gets between his legs,
and nearly throws him down. Confused and
ashamed, he stumbles to the upper end of the
room, and seats himself in the very chair he should
not. He there begins playing with his hat, which
he presently drops; and recovering his hat, he lets
fall his cane; and in picking up his cane, down
goes his hat again: thus it is a considerable time
before he is adjusted. When his tea or coffee is
handed to him, he spreads his handkerchief upon
his knees, scalds his mouth, drops either the cup
or the saucer, and spills the tea or coffee in his lap.
At dinner he is more uncommonly awkward : there
he tucks his napkin through a button-hole, which
tickles his chin, and occasions him to make a varie
ty of wry faces; he seats himself upon the edge of
the chair, at so great a distance from the table that
he frequently drops his meat between his plate and
his mouth ; he holds his knife, fork, and spoon, dif

ferently from other people; eats with his knife, to
the manifest danger of his mouth; picks his teeth
with his fork, rakes his mouth with his finger, and
puts his spoon, which has been in his throat a
dozen times, into the dish again. If he is to carve,
he cannot hit the joint, but, in laboring to cut
through the bone, splashes the sauce over every
body's clothes. He generally daubs himself all
over, his elbows are in the next person's plate, and
he is up to the knuckles in soup and grease. If he
drinks, it is with his mouth full, interrupting the
whole company with, " to your good health, sir ;"
and " my service to you;" perhaps coughs in his
glass, and besprinkles the whole table. Further,
he has, perhaps, a number of disagreeable tricks ;
he snuffs up his nose, picks it with his fingers,
blows it, and looks in his handkerchief; crams his
hands first into his bosom, and next into his
breeches. In short, he neither dresses nor acts
like any other person, but is particularly awkward
in every thing he does. All this, we own, has nothing in it criminal; but it is such an offence to
good manners and good breeding, that it is universally despised; it makes a man ridiculous in every
company, and, of course, ought carefully to be
avoided by every one who would wish to please.

From this picture of the ill-bred man, you will
easily discover that of the well-bred; for you may
readily judge what you ought to do, when you
are told what you ought not to do; a little attention to the manners of those who have seen the
world will make a proper behavior habitual and
familiar to you.

Actions that would otherwise be pleasing, frequently become ridiculous by your manner of doing
them. If a lady drops her fan in company, the

worst-bred man would immediately pick it up, and
give it to her; the best-bred man can do no more;
but then he does it in a graceful manner, which is
sure to please; whereas the other would do it so
awkwardly as to be laughed at.

You may also know a well-bred person by his
manner of sitting. Ashamed and confused, the
awkward man sits in his chair stiff and bolt upright; whereas the man of fashion is easy in every
position; instead of lolling or lounging as he sits,
he leans with elegance, and, by varying his attitudes, shows that he has been used to good company. Let it be one part of your study then, to
learn to sit genteelly in different companies, to loll
gracefully, where you are authorized to take that
liberty, and to sit up respectfully, where that free
dom is not allowable.

In short, you cannot conceive how advantageous
a graceful carriage and a pleasing address are,
upon all occasions; they ensnare the affections,
steal a prepossession in our favor, and play about
the heart till they engage it.

Now, to acquire a graceful air, you must attend
to your dancing; no one can either sit, stand, or
walk well, unless he dances well. And in learning
to dance, be particularly attentive to the motion of
your arms, for a stiffness in the wrist will make
any man look awkward. If a man walks well,
presents himself well in company, wears his hat
well, moves his head properly and his arms gracefully, it is almost all that is necessary.

There is also an awkwardness in speech, that
naturally falls under this head, and may and ought
to be guarded against; such as forgetting names,
and mistaking one name for another; to speak of
Mr. What-d'ye-call-him, or You-know-who, Mrs.

N

Thingum, What's-her-name, or How-d'ye-call-her, is exceedingly awkward and vulgar. It is the same to address people by improper titles, as *sir* for *my lord;* to begin a story without being able to finish it, and break off in the middle with " I have forgotten the rest."

Our voice and manner of speaking should like-wise be attended to. Some will mumble over their words so as not to be intelligible, and others will speak so fast as not to be understood; and, in do-ing this, will sputter and spit in your face: some will bawl as if they were speaking to the deaf; others will speak so low as scarcely to be heard; and many will put their face so close to yours as to offend you with their breath. All these habits are horrid and disgusting, but may easily be got the better of, with care. They are the vulgar char-acteristics of a low-bred man, or are proofs that very little pains have been bestowed on his educa-tion. In short, an attention to these little matters is of greater importance than you are aware of; many a sensible man having lost ground for want of these little graces, and many, possessed of these perfections alone, having made their way through life, who otherwise would not have been noticed.

CLEANLINESS OF PERSON.

But, as no one can please in company, nowever graceful his air, unless he be clean and neat in his person, this qualification comes next to be consid-ered. For though your clothes be plain, if they be clean, and your linen white, it matters not that they be rich: you will be respectable without it.

Negligence of one's person not only implies an insufferable indolence, but an indifference whether

we please or not. In others, it betrays an insolence and affectation, arising from a presumption
that they are sure of pleasing, without having recourse to those means which many are obliged to
use.

He who is not thoroughly clean in his person,
will be offensive to all he converses with. A particular regard to the cleanness of your mouth,
teeth, hands, and nails, is but common decency. A
foul mouth and unclean hands, are certain marks
of vulgarity; the first is the cause of an offensive
breath, which nobody can bear, and the last is de-
clarative of dirty work; one may always know a
gentleman by the state of his hands and nails.
The flesh at the roots should be kept back, so as to
show the semicircles at the bottom of the nails;
the edges of the nails should never be cut down
below the ends of the fingers, nor should they be
suffered to grow longer than the fingers. When
the nails are cut down to the quick, it is a shrewd
sign that the man is a laborer, to whom long nails
would be troublesome, or that he gets his bread by
fiddling; and if they are longer than his fingers'
ends, and encircled with a black rim, it foretells
he has been laboriously and meanly employed, and
too fatigued to clean himself: a good apology for
want of cleanliness in a laborer, but the greatest
disgrace that can attend a gentleman.

These things may appear too insignificant to be
mentioned; but when it is considered that a thousand little nameless things, which every one feels
but no one can describe, conspire to form that
whole of pleasing, we hope you will not call them
trifling. Besides, a clean shirt and a clean person
are as necessary to health, as not to offend other
people. It is a maxim, which I have lived to see

verified, that he who is negligent at twenty years of age, will be a sloven at forty, and intolerable at fifty.

Neatness of person, we observed, was as necessary as cleanliness ; of course, some attention must be paid to your dress.

Such is the absurdity of the times, that, to pass well with the world, we must adopt some of its customs, be they ridiculous or not.

In the first place, to neglect one's dress, is to affront all the female part of our acquaintance. The women in particular pay an attention to their dress ; therefore to neglect yours will displease them, as it would be tacitly taxing them with vanity, and declaring that you thought them not worth that respect which every body else does. And, as we have mentioned before, as it is the women who stamp a young man's credit in the fashionable world, if you do not make yourselves agreeable to the women, you will assuredly lose ground among the men.

Dress, as trifling as it may appear to a man of understanding, prepossesses on the first appearance, which is frequently decisive. And, indeed, we may form some opinion of a man's sense and character from his dress. Any exceeding of the fashion, or any affectation in dress whatever, argues a weakness in understanding ; and nine times out of ten it will be found so.

We should likewise proportion our dress to our persons ; we cannot be neat without it. Should the fashion make every thing large, a little man is to keep a mediocrity, or he will be laughed at.

Suppose it was the fashion to wear large capes; were a little man to wear a large cape too, he would be nothing but cape; if, when others' hats are broad-brimmed, his should be so too, the man would be lost, and the hat (not he) be thought to walk about the streets; which would be as ridiculous to the eye, as for a painter (contrary to all rules of proportion) to draw a large arm to a little man, or a little leg to a great one.

There are but few young men who do not display some character or other in their dress. Some would be thought fearless and brave : these wear a black cravat, a short coat and waistcoat, and a large hat fiercely cocked, and are *flash* all over. Others paint and powder themselves so much, and dress so finically, as leads us to suppose they are only women in boys' clothes. Now, a sensible man carefully avoids all this, or any other affectation. He dresses as fashionably and as well as persons of the best families and best sense : if he exceeds them, he is a coxcomb; if he dresses worse, he is unpardonable.

Dress yourself fine, then, if possible, or plain, agreeably to the company you are in ; that is, conform to the dress of others, and avoid the appearance of being tumbled. Imitate those reasonable people of your own age, whose dress is neither remarked as too neglected, or too much studied. Take care to have your clothes well made, in the fashion, and to fit you, or you will, after all, appear awkward. When once dressed, think no more of it ; show no fear of discomposing your dress, but let all your motions be as easy and unembarrassed as if you were at home in your dishabille.

ELEGANCE OF EXPRESSION.

Having mentioned elegance of person, we will proceed to elegance of expression.

It is not one or two qualifications alone, that will complete the gentleman: it must be an union of many; and gracefulness of speaking is as essential as gracefulness of person. Every man cannot be an harmonious speaker; a roughness or coarseness of voice may prevent it; but if there are no natural imperfections, if a man does not stammer or lisp, or has not lost his teeth, he may speak gracefully; nor will all these defects, if he has a mind to it, prevent him from speaking correctly.

Nobody can attend with pleasure to a bad speaker. One who tells his story ill, be it ever so important, will tire even the most patient. If you have been present at the performance of a good tragedy, you have doubtless been sensible of the good effects of a speech well delivered; how much it has interested and affected you; and on the contrary, how much an ill spoken one has disgusted you. It is the same in common conversation; he who speaks deliberately, distinctly, and correctly; he who makes use of the best words to express himself, and varies his voice according to the nature of the subject, will always please: while the thick or hasty speaker, he who mumbles out a set of ill-chosen words, utters them ungrammatically, or with a dull monotony, will tire and disgust. Be assured, then, the air, the gesture, the looks of a speaker, a proper accent, a just emphasis and tuneful cadence, are full as necessary to please and to be attended to, as the subject matter itself.

People may talk what they will of solid reasoning and sound sense; without the graces and ornaments of language, they will neither please nor persuade. In common discourse, even trifles, elegantly expressed, will be better received than the best of arguments, homespun and unadorned.

A good way to acquire a graceful utterance, is to read aloud to some friend every day, and beg of him to set you right in case you read too fast, do not observe the proper stops, lay wrong emphasis, or utter your words indistinctly. You may even read aloud to yourself, where such a friend is not at hand, and you will find your own ear a good corrector. Take care to open your teeth when you read or speak, and articulate every word distinctly · which last cannot be done, but by sounding the final letter. But above all, endeavor to vary your voice, according to the matter, and avoid a monotony. By a daily attention to this, it will, in a little time, become easy and habitual to you.

Pay attention also to your looks and your gesture, when talking even on the most trifling subjects; things appear very different according as they are expressed, looked, or delivered.

Now, if it is necessary to attend so particularly to our *manner* of speaking, it is much more so with respect to the *matter*. Fine turns of expression, a genteel and correct style, are ornaments as requisite to common sense, as polite behaviour and an elegant address are to common good manners · they are great assistants in the point of pleasing. A gentleman, it is true, may be known in the meanest garb; but it admits not of a doubt, that he would be better received into good company, genteelly and fashionably dressed, than were he to appear in dirt and tatters.

Be careful, then, of your style upon all occasions; whether you write or speak, study for the best words and best expressions, even in common conversation or the most familiar letters. This will prevent you from speaking in a hurry, than which nothing is more vulgar : though you may be a little embarrassed at first, time and use will render it easy. It is no such difficult thing to express ourselves well on subjects we are thoroughly acquainted with, if we think before we speak ; and no one should presume to do otherwise. When you have said a thing, if you did not reflect before, be sure to do it afterwards ; consider with yourself, whether you could not have expressed yourself better : and if you are in doubt of the propriety or elegance of any word, search for it in some dictionary, or some good author, while you remember it : never be sparing of your trouble while you would wish to improve, and you may be assured, a very little time will make this matter habitual.

In order to speak grammatically, and to express yourself pleasingly, we would recommend it to you to translate often any language you are acquainted with into English, and to correct such translation, till the words, their order, and the periods, are agreeable to your own ear.

Vulgarism in language, is another distinguishing mark of bad company and education. Expressions may be correct in themselves, and yet be vulgar, owing to their not being fashionable ; for language, as well as manners, are both established for the usage of people of fashion.

The conversation of a low-bred man is filled up with proverbs and hackneyed sayings. Instead of observing that tastes are different, and that most

men have one peculiar to themselves, he will give
you,—" What is one man's meat is another man's
poison :" or, " Every one to their liking, as the old
woman said, when she kissed her cow." He has
ever some favorite word, which he lugs in upon all
occasions, right or wrong : such as *vastly* angry,
vastly kind ; *devilish* ugly, *devilish* handsome ; *immensely* great, *immensely* little. In a dispute, he
will tell you that, *I-fackings* such a thing is true ;
and if you warm him a little, he will cry, *odds-bodi-
kins*, you are wrong. Even his pronunciation carries the mark of vulgarity along with it ; he calls
the earth, *yearth ;* finan' ces, *fin' ances ;* he goes
to wards, and not towards such a place. He affects
to use hard words, to give him the appearance of
a man of learning, but frequently mistakes their
meaning ; and seldom, if ever, pronounces them
properly.

All this must be avoided, if you would not be
supposed to have kept company with footmen and
housemaids. Never have recourse to proverbial or
vulgar sayings ; use neither favorite nor hard words,
but seek for the most elegant ; be careful in the
management of them, and depend on it, your labor
will not be lost ; for nothing is more engaging than
a fashionable and polite address.

Were every one to think before they speak, they
would seldom speak improperly ; but the misfortune is, that they speak before they think. As this
therefore is a fault, so is it to be tediously studying
every thing we say. There is a sort of people who
affect to be extremely nice in their language, and
whose words follow so slow, that we often lose the
connexion before we have heard them out. These
men are in constant labor, and we are obliged to
wait till they are delivered of their notions ; they

are made up of phrases and quaint turns, as singular as their gestures and their carriage; and in affecting to be thought men of sense, they become exceedingly ridiculous.

ADDRESS, PHRASEOLOGY, AND SMALL TALK.

In all good company, we meet with a certain manner, phraseology, and general conversation, that distinguish the man of fashion. This can only be acquired by frequenting good company, and being particularly attentive to all that passes there.

When invited to dine or sup at the house of any well-bred man, observe how he does the honors of his table, and mark his manner of treating his company.

Attend to the compliments of congratulation or condolence that he pays; and take notice of his address to his superiors, his equals, and his inferiors: nay, his very looks and tone of voice are worthy your attention, for we cannot please without a union of them all.

There is a certain distinguishing diction that marks the man of fashion, a certain language of conversation, that every gentleman should be master of. Saying to a man just married, " I wish you joy ;" or to one who has lost his wife, " I am sorry for your loss ;" and both, perhaps, with an unmeaning countenance; may be civil, but it is nevertheless vulgar. A man of fashion will express the same thing more elegantly, and with a look of sincerity that shall attract the esteem of the person he speaks to. He will advance to the one, with warmth and cheerfulness, and, perhaps, squeezing him by the hand, will say, " Believe me,

my dear sir, I have scarce words to express the
joy I feel, upon your happy alliance with such or
such a family," &c.; to the other, in affliction, he
will advance slower, and with a peculiar compo-
sure of voice and countenance, begin his compliments of condolence with " I hope, sir, you will do
me the justice to be persuaded, that I am not insensible of your unhappiness, that I take part in
your distress, and shall ever be affected when *you*
are so." Some will tell you, that these are merely
compliments, and as such, it is dissimulation; if
dissimulation in this sense be a fault, it is a fault
on the right side : thus compliments are considered as words of course, and therefore lead into no
error. We are not to expect friendship from every
man we meet, but we may expect civility, and a
polished behaviour. A certain mode of compli-
menting, then, marks the man of fashion from the
vulgar, and we may learn what company the man
has kept, by his words and phrases. Slight, genteel compliments are acceptable, but fulsome ones
are nauseous, and create disgust. It provokes
contempt rather than pity, to hear what solemn expressions of respect and kindness will pass between
men, upon the most trivial occasion : what vast
esteem they have for one, whom perhaps they never
saw before ; how entirely they are devoted to his
service, suddenly, perhaps, and for no reason ; how
infinitely they are obliged to him, and for no benefit ; and how extremely they are concerned for
him, and afflicted too, for no cause. Such trifling
with common sense should be avoided and detested;
we should never compliment away our integrity,
or speak so as to deceive; but the polite diction,
the compliments we are recommending, are mere
complaisances, such as make all conversation agree-

able, and may be defined a constant endeavor to please those we address, so far as we can do it innocently. It renders a superior amiable, an equal agreeable, an inferior acceptable, and makes every one in the company pleased with himself.

Your first address to, and indeed all your conversation with your superiors, should be open, cheerful, and respectful; with your equals, warm and animated; with your inferiors, hearty, free, and unreserved.

There is a fashionable kind of small talk, which, however trifling it may be thought, has its use, in mixed companies: of course, you should endeavor to acquire it. By small talk, we mean a great deal to say on unimportant matters; for example, food, the flavor and growth of wines, and the chit-chat of the day. Such conversation will serve to keep off serious subjects, which might sometimes create disputes.

OBSERVATION OF MANNERS.

As the art of pleasing is to be learnt only by frequenting the best companies, we must endeavor to pick it up in such companies by observation; for it is not sense and knowledge alone, that will acquire esteem; these certainly are the first and necessary foundations for pleasing, but they will by no means do, unless attended with manners and attention.

There have been people who have frequented the first companies all their life-time, and yet have never got rid of their natural stiffness and awkwardness; but have continued as vulgar as if they were never out of a servants' hall: this has been

owing to carelessness, and a want of attention to
the manners and behavior of others.

There are likewise many people who busy themselves the whole day, and who, in fact, do nothing.
They have possibly taken up a book for two or
three hours, yet from a certain inattention, that
grows upon them the more it is indulged, know no
more of the contents, than if they had not looked
into it; nay, it is impossible for any one to retain
what he reads, unless he reflects and reasons upon
it as he goes on. When they have thus lounged
away an hour or two, they will saunter into company without attending to any thing that passes
there; but, if they think at all, are thinking of
some trifling matter that ought not to occupy
their attention ; thence perhaps they go to the play,
where they stare at the company and the lights,
without attending to the piece, the very thing
they went to see. In this manner they while away
their hours, that might otherwise be employed to
their improvement and advantage. This silly sus-
pension of thought they would have pass for *absence of mind*—Ridiculous ! Wherever you are,
let us recommend you to pay an attention to all
that passes ; observe the characters of the persons
you are with, and the subjects of their conversation ; listen to every thing that is said, see every
thing that is done, and (according to the vulgar
saying) have your eyes and your ears about you.

A continual inattention to matters that occur is
the characteristic of a weak mind; the man who
gives way to it is little else than a trifler, a blank
in society, which every sensible person overlooks;
surely what is worth doing deserves to be done
well, and nothing can be well done if not properly
attended to. When one hears a man say, on being

asked about any thing that was said or done in his presence, "that truly he did not mind it," one is ready to knock the fool down. *Why* did he not mind it ?—What had he else to do ?—A man of sense never makes use of this paltry plea; he never complains of a treacherous memory; but attends to, and remembers every thing that is either said or done.

Whenever, then, you go into good company, that is, the company of people of fashion, observe carefully their behavior, their address, and their manner; imitate it as far as in your power. Your attention, if possible, should be so ready as to observe every person in the room at once, their motions, looks, and turns of expression, and that without staring, or seeming to be an observer. This kind of observation may be acquired by care and practice, and will be found of the utmost advantage to you in the course of life.

ABSENCE OF MIND.

Having mentioned absence of mind, let me be more particular concerning it.

What the world calls an absent man, is generally either a very affected one or a very weak one; but whether weak or affected, he is, in company, a very disagreeable man. Lost in thought, or possibly in no thought at all, he is a stranger to every one present, and to every thing that passes; he knows not his best friends, is deficient in every act of good manners, unobservant of the actions of the company, and insensible to his own. His answers are quite the reverse of what they ought to be; talk to him of one thing, he replies as of another. He forgets what he said last, leaves his hat

in one room, his cane in another, and his sword in
a third. Neither his arms nor his legs seem to be
a part of his body, and his head is never in a right
position. He joins not in the general conversation,
except it be by fits and starts, as if awaking from
a dream : this is either weakness or affectation.
His shallow mind is possibly not able to attend to
more than one thing at a time; or he would be
supposed wrapped up in the investigation of some
very important matter. Such men as Sir Isaac
Newton or Mr. Locke might occasionally have
some excuse for absence of mind; it might proceed from that intenseness of thought which was
necessary, at all times, for the scientific subjects
they were studying; but, for a young man, and a
man of the world, who has no such plea to make,
absence of mind is a rudeness to the company, and
deserves the severest censure.

However insignificant a company may be, however trifling their conversation, while you are with
them do not show them, by inattention, that you
think them trifling : that can never be the way to
please; but rather fall in with their weakness than
otherwise; for to mortify, or show the least contempt to those we are in company with, is the
greatest rudeness we can be guilty of, and what
few can forgive.

We never yet found a man inattentive to the
person he feared, or the woman he loved; which
convinces us, that absence of mind is to be got the
better of, if we think proper to make the trial; and
it is always worth the attempt.

Absence of mind is a tacit declaration that those
we are in company with are not worth attending
to; and what can be a greater affront ? Besides,
can an absent man improve by what is said or

done in his presence? No; he may frequent the best companies for years together, and all to no purpose. In short, a man is neither fit for business nor conversation, unless he can attend to the object before him, be that object what it may.

KNOWLEDGE OF THE WORLD.

A knowledge of the world, by our own experience and observation, is so necessary, that without it we shall act very absurdly, and frequently give offence when we do not mean it. All the learning and parts in the world will not secure us from it. Without an acquaintance with life a man may say very good things, but time them so ill, and address them so improperly, that he had much better be silent. Full of himself and his own business, and inattentive to the circumstances and situations of those he converses with, he vents it without the least discretion, says things that he ought not to say, confuses some, shocks others, and puts the whole company in pain, lest what he utters next should prove worse than the last. The best direction we can give you in this matter is, rather to fall in with the conversation of others than start a subject of your own; rather strive to put them more in conceit with themselves than to draw their attention to you.

A novice in life, he who knows little of mankind but what he collects from books, lays it down as a maxim, that most men love flattery; in order, therefore, to please, he will flatter: but how?— Without regard either to circumstances or occasion. Instead of those delicate touches, those soft tints, that serve to heighten the piece, he lays on his colors with a heavy hand, and daubs where he

means to adorn; in other words, he will flatter so
unseasonably, and at the same time so grossly,
that while he wishes to please he puts out of countenance, and is sure to offend. On the contrary,
a man of the world, one who has made life his
study, knows the power of flattery as well as he;
but then he knows how to apply it; he watches
the opportunity, and does it indirectly, by inference,
comparison and hint.

Man is made up of such a variety of matter,
that, to search him thoroughly, requires time and
attention; for, though we are all made of the same
materials, and have all the same passions, yet,
from a difference in their proportion and combina-
tion, we vary in our dispositions; what is agreeable to one is disagreeable to another, and what
one approves of, another will condemn. Reason is
given us to control these passions, but it seldom
does. Application, therefore, to the reason of any
man will frequently prove ineffectual, unless we
endeavor at the same time to gain his heart.

Wherever, then, you are, search into the characters of men; find out, if possible, their foible,
their governing passion, or their particular merit;
take them on their weak side, and you will generally succeed; their prevailing vanity you may
readily discover, by observing their favorite topic
of conversation; for every one talks most of what
he would be thought most to excel in.

The time should also be judiciously made choice
of. Every man has his particular times when he
may be applied to with success, the *mollia tempora
fandi;* but these times are not all day long,—they
must be found out, watched, and taken advantage
of. You could not hope for success in applying to
a man about one business when he was occupied

O

with another; or when his mind was affected with excess of grief, anger, or the like.

You cannot judge of other men's minds better than by studying your own; for, though some men have one foible, and others another, yet men, in general, are very much alike. Whatever pleases or offends you, will, in similar circumstances, please or offend others : if you find yourself hurt when another makes you feel his superiority, you will certainly, upon the common rule of right, *Do as you would be done by*, take care not to let another feel *your* superiority, if you have it; especially if you wish to gain his interest or esteem. If disagreeable insinuations, open contradictions, or oblique sneers, vex and anger you, would you use them where you wished to please? Certainly not. Observe, then, with care, the operations of your own mind, and you may, in a great measure, read all mankind.

We will allow, that one bred up in a cloister or college may reason well on the structure of the human mind; he may investigate the nature of man, and give a tolerable account of his head, his heart, his passions, and his sentiments; but at the same time he may know nothing of him; he has not lived with him, and of course can know but little how those sentiments or passions will work. He must be ignorant of the various prejudices, propensities, and antipathies that always bias, and frequently determine him. His knowledge is acquired only from theory, which differs widely from practice; and if he form his judgment from that alone, he must often be deceived; whereas a man of the world, one who collects his knowledge from personal experience and observation, is seldom wrong; he is well acquainted with the operations of the human mind, examines the heart of man; reads his words before they are uttered; sees his actions before they are performed; knows what will please and what will displease, and foresees the event of most things.

Labor, then, to acquire this intuitive knowledge; attend carefully to the address, the arts, and manners of those acquainted with life, and endeavor to imitate them. Observe the means they take to gain the favor and conciliate the affections of those they associate with; pursue those means, and you will soon gain the esteem of all who know you.

How often have we seen men governed by persons very much their inferiors in point of understanding, and even without their knowing it! A proof that some men have more worldly dexterity than others; they find out the weak and unguarded part, make their attack there, and the man surrenders.

Now, from a knowledge of mankind we shall learn the advantage of two things, the command of our tempers and countenances; a trifling, disagreeable incident shall perhaps anger one unacquainted with life, or confound him with shame; shall make him rave like a madman, or look like a fool: but a man of the world will never understand what he cannot or ought not to resent. If he should chance to make a slip himself, he will stifle his confusion, and turn it off with a jest; recovering it with coolness.

Many people have sense enough to keep their own secrets; but, from being unused to a variety of company, have unfortunately such a tell-tale countenance that it involuntarily declares what they would wish to conceal. This is a great unhappiness, and should, as soon as possible, be got the better of.

That coolness of mind and regularity of countenance which prevents a discovery of our sentiments by our words, our actions, or our looks, is too necessary to pass unnoticed. A man who cannot hear displeasing things without visible marks of anger or uneasiness, or pleasing ones without a sudden burst of joy, a cheerful eye, or an expanded face, is at the mercy of every knave; for either they will designedly please or provoke you themselves, to catch your unguarded looks, or they will thus seize the opportunity to read your very heart, when any other shall do it. You may possibly say, that this coolness must be natural, for, if not, you can never acquire it. We will admit the force of constitution; but people are very apt to blame that for many things they might readily avoid. Care, with a little reflection, will soon give you this mastery of your temper and countenance. If you find yourself subject to sudden starts of passion, determine with yourself not to utter a single word till your reason has recovered itself; and resolve to keep your countenance as unmoved as possible. As a man who, at a card-table, can preserve a serenity in his looks under good or bad luck, has considerably the advantage of one who appears elated with success, or cast down with ill fortune, from our being able to read his cards in his face: so the man of the world, having to deal with one of these babbling countenances, will take care to profit by the circumstance, let the consequence to him with whom he deals be as injurious as it may.

In the course of life we shall find it necessary often to bear with very ill tempers, as we do with copper money for the benefit of commerce, and to put on a pleasing countenance when we are exceedingly displeased ; we must frequently seem friendly when we are quite otherwise. We admit it is difficult to accost a man with smiles whom we know to be our enemy ; but what is to be done ? On receiving an affront, if you cannot be justified in knocking the offender down, you must not notice the offence ; for, in the eye of the world, taking an affront calmly is considered as cowardice.

If fools should at any time attempt to be witty upon you, the best way is not to know their witticisms are levelled at you, but to conceal any uneasiness it may give you : but should they be so plain that you cannot be thought ignorant of their meaning, we would recommend, rather than quarrel with the company, joining even in the laugh against yourself ; allow the jest to be a good one, and take it in seeming good humor. Never attempt to retaliate in the same way, as that would imply you were hurt.

Wrangling and quarrelling are characteristics of a weak mind ; leave that to blockheads, be *you* always above it. Do not enter into sharp contests, and pride yourself in showing, if possible, more civility to your antagonist than to any other in the company ; this will infallibly bring over all the laughers to your side ; and the person you are contending with will be very likely to confess you have behaved handsomely throughout the whole affair.

Experience will teach us, that though all men consist principally of the same materials, as we before noticed, yet, from a difference in their proportion, no two men are uniformly the same : we differ from one another, and we often differ from ourselves; that is, we sometimes do things utterly inconsistent with the general tenor of our characters. The wisest man will occasionally do a weak thing; the most honest man a wrong thing; the proudest man a mean thing; and the worst of men will sometimes do a good thing. On this account, our study of mankind should not be general; we should take a frequent view of individuals; and though we may, upon the whole, form a judgment of the man from his prevailing passion or general character, yet it will be prudent not to determine till we have waited to see the operations of his subordinate appetites and humors.

For example, a man's general character may be that of strictly honest. We would not dispute it, because we would not be thought envious or malevolent; but we would not rely upon this general character, so as to intrust him with our fortune or our life. Should this honest man, as is not uncommon, be a rival in power, interest, or love, he may possibly do things that, in other circumstances, he would abhor; and power, interest, and love, will often put honesty to the severest test, and frequently overpower it. We must then ransack this honest man to the bottom if we wish to trust him, and as we find him, place our confidence accordingly.

There is a kind of short-lived friendship that takes place among young men, from a connexion in their pleasures only; a friendship too often attended with bad consequences. This companion of your pleasures, young and inexperienced, will probably, in the heat of convivial mirth, vow a perpetual friendship, and unfold himself to you without the least reserve; but new associations, change of fortune, or change of place, may soon break this ill-timed connexion, and an improper use may be made of it. Be one, if you will, in young companies, and bear your part like others in the social festivity of youth; nay, trust them with your innocent frolics, but keep the serious matters to yourself; and if you must at any time make *them* known, let it be to some tried friend of great experience; and that nothing may tempt him to become your rival, let that friend be in a different walk of life from yourself.

Were we to hear a man making strong protestations, and swearing to the truth of a thing that is in itself probable, and very likely to be, we should doubt his veracity; for when he takes such pains to make us believe, it cannot be with a good design.

There is a certain easiness or false modesty in most young people, that either makes them unwilling or ashamed to refuse any thing that is asked of them. There is also an unguarded openness about them that makes them the ready prey of the artful and designing. They are easily led away by the feigned friendships of a knave or fool, and too rashly place a confidence in them, that terminates in their loss, and frequently in their ruin. Beware, therefore, of these proffered friendships; repay them with compliments, but not with confidence. Never let your vanity make you suppose that people become your friends upon a slight acquaintance, for good offices must be shown on both sides to create a friendship: it will not thrive unless its love be mutual; and it requires time to ripen it.

There is among young people another kind of friendship merely nominal, warm indeed for the time, but fortunately of short duration. This friendship takes its rise from their pursuing the same course of riot and debauchery; their purses are open to each other, they tell one another all they know, they embark in the same quarrels, and stand by each other on all occasions. We should rather call this a confederacy against good morals and manners, and think it deserves the severest lash of the law; but they have the impudence to call it friendship. However, it is often as suddenly dissolved as it is hastily contracted; some accident disperses them, and they presently forget each other, except it is to betray and laugh at their own egregious folly.

In short, the sum of the whole is, to make a wide difference between companions and friends; for a very agreeable companion has often proved a very dangerous friend.

CHOICE OF COMPANY.

The next thing to the choice of friends is the choice of your company.

Endeavor, as much as possible, to keep good company, and let it be that of your superiors; for you will be held in estimation according to the company you keep. By superiors, we do not mean so much with regard to birth as merit, and the light in which they are considered by the world.

There are two sorts of good company: the one consists of persons of birth, rank, and fashion; the other, of those who are distinguished by some peculiar merit in any liberal art or science: as men of letters, &c.; and a mixture of these is what we would have understood by good company; for it is not what particular sets of persons shall call themselves, but what the people in general acknowlodge to be so, and are the accredited good company of the place.

Now and then persons without either birth, rank, or character, will creep into good company, under the protection of some considerable personage; but, in general, none are admitted of mean degree, or infamous moral character.

In this fashionable good company alone can you learn the best manners and politest language; for, as there is no legal standard to form them by, it is here they are established.

It may possibly be questioned, whether a man has it always in his power to get into good company; undoubtedly, by deserving it he has; provided he is in circumstances which enable him to live and appear in the style of a gentleman. Knowledge, modesty, and good breeding will endear him to all that see him; for without politeness the scholar is no better than a pedant, the philosopher than a cynic, the soldier than a brute, nor any man than a clown.

Though the company of men of learning and genius is highly to be valued, and occasionally coveted, we would by no means have you always found in such company: as they do not live in the world, they cannot have that easy manner and address which we would wish you to acquire. If you can bear a part in such company, it is certainly advisable to be in it sometimes, and you will be the more esteemed in other companies by being so; but do not let it engross you, lest you be considered as one of the *literati*, which, however respectable in name, is not the way to rise or shine in the fashionable world.

But the company which of all others you should carefully avoid, is that which, in every sense of the word, may be called *low :* low in birth, in rank, in parts, and in manners;—the company of those who, insignificant and contemptible in themselves, think it an honor to be seen with *you*, and who will flatter your follies, nay your very vices, to keep you with them.

Though *you* may think such a caution unneces- sary, we do not; for many a young gentleman of sense and rank has been led by his vanity to keep such company, until he has been degraded, vilified, and ruined.

The vanity we mean is, that of being the first of the company. This pride, though too common, is idle to the last degree; nothing in the world lets a man down so much; for the sake of dicta- ting, being applauded and admired by this low company, he is disgraced and disqualified for bet- ter. Depend upon it, in the estimation of mankind, you will sink or rise to the level of the company you keep.

Be it then your ambition to get into the best company; and when there, imitate their virtues, but not their vices.

Imitate, then, only the perfections you meet with; copy the politeness, address, and easy man- ners of well-bred people; and remember, let them shine ever so bright, if they have any vices, they are so many blemishes, which it would be as ridi- culous to imitate as it would to make an artificial wart upon one's face, because some very handsome man had the misfortune to have a natural one upon his.

SUNDRY LITTLE ACCOMPLISHMENTS.

We have had reason to observe before, that various little matters, apparently trifling in themselves, conspire to form the *whole* of pleasing ; as, in a well-finished portrait, a variety of colors combine to complete the piece. It not being necessary to dwell much upon them, we shall content ourselves with just mentioning them as they occur.

1. To do the honors of a table gracefully is one of the outlines of a well-bred man ; and to carve well is an article, little as it may seem, that is useful at least once every day, and the doing of which ill, is not only troublesome to one's self, but renders us disagreeable and ridiculous to others. We are always in pain for a man who, instead of cutting up a fowl genteelly, is hacking for half an hour across the bone, greasing himself and bespattering the company with the sauce. Use, with a little attention, is all that is requisite to acquit yourself well in this particular.

2. To be well received, you must always pay some attention to your behavior at table, where it is exceedingly rude to scratch any part of your body, to spit, or blow your nose, if you can possibly avoid it, to eat greedily, to lean your elbows on the table, to pick your teeth before the dishes are removed, or to leave the table before grace be said.

3. A polite manner in refusing to comply with the solicitations of a company is also very necessary to be learnt ; for a young man who seems to have no will of his own, but does every thing that is asked of him, may be a good-natured fellow, but is a very foolish one. If you are invited to drink, at any man's house, more than you think is wholesome, you may say, " You wish you could, but a little makes you both intoxicated and sick, and that you should only be bad company by doing it ; of course beg to be excused." If desired to

play at cards deeper than you would, refuse it lu
dicrously; tell them, "If you were sure to lose,
you might possibly sit down; but that as fortune
may be favorable, you dread the thought of having
too much money, ever since you found what an encumbrance it was to poor Harlequin, and therefore
you are resolved never to put yourself in the way
of winning more than a certain sum per day."
This light way of declining invitations to vice and
folly is more becoming a young man than philosophical or sententious refusals, which would only
be laughed at.

4. There can be no greater instance of a weak
and pusillanimous temper, than for a man to pass
the whole of his life in opposition to his own un
derstanding, and not dare to be what he thinks he
ought to be, in the order of nature. Nothing betrays a man into so many errors and inconveniences as the desire of not appearing singular; for
which reason it is necessary to form a right idea
of singularity, that we may know when it is laudable and when otherwise. Singularity, then, is
always laudable; when, in contradiction to the
multitude, it adheres to the dictates of honor, conscience, and morality; and is only vicious when it
makes men act contrary to reason, or when it puts
them upon distinguishing themselves by trifles
and follies: for example, it is vicious in a modest
young gentleman, who has not the confidence to
refuse his glass at an entertainment till he grows
so heated and flushed with wine that he takes all
the talk at the table into his own hands, and
abuses every one present: it is vicious in any
young man that is afraid to refuse an invitation to
a tavern to dinner, to drink to excess if desired,
to go into any improper place, or to commit any

other extravagance proposed; and this under a fear of being thought covetous, to have no money, or to be under the control of his parents or friends: when, in fact, his pride should be in the free exercise of his understanding, and in daring to declare his real sentiments upon the occasion. Never suffer yourself, then, to be tempted by the bad examples of other young men, nor be laughed out of what your own judgment tells you is right. Resolution is the foundation of every virtue; without it there is none: even those who may presume to ridicule or laugh at you at first, will soon treat you with greater respect than they do each other, when they perceive that your conduct is always uniform, steady, and firm. Rest assured you will be respected by others when they find that you respect yourself. Let a good resolution, therefore, be your rule of conduct.

5. To write well and correctly, and in a pleasing style, is another part of polite education. Every man who has the use of his eyes and his right hand, can write whatever hand he pleases; nothing is so illiberal as a school-boy's scrawl. We would not have you learn a stiff, formal hand-writing, like that of a school-master, but a genteel, legible, and liberal hand, and be able to write quick. As to the correctness and elegancy of your writing, attention to grammar does the one, and to the best authors the other. Epistolary correspondence should not be carried on in a studied or affected style, but the language should flow from the pen as naturally and easily as it would from your mouth. In short, a letter should be penned in the same style as you would talk to your friend if he were present.

6. If writing will show the gentleman, much

more does spelling well. It is essentially necessary for a gentleman, or a man of letters, as one
mis-spelt word may fix a ridicule on him for the
remainder of his life. Words in books are generally well spelled, according to the orthography of
the age; reading, therefore, with attention, will
teach every one to spell right. It sometimes happens that words are spelt differently by different
authors; but, if you spell them upon the authority
of one in estimation of the public, you will escape
ridicule. Where there is but one way of spelling
a word, by your spelling it wrong you will be sure
to be laughed at. For a *woman* of a tolerable education would laugh at, and despise her lover, if he
wrote to her, and the words were mis-spelled. Be
particularly attentive then to your spelling.

7. There is nothing that a young man, on his
first appearance in life, ought more to dread than
having any ridicule fixed on him. In the estimation even of the most rational men it will lessen
him, but ruin him with all the rest. Many a
man has been undone by a ridiculous nick-name.
The causes of nick-names among well-bred men,
are generally the little defects in manner, air, or
address. To have the appellation of ill-bred, awkward, muttering, left-legged, or any other, tacked
always to your name, would injure you more than
you are aware of; avoid these little defects (and
they are easily avoided), and you need never fear
a nick-name.

8. Secrecy is another characteristic of good
breeding. Be careful never to tell in one company what you see or hear in another; much less
to divert the present company at the expense of
the last. Things apparently indifferent may, when
often repeated, and told abroad, have much more

serious consequences than are imagined. In conversation, there is generally a tacit reliance, that what is said will not be repeated; and a man, though not enjoined to secrecy, will be excluded company, if found to be a tattler: besides, he will draw himself into a thousand scrapes, and every one will be afraid to speak before him.

9. Pulling out your watch in company, unasked, either at home or abroad, is a mark of ill breeding; if at home, it appears as if you were tired of your company, and wished them to be gone; if abroad, as if the hours dragged heavily on, and you wished to be gone yourself. If you want to know the time, withdraw; besides, as the taking of what is called French leave was introduced, that on one person's leaving the company the rest might not be disturbed, looking at your watch does what that piece of politeness was designed to prevent; it is a kind of dictating to all present, and telling them it is time, or almost time, to break up.

10. Among other things, let us caution you against ever being in a hurry; a man of sense may be in haste, but he is never in a hurry; convinced that hurry is the surest way to make him do ill what he undertakes. To be in a hurry, is a proof that the business we embark in is too much for us; it is the mark of little minds, that are puzzled and perplexed when they should be cool and deliberate; they wish to do every thing at once, and are thus unable to do any thing. Be steady, then, in all your engagements; look round you before you begin, and remember that you had better do half of them well, and leave the rest undone, than do the whole indifferently.

11. From a kind of false modesty, most young

men are apt to consider familiarity as unbecoming.
Forwardness, we allow, is so; but there is a decent
familiarity which is necessary in the course of
life. Mere formal visits, upon ceremonious invitations, are not the thing; they create no connex
ion, nor will they prove of service to you: it is the
careless and easy ingress and egress, at all hours,
that secures an acquaintance to our interest:
and this is acquired by a respectful familiarity,
entered into without forfeiting your consequence.

12. In acquiring new acquaintance, be careful
not to neglect your old, for an action of this kind
is seldom forgiven. If you cannot be with your
former acquaintance so often as you used to be,
when you had no others, take care not to give
them cause to think you neglect them; call upon
them frequently, though you cannot stay long with
them; tell them you are sorry to leave them so
soon, and nothing should take you away but certain engagements, which good manners oblige you
to attend to; for it will be your interest to make
all the friends you can, and as few enemies as possible. By friends, we would not be understood to
mean confidential ones; but persons who speak
of you respectfully, and who, consistently with
their own interest, would wish to be of service to
you, and would rather do you good than harm.

13. Another thing we must recommend to you
as characteristic of a polite education, and of having kept good company; namely, a graceful manner of conferring favors. The most obliging things
may be done so awkwardly as to give offence,
whilst the most disagreeable things may be done
so agreeably as to please. One will refuse a favor
asked, more handsomely than another will grant it,
and some there are, who make us ask so often,

give so coldly, and clog their grants with such disagreeable conditions, that the greatest favor would
be, to excuse us from receiving any. It is more
difficult for superiors to conduct themselves in
granting favors to inferiors. To receive a solicita-
tion well, you ought to know to whom you speak,
and be thoroughly acquainted with the matter in
question. To this end, watch and attend; neither
discourage nor flatter with hopes; but hearken,
and, if necessary, bring the solicitor to the point,
always avoiding all appearance of unfavorable pre-
possessions; and, finally, promise nothing but
what you are sure to perform, and give no hopes
but such as are just and reasonable.

14. A few more articles of general advice, and
we have done : the first is on the subject of vanity;
which is the common failing of youth, and as such,
ought to be carefully guarded against. The vanity
we mean, is that which, if given way to, stamps a
man as a coxcomb; a character he will find a difficulty to get rid of, perhaps, as long as he lives.
Now, this vanity shows itself in a variety of shapes;
one man shall pride himself in taking the lead in
all conversations, and peremptorily deciding upon
every subject; another, desirous of appearing successful among the women, shall insinuate the en-
couragement he has met with, and the conquests
he makes, and perhaps boasts of favors he never
received. If he speak truth, he is ungenerous;
if false, he is a villain; but whether true or false,
he defeats his own purposes, overthrows the reputation he wishes to erect, and draws upon himself
contempt in the room of respect. Some men will
boast of the great respect that is paid them upon
all occasions, and the number of invitations sent
them from all quarters. Such will disturb a whole

P

company at their entrance, and beg there may be no ceremony; call themselves the saddest fellows, for disappointing so many places to which they had been invited; and tell you, that out of ten cards they have received for dinners, (though perhaps they have not received one,) they have given yours the preference. Some again are vain enough to think they acquire consequence by alliance or acquaintance with persons of distinguished character or abilities; hence they are eternally talking of their grandfather, Judge such-a-one; their kinsman, Colonel such-a-one; or their intimate friend, Dr. Such-a-one, with whom, perhaps, they are scarcely acquainted. If they are ever found out, (and that they are sure to be, some time or other,) they appear ridiculous and contemptible; but even admitting that what they say be true, what then? A man's intrinsic merit does not arise from an ennobled alliance, or a reputable acquaintance. A rich man never borrows. When angling for praise, modesty is the surest bait. If we wish to shine in any particular character, we must never affect that character. An affectation of courage will make a man pass for a bully; an affectation of wit, for a coxcomb; and an affectation of sense, for a fool. Not that we would recommend bashfulness or timidity; no, we would have every one know his own value, yet not discover that he knows it, but leave his merits to be found out by others.

15. Another thing worthy your attention is, if in company with an inferior, not to let him feel his inferiority; if he discover it himself, without your endeavors, the fault is not yours, and he will not blame you; but if you take pains to mortify him, or to make him feel himself inferior to you in abilities fortune, or rank, it is an insult

that will not readily be forgiven. In point of abilities it would be unjust, as they are out of his power; in point of rank or fortune, it is ill-natured and ill-bred. This rule is never more necessary than at table, where there cannot be a greater insult than to help an inferior to a part he dislikes, or to a part that may be worse than ordinary, and to take the best yourself. If you at any time invite an inferior to your table, you put him, during the time he is there, upon an equality with yourself, and it is an act of the highest rudeness to treat him in any respect slightingly. We would rather double our attention to such a person, and treat him with additional respect, lest he should even suppose himself neglected. There cannot be a greater savageness, or cruelty, or any thing more degrading to a man of fashion, than to put upon, or take unbecoming liberties with *him* whose modesty, humility, or respect, will not suffer him to retaliate. True politeness consists in making every body happy about you; and as to mortify is to render unhappy, it can be nothing but the worst of breeding. Make it a rule rather to flatter a man's vanity than otherwise; make him, if possible, more in love with himself, and you will be certain to gain his esteem; never tell him any thing he may not like to hear, nor say any thing that will put him out of countenance; but let it be your study, on all occasions, to please; this will be making friends instead of enemies, and be a means of serving yourself in the end.

16. Never say an ill-natured thing, nor be witty, at the expense of any one present; nor gratify that idle inclination, which is too strong in most young men, we mean, laughing at or ridiculing the weaknesses or infirmities of others, by way of diverting

the company, or displaying your own superiority
Most people have their weaknesses, their peculiar
likings and aversions. Some cannot bear the sight
of a cat; others, the smell of cheese, and so on.
were you to laugh at these men, for their antipathies, or, by design or inattention, to bring them
in their way, you could not insult them more
You may possibly thus gain the laugh on your
side for the present, but it will make the person,
perhaps, at whose expense you are merry, your
enemy for ever after; and even those who laugh
with you, will, on a little reflection, fear you, and
probably despise you; whereas, to procure what
one likes, and to remove what the *other* hates,
would show them that they were the objects of
your attention, and possibly make them more your
friends than much greater services would have
done. If you have wit, use it to please, and not to
hurt. You may shine, but take care not to scorch.
In short, never seem to see the faults of others.
Though among the mass of men there are, doubtless, numbers of fools and knaves, yet were we to
tell every one of these we meet with, that we know
them to be such, we should be in perpetual war.
We should detest the knave, and pity the fool,
wherever we find him; but we should let neither
of them know, unnecessarily, that we do so; as we
would not be industrious to make ourselves enemies. As one must please others, then, in order
be pleased one's self, consider what is agreeable to
you must be agreeable to them, and conduct yourself accordingly.

17. Raillery in conversation is frequently considered agreeable; but to make it so, a man must
either not know he is rallied, or think never the
worse of himself if he sees it; nor should the rail-

lery be continued too long: and as every one is
not sufficient master of this talent to rally agreeably, it is better never to attempt it. For, as the
first point to be aimed at in society is to gain the
good will of those with whom we converse, by
showing that we are well inclined towards them;
so is it an unpardonable offence to show a man,
that we do not care whether he is pleased or displeased at what we say. Not that we condemn an
innocent jest, provided it does not create uneasiness. To provoke was never the design of jesting;
nor does intimacy or friendship give a privilege to
say things with a design to shock. It is a maxim
in raillery, never to venture on it but with the
polite and witty; for countrymen and fools are
apt to take pet, and fancy you despise and laugh
at them.

18. When any thing curious is produced in
company, it is very ill manners to clap your hands
upon it first; moderate your impatience, and wait
till it comes to your turn; and when you have it
in hand, be cautious of admiring it too much, or
flying out into an extravagant commendation, lest
you should discover a weakness of judgment, or of
not having been used to see curious things; on the
other hand, if the thing shown be really valuable,
you should not be too cold or indifferent in commending it, lest you should be thought to repine at
the felicity of the owner, which is unbecoming
the character of a gentleman.

19. Whispering in company is another act of
ill manners: it seems to insinuate, either that the
persons whom we would not wish should hear,
are unworthy of our confidence, or it may lead
them to suppose we are speaking improperly of
them; on both accounts, therefore, abstain from it.

20. Pulling out one letter after another, and reading them in company, or cutting and paring one's nails, is unpolite and rude. It seems to say, we are weary of the conversation, and are in want of some amusement to pass away the time.

21. To peep over the shoulder of a person reading or writing a letter, or to open any papers you may find on the table of one you go to see, is also rude; it is of a piece with inquiring into the secrets of others. "I would say more to you," says a person writing to his friend, when a rude fellow was peeping into the letter, over his shoulder, "if an inquisitive blockhead was not looking over me." A gentleman will also be careful of going too near any one who is counting of money, or any cabinet or closet open, containing jewels or things of value, lest the owner should show any signs of mistrust, which would be an affront. To turn over any man's books, unless it be in his study, is also a liberty that few persons like; of course, every gentleman will attend to it.

22. Humming a tune to ourselves, drumming with our fingers on the table, making a noise with our feet, and such like, are all breaches of good manners, and indications of contempt for the persons present; therefore they should not be indulged.

23. Staring at any person you meet, full in the face, is also an act of ill manners; it looks as if you saw something wonderful in his appearance; and is therefore a tacit reprehension.

24. Eating quick, or very slow, at meals, is characteristic of the vulgar; the first infers poverty, that you have not had a good meal for some time; the last, if abroad, that you dislike your en.

tertainment; if at home, that you are rude enough to set before your friends what you cannot eat yourself. So again, eating your soup with your nose in the plate is vulgar. If it be necessary, then, to avoid this, it much more so that of,

25. Smelling at the meat while on the fork, before you put it into your mouth. We have seen many an ill-bred person do this, and have been so angry, that we could have kicked him from the table. If you dislike what you have upon your plate, leave it; but on no account, by smelling at, or examining it, charge your friend with putting unwholesome provisions before you.

26. Spitting on the carpet is a nasty practice, and shocking in a man of liberal education. Were this to become general, it would be as necessary to change the carpets, as the table-cloths; besides, it will lead our acquaintance to suppose, that we have not been used to genteel furniture: for this reason alone, if for no other, by all means avoid it. If you must spit, let it be in your handkerchief; and now we are speaking of a handkerchief, we must observe, that it is not decent to offer it to any one to use, be it ever so clean, unless it be expressly desired.

27. We would recommend it to every young gentleman, to avoid taking snuff or chewing tobacco; the latter is characteristic of vulgarity, and the first, though a fashionable affectation, is a filthy practice; they both tend to sully the mouth, and make it look dirty, than which there cannot be a more disagreeable thing. Besides, snuff-takers are generally very dull and shallow people, and have recourse to it merely as a fillip to the brain : by all means, therefore, avoid the filthy custom.

28. If the necessities of nature oblige you at **any**

time to withdraw from the company you are in,
endeavor to steal away unperceived, or make some
excuse for retiring, that may keep your motive for
withdrawing a secret; and, on your return, be
careful not to announce that return, or suffer any
adjusting of your dress, or replacing of your watch,
to say from whence you came. To act otherwise
is indelicate and rude.

29. Let us say a word or two here on indelicate
conversation. Though indecent discourse has
been too much the topic of fashionable men when
together, it is to be hoped, that, like smoking and
swearing, it will soon be excluded from good company; indeed, it is dying away apace; for to betray in a man's talk a corrupted imagination, is
a much greater offence against the conversation
of gentlemen than negligence of dress. It is one
of the first distinctions of a well-bred man, to express every thing that has the most remote appearance of being obscene, in distant phrases and
modest terms; not that this should be carried to
excess, so as to render conversation formal and
precise, but we would, by all means, have coarse
and obscene terms avoided, and have every gentleman remember, that the clothing of his mind is as
necessary to be attended to, as that of his body;
and that when he makes use of coarse and filthy
language, he has dressed himself clean to very little purpose.

30. Keep yourself free from odd tricks or habits;
such as thrusting out your tongue continually,
snapping your fingers, rubbing your hands, sighing
aloud, an affected shivering of your body, gaping
with a noise, like a countryman that has been
sleeping in a hay-loft, or indeed with any noise,
and many others, which we have before noticed

these are imitations of the manners of the mob, and are degrading to a gentleman.

A very little attention will get the better of all these ill-bred habits, and, be assured, you will find your benefit by it.

DIGNITY OF MANNERS.

There is a certain dignity of manner, without which the very best characters will not be valued.

Romping, loud and frequent laughing, punning, joking, mimicry, waggery, and too great and indiscriminate familiarity, will render any man contemptible, in spite of all his knowledge or merit. These may constitute a merry fellow, but a merry fellow was never considered respectable. Indiscriminate familiarity will either offend your superiors, or make you pass for their dependant or toad-eater, and it will put your inferiors on a degree of equality with you, that may be troublesome. Besides, a gentleman should know, that a fine coat is a livery, when the person who wears it discovers no higher sense than that of the meanest servant in his retinue. A joke, if it carries a sting with it, is no longer a joke, but an affront; and even if it has no sting, unless its witticism is delicate and facetious, instead of giving pleasure it will disgust; or, if the company *should* laugh, they will probably do so at the jester rather than the jest.

Punning is a mere playing upon words, and far from being a mark of sense : thus, were we to say such a dress is *commodious*, one of these wags would answer *odious;* or, that, whatever it has been, it is now be-*com odious*. Others will give us an answer different from what we should expect,

without either wit, or the least beauty of thought
as, "Where is Mr. B.?"—"In his clothes, unless
he is in bed." "How does this wine taste?"—"A
little moist, I think." "How is this to be eaten?"
—"With your mouth:" and such like, all which
(you will readily apprehend) are low and vulgar. If your witticisms are not instantly approved by the laugh of the company, do not attempt to be witty in future, for you may take it
for granted the defect is in yourself, and not in
your hearers.

Mimicry, the favorite amusement of weak minds,
has ever been the contempt of noble ones. Never
give way to it yourself, nor encourage it in others;
it is the most illiberal of all buffoonery: it is an
insult on the person you mimic; and insults, as
we have already told you, are seldom forgiven.

A wag is one who laughs at the first thing he
hears; not because it is ridiculous, but because he
is under the necessity of laughing, to keep himself in countenance; and his gaiety consists in a
certain professed ill breeding, as if it were an excuse for a fault, that a man knows he has committed one. Being too shallow to draw any occasion
for merriment out of his own thoughts, his mind
is always prepared to receive some occasion from
others; and rather than not be grinning, he will seek
that occasion at a great distance. He is ever guess-
ing how well such a lady slept last night, what
she dreamt of; and how much such a young fellow
is pleased with himself, on account of a smile from
his sweetheart, or the new-fashioned cut of his
coat. In short, he is a ridiculous fool, whom every
man of sense must secretly despise.

A mimic or a wag, then, being little else than a
buffoon, who will distort his mouth and eyes to

make people laugh, be very careful to avoid the
imputation. Be assured, no one person ever de-
meaned himself to please the rest, unless he wished
to be thought the fiddle or Merry-Andrew of the
company ; and whether this character is respectable we will leave you to judge.

If a man's company is coveted on any other account than his knowledge, good sense, or manners,
he is seldom respected by those who invite him, but
made use of only to entertain. "Let us have such
a one, for he sings a good song," or, "He is always
joking and laughing ;" or, "Let us send for such
a one, for he is a good bottle companion :" these
are degrading distinctions, that preclude all respect
and esteem. Whoever is *had*, (as the phrase is,)
for the sake of any qualification singly, is merely that thing he is *had* for, is never considered
in any other light, and, of course, never properly
respected, let his intrinsic merits be what they
may.

You may possibly suppose this dignity of manners to border upon pride ; but it differs as much
from pride, as true courage from blustering. To
trifle with a good grace, is certainly pleasing, and
marks the man of fashion ; but it requires inven-
tion as well as politeness ; and to play handsomely
on little things cannot be done without a copious
fancy ; it is a kind of creation, making something
of nothing. If you cannot play your part well,
therefore, you had better drop the character.

To praise a person right or wrong is abject flattery, and to consent readily to every thing proposed by a company, be it silly or criminal, is full
as degrading as to dispute warmly upon every
subject, and to contradict upon all occasions. To
preserve dignity, we should modestly assert our

own sentiments, though we politely acquiesce in those of others.

So again, to support dignity of character we should neither be frivolously curious about trifles, nor laboriously intent on small objects, that deserve not a moment's attention; for this implies an incapacity in matters of greater importance.

A good deal likewise depends upon our air, address, and expressions; an awkward address and vulgar expressions infer either a low turn of mind, or a low education.

So also in our salutations, than which nothing is more worthy a gentleman's attention. Some men will salute or address another so coldly as to give offence at the very time they mean to be civil; others, on the contrary, will be so over-obsequious as to be extremely troublesome; so courteous as to venture their very necks to bow out of a coach in full speed; some again, through an insufferable vanity and futility of character, will affect to know every body, and for want of judgment in time and place, will bow and smile in the face of a judge upon the bench; sit in an opposite gallery, and smile in the minister's face as he gets up into the pulpit, and a thousand such insolent and ill-bred things.

Insolent contempt, or low envy, is also incompatible with dignity of manners. Low-bred persons, fortunately lifted up in the world, in fine clothes and equipages, will insolently look down on all those who cannot afford to make as good an appearance; and they openly envy those who perhaps make a better. They also dread the idea of being slighted; of course, are suspicious and captious; are uneasy themselves, and make every body else so about them.

A certain degree of outward seriousness in looks
and actions gives dignity, while a constant smirk
upon the face (that insipid smile or laugh, called a
companionable laugh, which fools have when they
would be civil), and whiffling motions, are strong
marks of futility.

But above all, a dignity of character is to be
acquired best by a certain firmness in all our actions. A mean, timid, and passive complaisance
lets a man down more than he is aware of; but
still his firmness or resolution should not extend
to brutality, but be accompanied with a peculiar
and engaging softness, or mildness. In short, he
should be modest without bashfulness; frank and
affable without impertinence; obliging and com-
plaisant without servility; cheerful and good-hu-
mored without either noise or bluster.

If you discover any hastiness in your temper,
and find it apt to break out into rough and unguarded expressions, watch it narrowly, and endeavor to curb it; for as a gentleman cannot take
an affront, he should be very cautious how he gives
one. Let no complaisance, however, no weak desire of pleasing, no wheedling, urge you to do that
which discretion forbids; but persist and persevere
in all that is right. In your connexions and friendships you will find this rule of use to you. Invite
and preserve attachments by your firmness; but
labor to keep clear of enemies by a mildness of
behavior. Disarm those enemies you may unfortunately have (and few are without them), by a
gentleness of manner, but make them feel the
steadiness of your just resentment; for there is a
wide difference between bearing malice and a determined self-defence; the one is imperious, but
the other is prudent and justifiable.

In directing your servants, or any persons you
have a right to command, if you deliver your orders mildly, and in that engaging manner which
every gentleman should study to do, you will be
cheerfully, and, consequently, well obeyed; but if
tyrannically, you will be very unwillingly served,
if served at all. A cool, steady determination
should show that you *will* be obeyed; but a gentleness in the manner of enforcing that obedience
should make service a cheerful one. Thus will
you be loved without being despised, and feared
without being hated.

RULES FOR CONVERSATION.

Having now given you full and sufficient instructions for making you well received in the
best of companies, nothing remains but that we
should lay before you some few rules for your conduct in such company. Many things on this subject we have mentioned before, but some few matters still remain to be mentioned.

1. Talk, then, frequently, but not long together,
lest you tire the persons you are speaking to; for
few persons talk so well upon a subject as to keep
up the attention of their hearers for any length of
time. Discourse in general ought to be modest
and humble, as full of matter and substance as you
will, but always delivered with respect and deference to the company.

2. Avoid telling stories in company, unless they
are very short indeed, and very applicable to the
subject you are upon; in this case, relate them in
as few words as possible, without the least digres-
sion, and with some apology; as, that you hate the
telling of stories, but the shortness of it induced

you. And if your story has any wit in it, be particularly careful not to laugh at it yourself; it loses half its zest by so doing. Nothing is more tiresome and disagreeable than a long tedious narrative; it betrays a gossipping disposition, and a great want of imagination; and nothing is more ridiculous than to express an approbation of your own story by a laugh.

3. In relating any thing, keep clear of repetitions, or any hackneyed expressions, such as, *says he*, or *says she*. Some people will use these so frequently, as to take off the hearer's attention from the story; as, in an organ out of tune, one pipe shall perhaps sound the whole time we are playing, and confuse the piece so as not to be understood.

4. Digressions, likewise, should be guarded against. A story is always more agreeable without them. Of this kind are, "the gentleman I am telling you of is the son of Mr. Thomas ——, who lives in Harley street;—you must know him—his brother had a horse that won the sweepstakes at the last races—Zounds! if you do not know him, you know nothing." Or, "He was an upright, tall, old gentleman, who wore his own long hair; do not you recollect him?" There are also a species of story-tellers, who are religiously careful of keeping to the truth in every part of their narration, whether it be material or not; as, "I remember it was much about that time that a cousin-german of mine and I were at the Blue Boar Inn: no, I am wrong, it was at the Cross Keys,—but Jack Thompson was there, and he can tell;—however, I am sure it was somewhere thereabouts, for we used to drink a bottle there every evening; but no matter for all that, the thing is the same;—but—"

All this is unnecessary, is very tiresome and provoking, and would be an excuse for a man's behavior, if he was to leave us in the midst of our
narrative. There are others again equally troublesome, who will interrupt the story-teller, and
labor to raise an argument of no consequence
whatever; as, if he says, "I met Mr. Such-a-one
this morning, at nine o'clock, near St. James's, and
he was saying"——the interrupter will cry, " I
must beg your pardon, sir, for that; unwilling as
I am to contradict you, I must take the liberty to
tell you, it must have been after nine, for I saw him
at St. Paul's at that time."

5. Some people have a trick of holding the persons they are speaking to by the button, or the
hand, in order to be heard out; conscious, probably, that their tale is tiresome. Pray, never do
this: if the person you speak to is not as willing
to hear your story as you are to tell it, you had
much better break off in the middle; for if you
tire them once, they will be afraid to listen to you
a second time.

6. Others have a way of punching the person
they are talking to in the side, and at the end of
every sentence, asking him such questions as the
following, "Was not I right in that?—You know
I told you so?—What is your opinion?" and the
like; or, perhaps, they will be thrusting him, or
jogging him with their elbow. For mercy's sake
never give way to this; it will make your company dreaded.

7. Long talkers are frequently apt to single out
some unfortunate man present; generally the most
silent one of the company, or probably him who
sits next them. To this man, in a kind of half-
whisper, will they run on, for half an hour to-

gether. Nothing can be more ill bred. But, if one of these unmerciful talkers should attack you, if you wish to oblige him, we would recommend the hearing him with patience; seem to do so at least, for you could not hurt him more than to leave him in the middle of his story, or discover any impatience in the course of it.

8. Incessant talkers are very disagreeable companions; nothing can be more rude than to engross the conversation to yourself, or to take the words, as it were, out of another man's mouth. Every man in company has an equal claim to bear his part in conversation, and to deprive him of it is not only unjust, but a tacit declaration that he cannot speak so well upon the subject as yourself; you will therefore take it up. And what can be more rude? One would as soon forgive a man that should stop his mouth when he was gaping, as take his words from him while he was speaking them. Now, if this be unpardonable, it cannot be less so,—

9. To help out, or forestall the slow speaker, as if you alone were rich in expressions and he were poor. You may take it for granted, every one is vain enough to think he can talk well, though he may modestly deny it; helping a person out, therefore, in his expressions, is a correction that will stamp the corrector with impudence and ill manners.

10. Those who contradict others upon all occasions, and make every assertion a matter of dispute, betray, by this behavior, an unacquaintance with good breeding. He, therefore, who wishes to appear amiable with those he converses with, will be cautious of such expressions as these: "That cannot be true, sir." "The affair is as I

Q

say." "That must be false, sir." "If what you say is true," &c. You may as well tell a man he lies at once, as thus indirectly impeach his veracity. It is equally as rude to be provoking every trifling assertion with a bet or a wager. "I will bet you fifty of it," and so on. Then make it a constant rule, in matters of no great importance, complaisantly to submit your opinion to that of others; for a victory of this kind often costs a man the loss of a friend.

11. Giving advice unasked is another piece of rudeness; it is, in effect, declaring ourselves wiser than those to whom we give it; reproaching them with ignorance and inexperience. It is a freedom that ought not to be taken with any common acquaintance, and yet there are those who will be offended if their advice is not taken. "Such-a-one," say they, "is above being advised." "He scorns to listen to my advice;" as if it were not a mark of greater arrogance to expect every one to submit to their opinion, than for a man sometimes to follow his own.

12. There is nothing so unpardonably rude as a seeming inattention to the person who is speaking to you; though you may meet with it in others, by all means avoid it yourself. Some ill-bred people, while others are speaking to them, will, instead of looking at or attending to them, perhaps fix their eyes on the ceiling, or some picture in the room, look out of the window, play with a dog, their watch-chain, or cane, or probably pick their nails, or nose. Nothing betrays a more trifling mind than this; nor can any thing be a greater affront to the person speaking; it being a tacit declaration that what he is saying is not worthy of your attention. Consider with yourself how you

would like such treatment, and, we are persuaded, you will never show it to others.

13. Again, nothing is more simple than the pleasure some people take, in what they call speaking their minds. Such a man will say a rude thing for the mere pleasure of saying it, when an opposite behavior, fully as innocent, might have preserved his friend, or made his own fortune for ever. This error is often run into through an affectation of honesty, but, as it seldom fails of giving offence, it should be carefully avoided.

14. Surliness or moroseness is incompatible also with politeness. Such as, should any one say, "He was desired to present Mr. Such-a-one's respects to you;" to reply, "What the devil have I to do with his respects?" "The Governor inquired after you lately, and asked how you did;" to answer, "If he wishes to know, let him come and feel my pulse;" and the like. A good deal of this is often affected; but whether affected or natural it is always offensive. A man of this stamp will occasionally be laughed at as an oddity; but in the end will be despised.

15. We should suppose it unnecessary to advise you to adapt your conversation to the company you are in, and speak seasonably. You would not surely start the same subject, and discourse of it in the same manner with the old and with the young, with an officer, a clergyman, a philosopher, and a lady? No: your good sense would undoubtedly teach you to be serious with the old, gay with the young, and to trifle with the triflers.

16. In female conversation be as pleasant as possible; the very name of an argument frightens a woman, who is generally sooner convinced by a happy turn, or a witty expression, than by demon-

stration, or all the rules of logic. We must converse with them as a man would with those from whom he has an expectation, but without making requests. The great art among them is to be amiable without design, and whenever you commend, add your reasons for so doing. It is this that distinguishes the approbation of a man of sense from the admiration of fools and the flattery of sycophants.

17. Among other seasonable conversation, is carefully to avoid mentioning or reviving any circumstance or expression that may renew the affliction of any one present, or bring disagreeable subjects to their remembrance. How distressing would it be to say to an afflicted parent, "Such a thing happened the day after your son was buried." How mortifying to cry out, "Bless me, how ill you look to-day!" How rude to observe to a lady who would be thought young, "what a while it was, since you had the honor first to know her!" True politeness consists in putting every one in good humor with himself; of course, it is a mark of the greatest ill-breeding to say any thing that mortifies. In short, to speak of entertainments before the indigent, of sound limbs and health before the infirm, of houses and lands before one who has not so much as a dwelling, or of your prosperity before the miserable, is not only unpolite but cruel; and the comparison it gives rise to, between your condition and that of the person you speak to, is excruciating. He also offends against politeness who praises another's singing or touching an instrument, before such as he has obliged to sing or play for his diversion; or who commends another poet in the presence of one who reads him his verses.

18. There are certain expressions which are

exceedingly rude, and yet there are people of liberal education that sometimes use them; as, " You do not understand me, sir." " It is not so." " You mistake." " You know nothing of the matter," &c. Is it not better to say ? " I believe I do not express myself so as to be understood." " Let us consider it again, whether we take it right or not." It is much more polite and amiable to make some excuse for another, even in cases where he might justly be blamed, and to represent the mistake as common to both; rather than charge him with insensibility or incomprehension.

19. If any one should have promised you any thing, and not have fulfilled that promise, it would be very unpolite to tell him, he has forfeited his word; or if the same person should have disappointed you upon any occasion, would it not be better to say, " You are probably so much engaged, that you forgot my affair ;" or, " Perhaps it slipped your memory ;" rather than, " You thought no more about it ;" or, " You pay very little regard to your word ;" for expressions of this kind leave a sting behind them. They are a kind of provocation and affront, and very often bring on lasting quarrels.

20. Be careful not to appear dark and mysterious, lest you should be thought suspicious; than which there cannot be a more unamiable character. If you appear mysterious and reserved, others will be truly so with you; and in this case, there is an end to improvement, for you will gather no information. Be reserved, but never appear so.

21. There is a fault extremely common with some people, which we would have *you* avoid. When their opinion is asked upon any subject, they will give it with such apparent diffidence and

timidity, that one cannot listen to them with any pleasure; especially if they are known to be men of universal knowledge. "Pardon me," says one of this stamp, "if I should not be able to speak to the case in hand so well as might be wished." "I will venture to speak of this matter to the best of my poor abilities and dullness of apprehension." "I fear I shall expose myself, but in obedience to your commands." While they are making these apologies, they interrupt the business and tire the company.

22. Always look people in the face, when you speak to them, otherwise you will be thought conscious of some guilt; besides, you lose the opportunity of reading their countenances, from which you will learn much better the impression your discourse makes upon them, than you can possibly do from their words; for words are at the will of every one, but the countenance is frequently involuntary.

23. If, in speaking to a person, you are not heard, and should be desired to repeat what you said, do not raise your voice in the repetition, lest you should be thought angry at being obliged to repeat what you have said before; it being probably owing to the hearer's inattention. Indeed, loud speaking, at any time, is vulgar and rude; being little else than treating mankind as if they were all deaf.

24. One word only, as to swearing: those who addict themselves to it, and interlard their discourse with oaths, can never be considered as gentlemen; they are generally people of low education, and are unwelcome in what is called good company. It is a vice that has no temptation to

plead, but is, in every respect, as vulgar as it is wicked.

25. Never accustom yourself to scandal, nor listen to it; for though it may gratify the malevolence of some people, nine times out of ten it is attended with great disadvantages. The very persons you tell it to will, on reflection, entertain a mean opinion of you, and it will often bring you into very disagreeable situations. And as there would be no evil speakers if there were no evil hearers, it is in scandal as in robbery, the receiver is as bad as the thief. Besides, it will lead people to shun your company, supposing that you will speak ill of *them* to the next acquaintance you meet.

26. Carefully avoid talking either of your own or other people's domestic concerns. By doing the one you will be thought vain, by entering into the other you will be considered officious. Talking of yourself is an intrusion on the company; your affairs are nothing to them; besides, they cannot be kept too secret. And as to the affairs of others, what are they to you? In talking of matters in which you are not concerned, you are liable to commit blunders, and should you touch any one in a sore part, you may possibly lose his esteem. Let your conversation in mixed companies always be general : and if we resolve to please, let us never speak to gratify any particular vanity or passion of our own, but always with a design to divert or inform those we speak to.

27. Jokes, bon-mots, or the little pleasantries of one company, will not often bear to be told in another ; they are frequently local, and take their rise from certain circumstances a second company may not be acquainted with ; these circumstances,

and of course your story may be misunderstood, or want explaining; and if, after you have prefaced it with, "I will tell you a good thing," the sting should not be immediately received, you will appear exceedingly ridiculous, and wish you had not told it. Never, then, repeat in one place what you hear in another.

28. In most debates, take up the favorable side of the question; however, let me caution you against being clamorous; that is, never maintain an argument with heat, though you know yourself right; but offer your sentiments modestly and coolly; and if this does not prevail, give it up, and try to change the subject, by saying something to this effect: "I find we shall not convince one another, neither is there any necessity to attempt it; so let us talk of something else."

29. Not that we would have you give up your opinion, always; no, assert your own sentiments, and oppose those of others when wrong; but let your manner and voice be gentle and engaging, and in no way affected: but if you contradict, do it with, "I may be wrong, but—I will not be positive, but I really think,—I should rather suppose— If I may be permitted to say"—and close your dispute with good humor, to show that you are neither displeased yourself nor meant to displease the person you dispute with.

30. Acquaint yourself with the character and situations of the company you go into, before you give vent to your tongue; for should you enlarge on some virtue which any one present may notoriously want, or should you condemn some vice which any of the company may be particularly addicted to, they will be apt to think your reflections pointed and personal, and you will be sure to give

offence. This consideration will naturally lead you not to suppose things said in general to be levelled at you.

31. Low-bred people, when they happen occasionally to be in good company, imagine themselves to be the subject of every separate conversation. If any part of the company whispers, it is about them; if they laugh, it is at them; and if any thing is said which they do not comprehend, they immediately suppose it is meant of them. This mistake is admirably ridiculed in one of our celebrated comedies. "I am sure," says Scrub, "they were talking of me, for they laughed consumedly." A well-bred person never thinks himself disesteemed by the company, or laughed at, unless their reflections are so gross that he cannot be supposed to mistake them, and his honor obliges him to resent in a proper manner; however, be assured, gentlemen never laugh at, or ridicule one another, unless they are in joke, or on a footing of the greatest intimacy. If such a thing should happen once in an age, from some pert coxcomb, or flippant woman, it is better not to seem to know it, than to make any reply.

32. It is a piece of politeness not to interrupt a person in his story, whether you have heard it before or not. Nay, if a well-bred man is asked, whether he has heard it; he will answer no, and let the person go on, though he knows it already. Some are fond of telling a story, because they think they tell it well; others pride themselves on being the first tellers of it; and others are pleased at being thought intrusted with it. By answering yes, you would disappoint all these persons. And as we have said before, the greatest proof of politeness is to make every body happy about you, so one

would never deprive a person of any secret satisfaction of this sort, when he could gratify him by one minute's attention.

33. It is an old maxim, "that comparisons are odious." Never, therefore, compare a third person to the one you are speaking to. How dreadful would it be to tell a man, that the person alluded to "was gray-headed, or stooped like him;" or to say to a lady, "I know her well, she is as fat and swarthy as your ladyship!" Equally rude would it be to find fault with, or point out the defects of any one, in the presence of another who labors under the same misfortune. For example, to say, "it ill becomes a lady to pretend to beauty, with such a crooked nose as Mrs. ——'s;" or to cry, "it is pleasant indeed to see a lame person find fault with Miss ——'s dancing," and this before persons having the same imperfections. To deem it ill-bred is speaking too favorably of it; it is insolent and brutish.

34. Be not ashamed of asking questions, if they are such as lead to information; always accompany them with an apology, and you will never be reckoned impertinent. But abrupt questions, without some apology, by all means avoid, as they imply design. There is a way of fishing for facts, which, if done judiciously, will answer every purpose; such as, taking things you wish to know for granted; this will perhaps lead some officious person to set you right. So again, by saying you have heard so and so, and sometimes seeming to know more than you do, you will often get at information which you would lose by direct questions, as these would put people upon their guard, and frequently defeat the end you aim at.

35. Make it a rule never to reflect on any body

of people, for by this means you will create a number of enemies. There are good and bad of all professions—lawyers, soldiers, clergy, or citizens. They are all men, subject to the same passions, differing only in their manner, according to the way they have been bred up. For this reason, it is unjust, as well as indiscreet to attack them as a *corps* collectively. Many a young man has thought himself extremely clever in abusing the clergy. What are the clergy more than other men? Do you suppose a black gown can make any alteration in his nature? Fie, fie! think seriously, and you will never do it.

36. But above all, let no example, no fashion, no witticism, no foolish desire of rising above what knaves call prejudices, tempt you to excuse, extenuate, or ridicule the least breach of morality; but, upon every occasion, show the greatest abhorrence of such proceedings, and hold virtue and religion in the highest veneration.

37. It is a great piece of ill manners to interrupt any person while speaking, by speaking yourself, or calling off the attention of the company to any foreign matter. It is a secret known but to few, yet of no small use in the conduct of life, that when we fall into conversation with any person, the first thing we should consider is, whether that person is more inclined to hear us, or that we should hear him. Therefore, if you resolve to please, and good breeding is the art of pleasing, never, as we said before, speak to gratify any particular vanity or passion of your own, but always with a design either to amuse or inform those you speak to; but remember, that those to whom you speak are the best judges, whether what you say can either amuse or inform them. How disagreea-

ble and impertinent is that character also, who, in coming into company from 'Change, shall interrupt a discourse, by telling you, whether you will hear it or not, how the stocks go; or, if a young fellow from the other end of the town, by exclaiming, how handsome Miss Such-a-one is, because he had just seen her pass.

38. The last thing we shall mention, is that of concealing your learning, except upon particular occasions. Reserve this for learned men, and let them rather extort it from you, than be too willing to display it. Hence you will be thought modest, and to have more knowledge than you really have. Never seem more wise or learned than the company you are in. He who affects to show his learning will be frequently questioned; and if found superficial, will be sneered at; if otherwise, he will be deemed a pedant. Real merit will always show itself, and nothing can lessen it in the opinion of the world, but a man's exhibiting it himself. The word pedantry being seldom rightly understood, we will here explain it. Pedantry proceeds from much reading and shallow understanding; and a pedant, among men of learning and sense, is like an ignorant servant giving an account of a polite conversation. If a man can talk only on one subject, he is a pedant upon that subject, let it be what it will; whether on law, arms, books, or any other: deprive him of his favorite topic, and he has not a word to say; in short, a mere courtier, a mere soldier, a mere scholar, a mere any thing, is an insipid pedantic character, equally ridiculous amongst men of sound learning and good breeding, and consequently ought, in our oehavior, to be carefully avoided.

BEHAVIOR TO SUPERIORS.

THE principles of politeness here laid down, being designed for all classes of youth, it may not be amiss to show them how they are to conduct themselves when in the company of their superiors. Rowe says, " going into the company of great men, is like going into the other world, you ought to stay until you are called."

On paying a visit to a superior, where we are admitted, it is not respectful to enter his apartment, if you can help it, in dirty shoes, or in a great coat : take off your surtout before you enter, and leave it, with your hat, cane, and gloves, if your visit is to be of any length, in the antechamber ; but, if it be merely a visit of respect, or on business, that requires but a short stay, keep your gloves on, if you wear gloves, and your hat and cane in your hand.

If a servant is in the way, wait to be introduced, if not, knock gently ; and when admitted, and desired to sit, take a seat at the lower end of the room, and by no means in a great arm-chair, unless they are all so. If you meet the person you go to visit, in the open air, do not put on your hat until he puts his on, or until he begs you to be covered.

If the person you visit rises to speak to you, or takes off his hat, to bid him be covered, or beg him to sit, is a mark of ill manners ; for, as greater liberties can with propriety be taken by a supe rior towards an inferior, than by an inferior towards a superior, to direct him to be covered, &c., is putting yourself in his place, and him in yours.

If he desires you to sit, do so; if he offers you the upper hand, take it: if he urges you to approach, do it: but, do it all with a seeming reluctance; for, as a well-bred man would give his superior as little trouble as possible, to be too ceremonious is to be impertinent; and if, in the course of conversation, he rises to speak to you, you should do the same.

Your manner, tone of voice, language, and conversation, should be humble, modest, and respectful. To intrude upon, or interrupt the discourse, when a superior is speaking to another, unless you are appealed to, is want of respect; so it is to correct or assist his memory, this being little else than an indirect way of giving him the lie.

Though we have laid it down in this work, that a decent, respectful familiarity is necessary in the course of life, yet we must here observe, that, in the company of our superiors, unless commanded, it ought to be avoided. From a superior to an inferior, familiarity is not only tolerable, but obliging: but from an inferior to a superior, especially where there is no degree of intimacy, it is not only unbecoming, but insolent.

When you wait on a great person, be careful not to make your visit too long. The fool alone is troublesome; a man of sense perceives when he is agreeable or tiresome: he disappears the very minute he would have been thought to have staid too long. If the person you visit condescends to attend you to the door, do not interrupt him, but receive it modestly, as a mark of his respect.

In quitting one room for another, the company walk out according to their rank, the superior first. except he be master of the house, and then he is always the last.

In short, to point out all the particulars of your conduct in order to appear respectful, would be tedious to the last degree; it is best learnt by imitation. A young man should take notice how well-bred people act in company with their superiors, and endeavor, as far as possible, to follow their example.

———————

THE SECRET OF HAPPINESS.

The following observations of the admirable Paley are so full of practical wisdom and good sense, that we cannot refrain from inserting them. They relate to a subject equally interesting to all; but a subject on which the young are particularly apt to form absurd theories and visionary hopes, which, frequently, are not dissipated till it is too late to repair the errors to which they lead.

Let every young man read and ponder well the following chapter on human happiness.

The word *happy* is a relative term: that is, when we call a man happy, we mean that he is happier than some others with whom we compare him; than the generality of others; or than he himself was in some other situation :—thus, speaking of one who has just compassed the object of a long pursuit, " Now," we say, " he is happy;" and in a like comparative sense, compared, that is, with the general lot of mankind, we call a man happy who possesses health and competency.

In strictness, any condition may be denominated happy, in which the amount or aggregate of pleasure exceeds that of pain; and the degree of happiness depends upon the quantity of this excess

And the greatest quantity of it ordinarily attainable in human life is what we mean by happiness, when we inquire or pronounce what human happiness consists in.

In which inquiry I will omit much usual declamation on the dignity and capacity of our nature; the superiority of the soul to the body, of the rational to the animal part of our constitution; upon the worthiness, refinement, and delicacy of some satisfactions, or the meanness, grossness, and sensuality of others; because I hold that pleasures differ in nothing but in continuance and intensity: from a just computation of which, confirmed by what we observe of the apparent cheerfulness, tranquillity, and contentment of men of different tastes, tempers, stations, and pursuits, every question concerning human happiness must receive its decision.

It will be our business to show, if we can,

1. What human happiness does not consist in:
2. What it does consist in.

FIRST, then, happiness does not consist in the pleasures of sense, in whatever profusion or variety they be enjoyed. By the pleasures of sense, I mean, as well the animal gratifications of eating, drinking, and that by which the species is continued, as the more refined pleasures of music, painting, architecture, gardening, splendid shows, theatric exhibitions; and the pleasures, lastly, of active sports, as of hunting, shooting, fishing, &c. For,

1st, These pleasures continue but a little while at a time. This is true of them all, especially of the grosser sort of them. Laying aside the preparation and the expectation, and computing strictly the actual sensation, we shall be surprised to find how inconsiderable a portion of our time they occupy, how few hours in the twenty-four they are able to fill up.

2dly, These pleasures, by repetition, lose their relish. It is a property of the machine, for which we know no remedy, that the organs by which we perceive pleasures are blunted and benumbed by being frequently exercised in the same way. There is hardly any one who has not found the difference between a gratification when new, and when familiar; or any pleasure which does not become indifferent as it grows habitual.

3dly, The eagerness for high and intense delights takes away the relish from all others; and as such delights fall rarely in our way, the greater part of our time becomes, from this cause, empty and uneasy.

There is hardly any delusion by which men are greater sufferers in their happiness than by their expecting too much from what is called pleasure; that is, from those intense delights which vulgarly engross the name of pleasure. The very expectation spoils them. When they do come, we are often engaged in taking pains to persuade ourselves how much we are pleased, rather than enjoying any pleasure which springs naturally out of the object. And whenever we depend upon being vastly delighted, we always go home secretly grieved at missing our aim. Likewise, as has been observed just now, when this humor of being prodigiously delighted has once taken hold of the imagination, it hinders us from providing for, or acquiescing in, those gently soothing engagements, the due variety and succession of which are the only things that supply a vein or continued stream of happiness.

What I have been able to observe of that part

R

of mankind, whose professed pursuit is pleasure
and who are withheld in the pursuit by no restraint of fortune, or scruples of conscience, cor-
responds sufficiently with this account. I have
commonly remarked in such men a restless and
inextinguishable passion for variety; a great part
of their time to be vacant, and so much of it irk-
some; and that, with whatever eagerness and expectation they set out, they become, by degrees,
fastidious in their choice of pleasures, languid in
their enjoyment, yet miserable under the want
of it.

The truth seems to be, that there is a limit at
which these pleasures soon arrive, and from which
they ever afterwards decline. They are by necessity of short duration, as the organs cannot
hold on their emotions beyond a certain length of
time; and if you endeavor to compensate for this
imperfection in their nature by the frequency
with which you repeat them, you suffer more than
you gain, by the fatigue of the faculties, and the
diminution of sensibility.

We have said nothing, in this account, of the
loss of opportunities or decay of faculties, which,
whenever they happen, leave the voluptuary destitute and desperate; teased by desires that can
never be gratified, and the memory of pleasures
which must return no more.

It will also be allowed by those who have expe-
-ienced it, and perhaps by those alone, that pleasure which is purchased by the encumbrance of
our fortune, is purchased too dear; he pleasure
never compensating for the perpetual irritation of
embarrassed circumstances.

These pleasures, after all, have their value; and
as the young are always too eager in their pursuit

of them, the old are sometimes too remiss, that is, too studious of their ease, to be at the pains for them which they really deserve.

Secondly; Neither does happiness consist in an exemption from pain, labor, care, business, suspense, molestation, and "those evils which are without;" such a state being usually attended, not with ease, but with depression of spirits, a tastelessness in all our ideas, imaginary anxieties, and the whole train of hypochondriacal affections.

For which reason, the expectations of those who retire from their shops and counting-houses, to enjoy the remainder of their days in leisure and tranquillity, are seldom answered by the effect; much less of such as, in a fit of chagrin, shut themselves up in cloisters and hermitages, or quit the world, and their stations in it, for solitude and repose.

Where there exists a known external cause of uneasiness, the cause may be removed, and the uneasiness will cease. But those imaginary distresses which men feel for want of real ones (and which are equally tormenting, and so far equally), as they depend upon no single or assignable subject of uneasiness, admit oftentimes of no application of relief.

Hence a moderate pain, upon which the attention may fasten and spend itself, is to many a refreshment: as a fit of the gout will sometimes cure the spleen. And the same of any less violent agitation of the mind, as a literary controversy, a lawsuit, a contested election, and, above all, gaming; the passion for which, in men of fortune and liberal minds, is only to be accounted for on this principle.

Thirdly; Neither does happiness consist in greatness, rank, or elevated station.

Were it true that all superiority afforded pleasure, it would follow, that by how much we were
the greater, that is, the more persons we were
superior to, in the same proportion, so far as depended upon this cause, we should be the happier;
but so it is, that no superiority yields any satisfaction, save that which we possess or obtain over
those with whom we immediately compare ourselves. The shepherd perceives no pleasure in his
superiority over his dog; the farmer, in his superiority over the shepherd; the lord, in his superiority over the farmer; nor the king, lastly, in his
superiority over the lord. Superiority, where there
is no competition, is seldom contemplated; what
most men are quite unconscious of.

But if the same shepherd can run, fight, or
wrestle, better than the peasants of his village; if
the farmer can show better cattle, if he keep a
better horse, or be supposed to have a longer purse,
than any farmer in the hundred; if the lord have
more interest in an election, greater favor at court,
a better house, or larger estate than any noble-
man in the country; if the king possess a more
extensive territory, a more powerful fleet or army,
a more splendid establishment, more loyal subjects,
or more weight and authority in adjusting the
affairs of nations, than any prince in Europe;—in
all these cases, the parties feel an actual satisfaction in their superiority.

Now the conclusion that follows from hence is
this; that the pleasures of ambition, which are
supposed to be peculiar to high stations, are in
reality common to all conditions. The farrier
who shoes a horse better, and who is in greater
request for his skill than any man within ten
miles of him, possesses, for all that I can see, the

delight of distinction and of excelling, as truly and substantially as the statesman, the soldier, and the scholar, who have filled Europe with the reputation of their wisdom, their valor, or their knowledge.

No superiority appears to be of any account, but superiority over a rival. This, it is manifest, may exist wherever rivalships do; and rivalships fall out amongst men of all ranks and degrees. The object of emulation, the dignity or magnitude of this object, makes no difference; as it is not what either possesses that constitutes the pleasure, but what one possesses more than the other.

Philosophy smiles at the contempt with which the rich and great speak of the petty strifes and competitions of the poor; not reflecting that these strifes and competitions are just as reasonable as their own, and the pleasures which success affords, the same.

Our position is, that happiness does not consist in greatness. And this position we make out by showing, that even what are supposed to be the peculiar advantages of greatness, the pleasures of ambition and superiority, are in reality common to all conditions. But whether the pursuits of ambition be ever wise, whether they contribute more to the happiness or misery of the pursuers, is a different question; and a question concerning which we may be allowed to entertain great doubt. The pleasure of success is exquisite; so also is the anxiety of the pursuit, and the pain of disappointment;—and what is the worst part of the account, the pleasure is short-lived. We soon cease to look back upon those whom we have left behind; new contests are engaged in, new prospects unfold themselves; a succession of struggles

is kept up, whilst there is a rival left within the
compass of our views and profession; and when
there is none, the pleasure of the pursuit is at an
end.

II. We have seen what happiness does not consist in. We are next to consider in what it does
consist.

In the conduct of life the greater matter is to
know· beforehand what will please us, and what
pleasure will hold out. So far as we know this,
our choice will be justified by the event. And
this knowledge is more scarce and difficult than
at first sight it may seem to be: for sometimes
pleasures, which are wonderfully alluring and flattering in the· prospect, turn out in the possession
extremely insipid; or do not hold out as we expected: at other times pleasures start up which
never entered into our calculation; and which we
might have missed by not foreseeing: whence we
have reason to believe, that we actually do miss
many pleasures from the same cause. I say to
know " beforehand;" for, after the experiment is
tried, it is commonly impracticable to retreat or
change; beside that shifting and changing is apt
to generate a habit of restlessness, which is destructive of the happiness of every condition.

By the reason of the original diversity of taste
capacity, and constitution, observable in the human species, and the still greater variety which
habit and fashion have introduced in these particulars, it is impossible to propose any plan of happiness which will succeed to all, or any method of
life which is universally eligible or practicable.

All that can be said is, that there remains a presumption in favor of those conditions of life, in
which men generally appear most cheerful and

contented. For though the apparent happiness of mankind be not always a true measure of their real happiness, it is the best measure we have.

Taking this for my guide, I am inclined to believe that happiness consists,

1. In the exercise of the social affections.

Those persons commonly possess good spirits who have about them many objects of affection and endearment, as wife, children, kindred, friends. And to the want of these may be imputed the peevishness of monks, and of such as lead a monastic life.

Of the same nature with the indulgence of our domestic affections, and equally refreshing to the spirits, is the pleasure which results from acts of bounty and beneficence, exercised either in giving money, or in imparting, to those who want it, the assistance of our skill and profession.

Another main article of human happiness is,

2. The exercise of our faculties, either of body or mind, in the pursuit of some engaging end.

It seems to be true, that no plenitude of present gratifications can make the possessor happy for a continuance, unless he have something in reserve—something to hope for, and look forward to. This I conclude to be the case, from comparing the alacrity and spirits of men who are engaged in any pursuit which interests them, with the dejection and *ennui* of almost all, who are either born to so much that they want nothing more, or who have *used up* their satisfactions too soon, and drained the sources of them.

It is this intolerable vacuity of mind which carries the rich and great to the horse course and the gaming table; and often engages them in contests and pursuits, of which the success bears no pro portion to the solicitude and expense with which it is sought. An election for a disputed borough shall cost the parties twenty or thirty thousand pounds each,—to say nothing of the anxiety, humiliation, and fatigue of the canvass; when a seat in the house of commons, of exactly the same value, may be had for a tenth part of the money, and with no trouble. I do not mention this to blame the rich and great (perhaps they cannot do better), but in confirmation of what I have advanced.

Hope, which thus appears to be of so much importance to our happiness, is of two kinds;—where there is something to be done towards attaining the object of our hope, and where there is nothing to be done. The first alone is of any value; the latter being apt to corrupt into impatience, having no power but to sit still and wait, which soon grows tiresome.

The doctrine delivered under this head may be readily admitted; but how to provide ourselves with a succession of pleasurable engagements, is the difficulty. This requires two things: judgment in the choice of *ends* adapted to our opportunities; and a command of imagination, so as to be able, when the judgment has made choice of an end, to transfer a pleasure to the *means:* after which, the end may be forgotten as soon as we will.

Hence those pleasures are most valuable, not which are most exquisite in the fruition, but which are most productive of engagement and activity in the pursuit.

A man who is in earnest in his endeavors after the happiness of a future state has, in this respect, an advantage over all the world; for he has constantly before his eyes an object of supreme im-

portance, productive of perpetual engagement and
activity, and of which the pursuit (which can be
said of no pursuit besides) lasts him to his life's
end. Yet even he must have many ends, besides
the *far end;* but then they will conduct to that,
be subordinate, and in some way or other capable
of being referred to that, and derive their satisfaction, or an addition of satisfaction, from that.

Engagement is every thing : the more significant, however, our engagements are, the better;
such as the planning of laws, institutions, manu-
factures, charities, improvements, public works,
and the endeavoring, by our interest, address, solicitations, and activity, to carry them into effect :
or, upon a smaller scale, the procuring of a main-
tenance and fortune for our families by a course
of industry and application to our callings, which
forms and gives motion to the common occupations
of life ; training up a child ; prosecuting a scheme
for his future establishment ; making ourselves
masters of a language or a science ; improving or
managing an estate ; laboring after a piece of pre-
ferment; and lastly, *any* engagement which is innocent is better than none; as the writing of a
book, the building of a house, the laying out of a
garden, the digging of a fishpond,—even the raising of a cucumber or a tulip.

Whilst our minds are taken up with the objects
or business before us, we are commonly happy,
whatever the object or business be ; when the mind
is *absent* and the thoughts are wandering to some
thing else than what is passing in the place in
which we are, we are often miserable.

3. Happiness depends upon the prudent constitution of the habits.

The art in which the secret of human happiness

in a great measure consists, is to *set* the habits in
such a manner, that every change may be a change
for the better. The habits themselves are much
the same; for whatever is made habitual becomes
smooth, and easy, and nearly indifferent. The return to an old habit is likewise easy, whatever the
habit be. Therefore the advantage is with those
habits which allow of an indulgence in the devia-
tion from them. The luxurious receive no greater
pleasures from their dainties than the peasant does
from his bread and cheese: but the peasant, whenever he goes abroad, finds a feast; whereas the
epicure must be well entertained to escape disgust.
Those who spend every day at cards, and those
who go every day to plow, pass their time much
alike; intent upon what they are about, wanting
nothing, regretting nothing, they are both for the
time in a state of ease: but then, whatever suspends the occupation of the card-player distresses
him; whereas to the laborer every interruption is
a refreshment: and this appears in the different
effects that Sunday produces upon the two, which
proves a day of recreation to the one, but a lamentable burden to the other. The man who has learned
to live alone, feels his spirits enlivened whenever
he enters into company, and takes his leave without regret; another, who has long been accustomed
to a crowd, or continual succession of company,
experiences in company no elevation of spirits, nor
any greater satisfaction than what the man of a
retired life finds in his chimney-corner. So far
their conditions are equal: but let a change of
place, fortune, or situation separate the companion
from his circle, his visitors, his club, common room,
or coffee-house; and the difference and advantage
in the choice and constitution of the two habits

will show itself. Solitude comes to the one clothed
with melancholy; to the other it brings liberty and
quiet. You will see the one fretful and restless, at
a loss how to dispose of his time till the hour comes
round when he may forget himself in bed : the
other, easy and satisfied, taking up his book or his
pipe as soon as he finds himself alone; ready to
admit any little amusement that casts up, or to
turn his hands and attention to the first business
that presents itself; or content, without either, to
sit still, and let his train of thought glide indolently
through his brain, without much use, perhaps, or
pleasure, but without *hankering* after any thing
better, or without irritation. A reader, who has
inured himself to books of science and argumentation, if a novel, a well-written pamphlet, an article of news, a narrative of a curious voyage, or a
journal of a traveller, fall in his way, sits down to
the repast with relish; enjoys his entertainment
while it lasts, and can return, when it is over, to
his graver reading without distaste. Another, with
whom nothing will go down but works of humor
and pleasantry, or whose curiosity must be interested by perpetual novelty, will consume a book
seller's window in half a forenoon; during which
time he is rather in search of diversion than diverted; and as books to his taste are few and short,
and rapidly read over, the stock is soon exhausted,
when he is left without resource from this principal supply of harmless amusement.

So far as circumstances of fortune conduce to
happiness, it is not the income which any man
possesses, but the increase of income, that affords
the pleasure. Two persons, of whom one begins
with a hundred, and advances his income to a
thousand pounds a year, and the other sets off with

a thousand, and dwindles down to a hundred, may, in the course of their time, have the receipt and spending of the same sum of money; yet their satisfaction, so far as fortune is concerned in it, will be very different: the series and sum total of their incomes being the same, it makes a wide difference at which end they begin.

4. Happiness consists in health.

By health I understand, as well freedom from bodily distempers, as that tranquillity, firmness, and alacrity of mind, which we call good spirits; and which may properly enough be included in our notion of health, as depending commonly upon the same causes, and yielding to the same management, as our bodily constitution.

Health, in this sense, is the one thing needful. Therefore no pains, expense, self-denial, or restraint to which we subject ourselves for the sake of health, is too much. Whether it require us to relinquish lucrative situations, to abstain from favorite indulgences, to control intemperate passions, or undergo tedious regimens; whatever difficulties it lays us under, a man, who pursues his happiness rationally and resolutely, will be content to submit.

When we are in perfect health and spirits, we feel in ourselves a happiness independent of any particular outward gratification whatever, and of which we can give no account. This is an enjoyment which the Deity has annexed to life; and it probably constitutes, in a great measure, the happiness of infants and brutes, especially of the lower and sedentary orders of animals, as of oysters, periwinkles, and the like; for which I have sometimes been at a loss to find out amusement.

The above account of human happiness will justify the two following conclusions, which, although found in most books of morality, have seldom, we think, been supported by any sufficient reason :—

FIRST, That happiness is pretty equally distributed amongst the different orders of civil society :

SECONDLY, That vice has no advantage over virtue, even with respect to this world's happiness.

TRAVELLING.

To derive any advantage from travelling, it is not sufficient to pass through different countries; we ought to know how to travel; we ought to make a proper use of our eyes, and turn them toward the most important objects. Many gain less information from travelling than from books: being ignorant of the art of thinking, their understanding is at least directed by the author when they read; whereas in travelling, for want of a guide they can discern nothing. Others do not improve because they do not take pains to acquire information. They are pursuing such different objects, that this never enters into their thoughts; and it is a great chance if they ever see what they do not care whether they see or not.

There is a great difference between travelling to see a country and travelling to see the inhabitants. With virtuosoes the former is always the chief object; the latter is a mere secondary consideration. He who wishes to be a philosopher must follow the very opposite plan. A child observes objects till he is able to observe men: a man ought to begin with studying his fellow-creatures, and then he may inquire into other things if he has leisure.

It is therefore a false conclusion to suppose that travelling is useless, because men do not in general travel with advantage. On the other hand, if the utility of travelling be granted, does it follow that it is desirable for every individual? By no means; travelling is perhaps suited to but very few people. No man should travel who does not possess suffi cient firmness of mind and steadiness of character to hear bad principles without being corrupted, and to see bad examples without copying them.

Travelling confirms the natural bent of the mind, and will either make a man good or bad. For when a man returns from his travels, his character is generally fixed for life; and there are more men come home bad than good, because the majority were inclined to evil before they set off. Young men who are badly brought up contract during their travels all the vices of those with whom they mix, without acquiring one of the vir- tues to which these vices are allied. But those who have really received a good education, whose good dispositions have been well cultivated, and who travel with a sincere desire to improve them- selves, return home better and wiser than they were before.

Whatever is done with design should be done by rule. Travelling, considered as a part of education, should be conducted according to some fixed plan. To travel for travelling sake is only to wander about like a vagabond. To travel for improve- ment is even too vague an object; for mere im- provement, without having some particular object in view, amounts to nothing. We would give a young man some strong motive for improving

himself, and this motive if well chosen will determine the nature of his studies.

One cause which renders travelling so useless
to the majority of the world, is the manner in
which it is conducted. Tutors generally think
more of their own amusement than of the improvement of their pupils. They take them from
city to city, from palace to palace, from assembly
to assembly; or if they happen to be learned themselves, consume their time in running from one
library to another, in visiting antiquities, in searching after old monuments, and in copying old in-
scriptions. In each country they occupy themselves about another age, which is the same thing
as to interest themselves about another country,
and after having been at a great expense to make
the tour of Europe, after having been ruined by
dissipation or tormented by *ennui*, they return
home without having seen any thing truly interesting, and without having gained any useful
knowledge.

All great cities are nearly alike, for there the
people of different nations associate together till
their manners are confounded. It is only at a
considerable distance from the capital, that the
national character can be discovered in its true
colors. The best method then of studying a people is to quit their great cities and observe them in
the distant provinces. Nor is it of any use to see
the apparent forms of government, with all the
parade and different costumes of the kings or chief
magistrates, or to listen to the jargon of their
ministers, if you do not also attend to the effects
they produce on the people and on the different
departments of the administration.

By a young man's spending but a short time in

great cities, of which the morals are generally very bad, he will be less exposed to be corrupted and depraved ; while among the inhabitants of the provinces, whose manners are more innocent and their societies less numerous, he will preserve a sounder judgment, a juster taste, and more amiable manners.

IMPORTANCE OF RELIGIOUS KNOWLEDGE.

RELIGION, on account of its intimate relation to a future state, is every man's proper business, and should be his chief care. Of knowledge in general, there are branches which it would be preposterous in the bulk of mankind to attempt to acquire, because they have no immediate connexion with their duties, and demand talents which nature has denied, or opportunities which Providence has withheld. But with respect to the primary truths of religion, the case is different; they are of such daily use and necessity, that they form not the materials of mental luxury, so properly, as the food of the mind. In improving the character, the influence of general knowledge is often feeble and always indirect; of religious knowledge the tendency to purify the heart is immediate, and forms its professed scope and design. *This is life eternal, to know thee the only true God, and Jesus Christ, whom thou hast sent.* To ascertain the character of the Supreme Author of all things, to know, as far as we are capable of comprehending such a subject, what is his moral disposition, what the situation we stand in towards him, and the principles by which he conducts his administration, will be allowed by every considerate person to be of the highest consequence. Compared to this, all other speculations or inquiries sink into insignificance; because every event that can befall us is in his hands, and by his sentence our final condition must be fixed. To regard such an inquiry with indifference is the mark not of a noble but of an abject mind, which, immersed in sensuality, or amused with trifles, *deems itself unworthy of eternal life.* To be so absorbed in worldly pursuits as to neglect future prospects, is a conduct that can plead no excuse until it is ascertained beyond all doubt or contradiction that there is no hereafter, and that nothing remains but that *we eat and drink, for to-morrow we die.* Even in that case to forego the hope of immortality without a sigh,—to be gay and sportive on the brink of destruction, in the very moment of relinquishing prospects on which the wisest and best in every age have delighted to dwell, is the indication of a base and degenerate spirit. If existence be a good, the eternal loss of it must be a great evil: if it be an evil, reason suggests the propriety of inquiring why it is so, of investigating the maladies by which it is oppressed. Amid the darkness and uncertainty which hang over our future condition, Revelation, by bringing life and immortality to light, affords the only relief. In the Bible alone we learn the real character of the Supreme Being; his holiness, justice, mercy, and truth; the moral condition of man considered in his relation to Him is clearly pointed out; the doom of impenitent transgressors denounced, and the method of obtaining mercy through the interposition of a divine mediator plainly revealed.

S

ANGER.

" BE ye angry, and sin not ;" therefore all anger
is not sinful : we suppose, because some degree of
it, and upon some occasions, is inevitable.

It becomes sinful, or contradicts, however, the
rule of Scripture, when it is conceived upon slight
and inadequate provocations, and when it con
tinues long.

1. When it is conceived upon slight provocations : for, " charity suffereth long, is not easily
provoked."—" Let every man be slow to anger."
Peace, long-suffering, gentleness, meekness, are
enumerated among the fruits of the Spirit, Gal. v.
22, and compose the true Christian temper, as to
this article of duty.

2. When it continues long : for, " let not the sun
go down upon your wrath."

These precepts, and all reasoning indeed upon
the subject, suppose the passion of anger to be
within our power : and this power consists not so
much in any faculty we possess of appeasing our
wrath at the time (for we are passive under the
smart which an injury or affront occasions, and
all we can then do is to prevent its breaking out
into action,) as in so mollifying our minds by
habits of just reflection, as to be less irritated by
impressions of injury, and to be sooner pacified.

Reflections proper for this purpose, and which
may be called the *sedatives* of anger, are the following : The possibility of mistaking the motives
from which the conduct that offends us proceeded ;
how often *our* offences have been the effect of inadvertency, when they were construed into indications of malice ; the inducement which prompted

our adversary to act as he did, and how powerfully
the same inducement has, at one time or other,
operated upon ourselves; that he is suffering perhaps under a contrition, which he is ashamed, or
wants an opportunity, to confess; and how ungenerous it is to triumph by coldness or insult over a
spirit already humbled in secret; that the returns
of kindness are sweet, and that there is neither
honor nor virtue nor use in resisting them;—for
some persons think themselves bound to cherish
and keep alive their indignation, when they find it
dying away of itself. We may remember that
others have their passions, their prejudices, their
favorite aims, their fears, their cautions, their interests, their sudden impulses, their varieties of
apprehension, as well as we: we may recollect
what hath sometimes passed in our own minds,
when we have gotten on the wrong side of a quarrel, and imagine the same to be passing in our adversary's mind now; when we became sensible of
our misbehavior, what palliations we perceived in
it, and expected others to perceive; how we were
affected by the kindness, and felt the superiority
of a generous reception and ready forgiveness;
how persecution revived our spirits with our enmity, and seemed to justify the conduct in ourselves which we before blamed. Add to this, the
indecency of extravagant anger; how it renders
us, whilst it lasts, the scorn and sport of all about
us, of which it leaves us, when it ceases, sensible
and ashamed; the inconveniences and irretrievable
misconduct into which our irascibility has sometimes betrayed us; the friendships it has lost us;
the distresses and embarrassments in which we
have been involved by it; and the sore repent-

ance which, on one account or other, it always costs us.

But the reflection calculated above all others to allay the haughtiness of temper which is ever finding out provocations, and which renders anger so impetuous, is that which the gospel proposes; namely, that we ourselves are, or shortly shall be, suppliants for mercy and pardon at the judgment-seat of God. Imagine our secret sins disclosed and brought to light; imagine us thus humbled and exposed; trembling under the hand of God; casting ourselves on his compassion; crying out for mercy:—imagine such a creature to talk of satisfaction and revenge; refusing to be entreated, disdaining to forgive; extreme to mark and to resent what is done amiss:—imagine, I say, this, and you can hardly frame to yourself an instance of more impious and unnatural arrogance.

The point is, to habituate ourselves to these reflections, till they rise up of their own accord when they are wanted, that is, instantly upon the receipt of an injury or affront, and with such force and coloring, as both to mitigate the paroxysms of our anger at the time, and at length to produce an alteration in the temper and disposition itself.

REVENGE.

ALL pain occasioned to another in consequence of an offence or injury received from him, further than what is calculated to procure reparation or promote the just ends of punishment, is so much revenge.

There can be no difficulty in knowing when we

occasion pain to another; nor much in distinguishing, whether we do so with a view only to the ends of punishment, or from revenge: for, in the one case we proceed with reluctance, in the other with pleasure.

It is highly *probable* from the light of nature, that a passion, which seeks its gratification immediately and expressly in giving pain, is disagreeable to the benevolent will and counsels of the Creator. Other passions and pleasures may, and often do, produce pain to some one; but then pain is not, as it is here, the object of the passion, and the direct cause of the pleasure. This *probability* is converted into a certainty, if we give credit to the Authority which dictated the several passages of the Christian Scriptures that condemn revenge, or, what is the same thing, which enjoin forgiveness.

We will set down the principal of these passages: and endeavor to collect from them, what conduct upon the whole is allowed towards an enemy, and what is forbidden.

" If ye forgive men their trespasses, your heavenly Father will also forgive you: but if ye forgive not men their trespasses, neither will your Father forgive your trespasses."—" And his lord was wroth, and delivered him to the tormenters, till he should pay all that was due unto him; so likewise shall my heavenly Father do also unto you, if ye from your hearts forgive not every one his brother their trespasses."—" Put on bowels of mercy kindness, humbleness of mind, meekness, long-suffering; forbearing one another, forgiving one another, if any man have a quarrel against any: even as Christ forgave you, so also do ye."—" Be patient towards all men; see that none render ev for evil to any man."—"Avenge not yourselves, but rather give place unto wrath: for it is written, Vengeance is mine; I will repay, saith the Lord. Therefore, if thine enemy hunger, feed him; if he thirst, give him drink: for in so doing thou shalt heap coals of fire on his head. Be not overcome of evil, but overcome evil with good."

We think it evident, from some of these passages taken separately, and still more so from all of them together, that *revenge* is forbidden in every degree, under all forms, and upon every occasion. We are likewise forbidden to refuse to an enemy even the most imperfect right; "if he hunger, feed him; if he thirst, give him drink;" which are examples of imperfect rights. If one who has offended us solicit from us a vote to which his qualifications entitle him, we may not refuse it from motives of resentment, or the remembrance of what we have suffered at his hands. His right, and our obligation which follows the right, are not altered by his enmity to us, or by ours to him.

On the other hand, we do not conceive that these prohibitions were intended to interfere with the punishment or prosecution of public offenders. In the eighteenth chapter of St. Matthew, our Savior tells his disciples; "If thy brother who has trespassed against thee neglect to hear the church, let him be unto thee as a heathen man, and a publican." Immediately after this, when St. Peter asked him, "How oft shall my brother sin against me, and I forgive him? till seven times?" Christ replied, "I say not unto thee until seven times, but until seventy times seven;" that is, as often as he repeats the offence. From these two adjoining passages, compared together, we are authorized to conclude, that the forgiveness of an enemy is not inconsistent with the proceeding against him as a public offender; and that the discipline established in religious or civil societies for the restraint or punishment of criminals ought to be upholden.

If the magistrate be not tied down with these prohibitions from the execution of his office, neither is the prosecutor; for the office of the prosecutor is as necessary as that of the magistrate.

Nor, by parity of reason, are private persons withholden from the correction of vice, when it is in their power to exercise it; provided they be assured that it is the guilt which provokes them, and not the injury; and that their motives are pure from all mixture and every particle of that spirit which delights and triumphs in the humiliation of an adversary

Thus, it is no breach of Christian charity to withdraw our company or civility when the same tends to discountenance any vicious practice. This is one branch of that extrajudicial discipline, which supplies the defects and the remissness of law; and is expressly authorized by St. Paul (1 Cor. v. 11): " But now I have written unto you not to keep company, if any man that is called a brother be a fornicator, or covetous, or an idolater, or a railer, or a drunkard, or an extortioner; with such an one, no not to eat." The use of this association against vice continues to be experienced in one remarkable instance, and might be extended with good effect to others. The confederacy amongst women of character, to exclude from their society kept-mistresses and prostitutes, contributes more perhaps to discourage that condition of life, and prevents greater numbers from entering into it, than all the considerations of prudence and religion put together.

We are likewise allowed to practise so much caution, as not to put ourselves in the way of injury, or invite the repetition of it. If a servant or tradesman has cheated us, we are not bound to trust him again: for this is to encourage him in his dishonest practices, which is doing him much harm.

Where a benefit can be conferred only upon one or few, and the choice of the person upon whom it is conferred is a proper object of favor, we are at liberty to prefer those who have not offended us to those who have; the contrary being nowhere required.

Christ, who estimated virtues by their solid utility, and not by their fashion or popularity, prefers this of the forgiveness of injuries to every other. He enjoins it oftener; with more earnestness; under a greater variety of forms; and with this weighty and peculiar circumstance, that the forgiveness of others is the condition upon which alone we are to expect, or even ask, from God, forgiveness for ourselves. And this preference is justified by the superior importance of the virtue itself. The feuds and animosities in families, and between neighbors, which disturb the intercourse of human life, and collectively compose half the misery of it, have their foundation in the want of a forgiving temper; and can never cease, but by the exercise of this virtue, on one side, or on both

DUELLING.

DUELLING as a punishment is absurd; because it is an equal chance, whether the punishment fall upon the offender, or the person offended. Nor is it much better as a reparation; it being difficult to explain in what the *satisfaction* consists, or how it tends to undo the injury, or to afford a compensation for the damage already sustained.

The truth is, it is not considered as either. A law of honor having annexed the imputation of cowardice to patience under an affront, challenges are given and accepted with no other design than to prevent or wipe off this suspicion; without malice against the adversary, generally without a wish to destroy him, or any other concern than to preserve the duellist's own reputation and reception in the world.

The unreasonableness of this rule of manners is one consideration; the duty and conduct of individuals, while such a rule exists, is another.

As to which, the proper and single question is this: whether a regard for our own reputation is, or is not, sufficient to justify the taking away the life of another?

Murder is forbidden; and wherever human life is deliberately taken away, otherwise than by public authority, there is murder. The value and security of human life make this rule necessary; for we do not see what other idea or definition of murder can be admitted, which will not let in so much private violence, as to render society a scene of peril and bloodshed.

If unauthorized laws of honor be allowed to create exceptions to Divine prohibitions, there is an end of all morality, as founded in the will of the Deity; and the obligation of every duty may, at one time or other, be discharged by the caprice and fluctuations of fashion.

" But a sense of shame is so much torture; and no relief presents itself otherwise than by an attempt upon the life of our adversary." What then? The distress which men suffer by the want of money is oftentimes extreme, and no resource can be discovered but that of removing a life which stands between the distressed person and his inheritance. The motive in this case is as urgent, and the means much the same as in the former: yet this case finds no advocate.

Take away the circumstance of the duellist's exposing his own life, and it becomes assassination; add this circumstance, and what difference does it make? None but this, that fewer perhaps will imitate the example, and human life will be somewhat more safe, when it cannot be attacked without equal danger to the aggressor's own. Experience, however, proves that there is fortitude enough in most men to undertake this hazard; and were it otherwise, the defence, at best, would be only that which a highwayman or housebreaker might plead, whose attempt had been so daring and desperate, that few were likely to repeat the same.

In expostulating with the duellist, we all along suppose his adversary to fall. Which supposition we are at liberty to make, because, if he have no right to kill his adversary, he has none to attempt it.

In return, we forbear from applying to the case of duelling the Christian principle of the forgiveness of injuries; because it is possible to suppose the injury to be forgiven, and the duellist to act entirely from a concern for his own reputation: where this is not the case, the guilt of duelling is manifest, and is greater.

In this view it seems unnecessary to distinguish between him who gives, and him who accepts, a challenge: for, on the one hand, they incur an equal hazard of destroying life; and on the other, both act upon the same persuasion, that what they do is necessary, in order to recover or preserve the good opinion of the world.

Public opinion is not easily controlled by civil institutions: for which reason we question whether any regulations can be contrived, of sufficient force to suppress or change the rule of honor, which stigmatizes all scruples about duelling with the reproach of cowardice.

The insufficiency of the redress which the law of the land affords, for those injuries which chiefly affect a man in his sensibility and reputation, tempts many to redress themselves. Prosecutions for such offences, by the trifling damages that are recovered, serve only to make the sufferer more ridiculous.—This ought to be remedied.

For the army, where the point of honor is cultivated with exquisite attention and refinement, we would establish *a Court of Honor*, with a power of awarding those submissions and acknowledgments, which it is generally the purpose of a challenge to obtain; and it might grow into a fashion, with persons of rank of all professions, to refer their quarrels to this tribunal.

Duelling, as the law now stands, can seldom be overtaken by legal punishment. The challenge, appointment, and other previous circumstances which indicate the intention with which the combatants met, being suppressed, nothing appears to a court of justice but the actual rencounter; and if a person be slain when actually fighting with his adversary, the law deems his death nothing more than manslaughter.

WE feel that an apology is due for the unusual length of the following extract. We hope that it will be excused when the reader considers that it is from Paley, and that the precepts it contains are of incalculable importance in directing the conduct of life.

PROMISES.

1. *From whence the obligation to perform prom ises arises.*
2. *In what sense promises are to be interpreted.*
3. *In what cases promises are not binding.*

1. *From whence the obligation to perform prom- ises arises.*

They who argue from innate moral principles suppose a sense of the obligation of promises to be one of them; but, without assuming this, or any thing else, without proof, the obligation to perform promises may be deduced from the necessity of such a conduct to the well-being, or the existence, indeed, of human society.

Men act from expectation. Expectation is in most cases determined by the assurances and engagements which we receive from others. If no dependence could be placed upon these assurances, it would be impossible to know what judgment to form of many future events, or how to regulate

our conduct with respect to them. Confidence,
therefore, in promises is essential to the intercourse
of human life; because, without it, the greatest
part of our conduct would proceed upon chance.
But there could be no confidence in promises if
men were not obliged to perform them: the obligation therefore to perform promises is essential
to the same ends, and in the same degree.

Some may imagine, that if this obligation were
suspended, a general caution and mutual distrust
would ensue, which might do as well: but this is
imagined, without considering how, every hour of
our lives, we trust to and depend upon others; and
how impossible it is to stir a step, or, what is worse,
to sit still a moment, without such trust and dependence. I am now writing at my ease, not
doubting (or rather never distrusting, and therefore never thinking about it,) that the butcher will
send in the joint of meat which I ordered; that
his servant will bring it; that my cook will dress
it; that my footman will serve it up; and that I
shall find it upon table at one o'clock. Yet have
I nothing for all this but the promise of the butcher, and the implied promise of his servant and
mine. And the same holds of the most important
as well as the most familiar occurrences of social
life. In the one the intervention of promises is
formal, and is seen and acknowledged: our instance, therefore, is intended to show it in the
other, where it is not so distinctly observed.

2. *In what sense promises are to be interpreted.*
Where the terms of promise admit of more
senses than one, the promise is to be performed
" in that sense in which the promiser apprehended,
at the time, that the promisee received it."

It is not the sense in which the promiser actually intended it that always governs the interpretation of an equivocal promise; because, at that rate, you might excite expectations which you never meant, nor would be obliged to satisfy. Much less is it the sense in which the promisee actually received the promise; for, according to that rule, you might be drawn into engagements which you never designed to undertake. It must therefore be the sense (for there is no other remaining) in which the promiser believed that the promisee accepted his promise.

This will not differ from the actual intention of the promiser, where the promise is given without collusion or reserve: but we put the rule in the above form, to exclude evasion in cases in which the popular meaning of a phrase, and the strict grammatical signification of the words, differ; or in general, wherever the promiser attempts to make his escape through some ambiguity in the expressions which he used.

Temures promised the garrison of Sebastia, that if they would surrender, *no blood should be shed.* The garrison surrendered; and Temures buried them all alive. Now Temures fulfilled the promise in one sense, and in the sense too in which he intended it at the time; but not in the sense in which the garrison of Sebastia actually received it, nor in the sense in which Temures himself knew that the garrison received it: which last sense, according to our rule, was the sense in which he was in conscience bound to have performed it.

From the account we have given of the obligation of promises, it is evident that this obligation depends upon the *expectations* which we knowingly and voluntarily excite. Consequently, any action or conduct towards another, which we are sensible excites expectations in that other, is as much a promise, and creates as strict an obligation, as the most express assurances. Taking, for instance, a kinsman's child, and educating him for a liberal profession, or in a manner suitable only for the heir of a large fortune, as much obliges us to place him in that profession, or to leave him such a fortune, as if we had given him a promise to do so under our hands and seals. In like manner, a great man, who encourages an indigent retainer; or a minister of state, who distinguishes and caresses at his levee one who is in a situation to be obliged by his patronage; engages, by such behavior, to provide for him.—This is the foundation of *tacit promises.*

You may either simply declare your present intention, or you may accompany your declaration with an engagement to abide by it, which constitutes a complete promise. In the first case, the duty is satisfied if you were *sincere* at the time; that is, if you entertained at the time, the intention you expressed, however soon, or for whatever reason, you afterwards change it. In the latter case, you have parted with the liberty of changing. All this is plain: but it must be observed, that most of those forms of speech, which, strictly taken, amount to no more than declarations of present intention, do yet, in the usual way of understanding them, excite the expectation, and therefore carry with them the force of absolute promises. Such as, " I intend you this place"—" I design to leave you this estate"—" I purpose giving you my vote"—" I mean to serve you." In which, although the " intention," the " design," the " purpose," the " meaning," be expressed in words of the present time yet you cannot afterwards recede from them without a breach of good faith. If you choose therefore to make known your present intention, and yet to reserve to yourself the liberty of changing it, you must guard your expressions by an additional clause, as, " I intend *at present*,"—" *If I do not alter*,"—or the like. And after all, as there can be no reason for communicating your intention, but to excite some degree of expectation or other, a wanton change of an intention which is once disclosed, always disappoints somebody ; and is always for that reason wrong.

There is, in some men, an infirmity with regard to promises, which often betrays them into great distress. From the confusion, or hesitation, or obscurity, with which they express themselves, especially when overawed or taken by surprise, they sometimes encourage expectations, and bring upon themselves demands, which, possibly, they never dreamed of. This is a want, not so much of integrity as of presence of mind.

3. *In what cases promises are not binding.*

1. Promises are not binding where the performance is *impossible*.

But observe, that the promiser is guilty of a fraud, if he be secretly aware of the impossibility at the time of making the promise. For, when any one promises a thing, he asserts his belief, at least, of the possibility of performing it ; as no one can accept or understand a promise under any other supposition. Instances of this sort are the following : The minister promises a place, which he knows to be engaged, or not at his disposal :— A father, in settling marriage articles, promises to leave his daughter an estate, which he knows to be entailed upon the heir male of his family :—A merchant promises a ship, or share of a ship, which he is privately advised is lost at sea:—An incumbent promises to resign a living, being previously assured that his resignation will not be accepted by the bishop. The promiser, as in these cases, with knowledge of the impossibility, is justly answerable in an equivalent; but otherwise not.

When the promiser himself occasions the impossibility, it is neither more nor less than a direct breach of the promise; as when a soldier maims or a servant disables himself, to get rid of his engagements.

2. Promises are not binding when the performance is *unlawful*.

There are two cases of this: one, where the unlawfulness is known to the parties at the time of making the promise; as, where an assassin promises his employer to dispatch his rival or his enemy; a servant to betray his master; a pimp to procure a mistress; or a *friend* to give his assistance in a scheme of seduction. The parties in these cases are not obliged to perform what the promise requires, *because they were under a prior obligation to the contrary.* From which prior obligation what is there to discharge them? Their promise—their own act and deed. But an obligation, from which a man can discharge himself by his own act, is no obligation at all. The guilt therefore of such promises lies in the making, not in the breaking of them; and if, in the interval betwixt the promise and the performance, a man so far recover his reflection as to repent of his engagements, he ought certainly to break through them.

The other case is, where the unlawfulness did not exist, or was not known, at the time of making the promise; as where a merchant promises his

T

correspondent abroad, to send him a ship-load of corn at a time appointed, and before the time ar rive an embargo is laid upon the exportation of corn:—A woman gives a promise of marriage; before the marriage, she discovers that her intended husband is too nearly related to her, or that he has a wife yet living. In all such cases, where the contrary does not appear, it must be presumed that the parties supposed what they promised to be lawful, and that the promise proceeded entirely upon this supposition. The lawfulness therefore becomes a condition of the promise; which condition failing, the obligation ceases. Of the same nature was Herod's promise to his daughter-in-law, "that he would give her whatever she asked, even to the half of his kingdom." The promise was not unlawful in the terms in which Herod delivered it; and when it became so by the daughter's choice, by her demanding "John the Baptist's head," Herod was discharged from the obligation of it, for the reason now laid down, as well as for that given in the last paragraph.

This rule, "that promises are void, where the performance is unlawful," extends also to imperfect obligations; for the reason of the rule holds of all obligations. Thus, if you promise a man a place, or your vote, and he afterwards render himself unfit to receive either, you are absolved from the obligation of your promise; or, if a better candidate appear, and if it be a case in which you are bound by oath, or otherwise, to govern yourself by the qualification, the promise must be broken through.

And here we would recommend, to young persons especially, a caution, from the neglect of which many involve themselves in embarrassment

and disgrace; and that is, "never to give a promise, which may interfere in the event with their
duty;" for, if it do so interfere, their duty must
be discharged, though at the expense of their
promise, and not unusually of their good name.

The specific performance of promises is reckoned a perfect obligation. And many casuists have
laid down, in opposition to what has been here as-
serted, that, where a perfect and an imperfect obligation clash, the perfect obligation is to be pre-
ferred. For which opinion, however, there seems
to be no reason, but what arises from the terms
"perfect" and "imperfect," the impropriety of
which has been remarked above. The truth is,
of two contradictory obligations that ought to prevail which is prior in point of time.

It is the *performance* being unlawful, and not
any unlawfulness in the subject or motive of the
promise, which destroys its validity : therefore a
bribe, after the vote is given; the wages of prosti-
tution; the reward of any crime, after the crime
is committed; ought, if promised, to be paid. For
the sin and mischief, by this supposition, are over;
and will be neither more nor less for the performance of the promise.

In like manner, a promise does not lose its obligation merely because it proceeded from an *unlawful motive*. A certain person, in the lifetime of
his wife, who was then sick, had paid his addresses
and promised marriage to another woman;—the
wife died; and the woman demanded performance
of the promise. The man, who, it seems, had
changed his mind, either felt or pretended doubts
concerning the obligation of such a promise, and
referred his case to Bishop Sanderson, the most
eminent, in this kind of knowledge, of his time.

Bishop Sanderson, after writing a dissertation upon the question, adjudged the promise to be void: in which, however, upon our principles, he was wrong; for, however criminal the affection might be which induced the promise, the performance, when it was demanded, was lawful; which is the only lawfulness required.

A promise cannot be deemed unlawful, where it produces, when performed, no effect beyond what would have taken place had the promise never been made. And this is the single case, in which the obligation of a promise will justify a conduct which, unless it had been promised, would be unjust. A captive may lawfully recover his liberty, by a promise of neutrality; for his conqueror takes nothing by the promise, which he might not have secured by his death or confinement; and neutrality would be innocent in him, although criminal in another. It is manifest, however, that promises, which come into the place of coercion, can extend no further than to passive compliances; for coercion itself could compel no more. Upon the same principle, promises of secrecy ought not to be violated, although the public would derive advantage from the discovery. Such promises contain no unlawfulness in them to destroy their obligation; for as the information would not have been imparted upon any other condition, the public lose nothing by the promise, which they would have gained without it.

3. Promises are not binding, where they *contradict a former promise;*

Because the performance is then unlawful; which resolves this case into the last.

4. Promises are not binding *before acceptance;* that is, before notice given to the promisee; for,

where the promise is beneficial, if notice be given, acceptance may be presumed. Until the promise be communicated to the promisee, it is the same only as a resolution in the mind of the promiser, which may be altered at pleasure. For no expectation has been excited, therefore none can be disappointed.

But suppose I declare my intention to a third person, who without any authority from me, conveys my declaration to the promisee; is that such a notice as will be binding upon me? It certainly is not: for I have not done that which constitutes the essence of a promise—I have not *voluntarily* excited expectation.

5. Promises are not binding which are *released by the promisee.*

This is evident; but it may be sometimes doubted who the promisee is. If I give a promise *to* A, of a place to vote for B; as to a father for his son; to an uncle for his nephew; to a friend of mine for a relation or friend of his; then A is the promisee, whose consent I must obtain, to be released from the engagement.

If I promise a place or vote to B *by* A, that is, if A be a messenger to convey the promise, as if I should say, " You may tell B that he shall have this place, or may depend upon my vote;" or if A be employed to introduce B's request, and I answer in any terms which amount to a compliance with it; then B is the promisee.

Promises to one person, for the benefit of another, are not released by the death of the promisee; for his death neither makes the performance impracticable, nor implies any consent to release the promiser from it.

6. *Erroneous* promises are not binding in certain cases; as,

1. Where the error proceeds from the mistake or misrepresentation of the promisee

Because a promise evidently supposes the truth of the account, which the promisee relates in order to obtain it. A beggar solicits your charity by a story of the most pitiable distress; you promise to relieve him if he will call again:—In the interval you discover his story to be made up of lies;—this discovery, no doubt, releases you from your promise. One who wants your service describes the business or office for which he would engage you;—you promise to undertake it: when you come to enter upon it, you find the profits less, the labor more, or some material circumstance different from the account he gave you:—In such case, you are not bound by your promise.

2. When the promise is understood by the prom isee to proceed upon a certain supposition, or when the promiser apprehended it to be so understood, and that supposition turns out to be false; then the promise is not binding.

This intricate rule will be best explained by an example. A father receives an account from oroad, of the death of his only son;—soon after which, he promises his fortune to his nephew. The account turns out to be false. The father, we say, is released from his promise; not merely because he never would have made it, had he known the truth of the case—for that alone will not do;—but because the nephew also himself understood the promise to proceed upon this supposition of his cousin's death; or, at least his uncle so thought he understood it, and could not think otherwise. The promise proceeded upon this supposition in the promiser's own apprehension, and, as he believed, n the apprehension of both parties; and this be

lief of his is the precise circumstance which sets
him free. The foundation of the rule is plainly
this: a man is bound only to satisfy the expectation
which he intended to excite; whatever condition
therefore he intended to subject that expectation
to, becomes an essential condition of the promise.

Errors, which come not within this description,
do not annul the obligation of a promise. I promise a candidate my vote;—presently another candidate appears, for whom I certainly would have
reserved it, had I been acquainted with his design.
Here therefore, as before, my promise proceeded
from an error; and I never should have given such
a promise, had I been aware of the truth of the
case, as it has turned out.—But the *promisee* did
not know this;—*he* did not receive the promise
subject to any such condition, or as proceeding
from any such supposition; nor did I at the time
imagine he so received it. This error, therefore,
of mine, must fall upon my own head, and the
promise be observed notwithstanding. A father
promises a certain fortune with his daughter, supposing himself to be worth so much—his circumstances turn out, upon examination, worse than he
was aware of. Here again the promise was erroneous, but, for the reason assigned in the last case,
will nevertheless be obligatory.

The case of erroneous promises is attended with
some difficulty: for, to allow every mistake, or
change of circumstances, to dissolve the obligation
of a promise, would be to allow a latitude, which
might evacuate the force of almost all promises:
and, on the other hand, to gird the obligation so
tight, as to make no allowances for manifest and
fundamental errors, would, in many instances, be
productive of great hardship and absurdity.

TEMPTATIONS ARISING FROM THE INDUL-
GENCE OF SOCIAL PLEASURES.

WHEREVER circumstances throw a large number of young men into each other's society, and
where similar pursuits naturally lead to a homo-
geneous character, temptations are forcible, and
often fatally successful. This happens in large
cities, and in literary institutions. In the former,
there is a vast concourse of young men assembled
from all parts of the country, who come together as
adventurers in the pursuit of affluence or pleasure.
Some of them bring into the metropolis a reputable character, and correct moral principles. Others
come to give loose to evil propensities, which, in
the country, and under the restraints of home, were
kept in some subordination.

When these characters mingle in a large and
bustling city, the *former* class will naturally be
exposed to the seductions of the latter. The pioneers
in wickedness, the practised and hardened crew,
who have abandoned themselves to the indulgence
of their passions, lie in ambush, to seize upon their
victim and hurry him to ruin. Hundreds of such,
with a comparatively plausible exterior, may be
found in the streets, and shops, and alleys of our
cities. Some of them manage to keep up an outward show of decency, and conduct their plans of
dissipation in so covert a manner, as neither to fall
into disgrace, nor excite suspicion or investigation. These are most to be dreaded. They who
have gone beyond the bounds of external decency,
and become so hardened as to feel no shame, have
less influence, in proportion to their loss of charac-
'er, and their notoriety in crime. A moral youth

feels contaminated by their approach. Any visible connexion with such, would be at once a forfeiture of character.

It is men of fair professions and unsuspected wickedness, plausible, but insidious, who are most to be feared, because most likely to be successful. Practised in the arts of temptation, they make a gradual advance upon the ingenuous and unsuspecting youth. They insinuate themselves into his confidence and friendship. When they have learned his scruples, and fathomed his character, they begin the work of drawing him on to their own desperate state of hypocrisy and crime. They will represent as mean, what is only frugal, and characterize as childish those scruples of conscience which it is their object to eradicate. They will first appeal to curiosity, and then make curiosity the avenue to crime. They will speak of the possibility of concealment, and insist that we could not have been endowed with propensities which it is unlawful to indulge. They will represent as manly, what is mean and debasing; and tauntingly ascribe to superstition, what is but the sober dictate of reason and religion. By every possible mode of attack, by persuasion and ridicule, by professions of friendship, and sneers of contempt, will they assail the principles and conduct of their victim, until reason and conscience give way, and like the bird lured on by the fowler, he goes directly into the fatal snare.

The indulgence, at first, will be only such as causes a twinge of conscience, or a secret misgiving of soul. The tempted youth will feel a sort of shame and self-contempt; and in the cool moment of reflection, will fix his resolution against all future attacks. But, alas! the first step in a retro-

grade course has been taken. Like the first step
in the retreat of an army, it is as dispiriting to the
vanquished, as it is invigorating to his foe. The
next attack is less likely to be resisted, for the
ability to resist decreases with every successful
temptation. The first sacrifice of conscience and
principle is like Samson giving up his locks. It is
in vain then to go out and shake yourself, in the
consciousness of your strength. The seducer will
be upon you. He will no longer fear, either the
force of principle, or the vigor of resolution. He
has carried his point; and one breach of obligation,
he well knows, will make way for another, until
your character and your destiny become identified
with his own. How many a young man has fallen
a victim to this process of temptation! How many,
with prospects of usefulness and success, and with
a character which might have insured respect,
have, by listening to the voice of the seducer, forfeited the confidence, and fallen under the pity and
contempt of the community. Yes, and with the
wreck of his own character and prospects, he has
become a source of mortification to his friends, and
perhaps " brought down the gray hairs of a parent
with sorrow to the grave."

These remarks apply, with equal force, to the
dangers and temptations of a college life. Human
nature is the same in both circumstances. Instances of successful temptation are very common
in our literary institutions. There is, there, the
absence of parental watchfulness, and the present-
ation of powerful inducements to ruin. There is,
there, a class of youth whose progress in dissipation is incredibly great. It is in inverse proportion to their years. Idle themselves, their study
is to make others so. Lost to morality and de-

cency themselves, they watch for opportunities to reduce their companions to the same degraded level. They endeavor not only to copy the man ners, but to ape the vices of older profligates; and the rapidity with which they make shipwreck of health, character, and conscience, is a most melancholy proof of the force of temptation, and the prevalence of youthful depravity.

O, ye reckless young men, let me reach your ear, and pour into it a note of friendly warning. If there be left in your heart any feeling; if the rapid abandonment of all that is sacred and honorable have not carried away every vestige of remorse; let me remind you of the claims of your relatives, your country, and your God. Your course will give a death-blow to a father's hopes, and a death-pang to a mother's heart. It will deprive your country of services which might adorn her annals. It will draw down upon you the displeasure of heaven, and, if persisted in, will cover you with ignominy, and ultimately consign you to the prison of despair. With such certain consequences of your dissipation staring you in the face, can you, *dare* you, rush on to the issue? Is it not time to pause—to repent—to break from the grasp of the destroyer?

If these pages meet the eye of one who is still on comparatively safe ground, who has not yet made a plunge into sensual and forbidden pleasures, we would bid him beware of the destroyer. For *you*, there is hope. If a freedom from gross vice, and an avoidance of the occasions of temptation, yet sustain you in the confidence of your friends, and in justifiable hopes of respectability and influence, again we say, beware of the destroyer. Place yourself in an attitude of defence.

Insidious foes lurk around your path. A dangerous enemy lies in ambush. Avoid a vicious companion, as you would avoid the fascination and the
fang of a serpent. His eye may attract, and his
movements may seem graceful; but his intentions
are deadly, and his venom fatal. "He that walk-
eth with wise men shall be wise, but a companion
of fools shall be destroyed."

TEMPTATIONS OF A CITY LIFE.

It cannot be denied that a residence in one of
our cities is attended with more danger to a youth
of inexperience, than where the population is more
sparse, and the temptations proportionably fewer.
The seducer does not work without his appropriate
tools, nor hope to compass his end without the aid
of intermediate agents.

The theatre, appealing to that curiosity and
fondness for excitement which strongly characterize the young, throws upon his eye, at every post
and corner of the streets, the announcement of
some splendid tragedy, or some popular performer.
The comparative respectability of this amusement
is plausibly urged, and the pittance for which it
can be enjoyed is so trifling, that, in the opinion
of the tempter, it would be a disgrace never to have
enjoyed the gratifications of the drama. Whilst
respectable names are brought forward as the warrant for an innocent attendance on this species of
amusement, the deadly concomitants are cautiously
kept out of view. It is not suggested that licentiousness appropriates to herself a large part of the
ground, and rallies there her sons and daughters,

who throw out their lures for the innocent and the unsuspecting. It is not mentioned that a sublime tragedy is generally followed by an obscene after-piece, graduated to the taste, and co-operating with the intentions of that licentious crew. The un-wary youth is not informed how many appendages of ruin are hung around the vestibule of this pol-luted temple, nor how easy is the transition from the court of Thespis to the revels of Bacchus, and the haunts of his dissolute train.

It will not do to talk of inculcating virtue from the stage, when even decency is often made to blush, and when some of the most acceptable pieces are fraught with immorality. Instead of being a " school of virtue," it is a school of vice, a hot-bed of iniquity, a pander to pollution and death. This is not idle declamation against a popular amusement. We speak a sentiment, to the truth of which the consciences, if not the lives, of thea-tre-going men, will bear us witness. Many a youth has found, by lamentable experience, that, in passing the threshold of a theatre, he bade adieu for ever to hope, reputation, and happiness.

The auxiliary, next in influence, which comes to aid the tempter in his malignant projects, is the gaming-table. This is an appendage to those houses of refreshment, whose ostensible object is to afford an occasional meal, and offer to the social club the means of social enjoyment. But it is scarcely necessary to enter these depraved dwell-ings, to understand that *this* is not their *only* ob-ject. Even in passing, you may hear the jarring strife, the intimidating threat, and the eager and malicious note of triumph, mingled with rattling balls, and the bedlam roar of merriment. The sickly light that twinkles, evening after evening, over the porch of this saturnalian abode, conducts the unwary feet first to the revel, and then to the gaming-table.

The gambling room is generally thrown in the back-ground, and sometimes shut out even from the light of day : thus indicating that designs so base, require, for their perpetration, appropriate darkness. There, in that artificial night, and around that fatal table, dwell the maddened sons of strife, practised in the arts of deception, and co-partners in the stakes which their adroitness ena-bles them to seize. There, they hover like so many vultures, circling and scanning their prey, until an opportunity enables them to swoop upon it, with the certainty of its destruction. From these men, all soul, all sympathy, is gone. They have an eye that measures the possessions of their victim, and a hand that can feel its way, unobserved, to the last cent in the pocket. Many of our young men are drawn into these scenes, and, after becoming once initiated, become permanent occupants of the card-table or the billiard-room.

There is still another dark porch which leads to certain ruin ; and he, whose feet cross its threshold, will discover the truth of the inspired declaration, " Her house is the way to hell, going down to the chambers of death." We would willingly pass over this unwelcome subject : we would gladly in-dulge the hope, that no young man, who shall have had decision enough to peruse these desultory re-marks, up to this point, possesses the hardihood which is requisite to the indulgence of so base and destructive a crime. We would gladly presume, that it is necessary only to allude to it, to fill the soul of my youthful reader with horror. But alas ! how many have gone to this fatal ground ! How many have found themselves bound by a fascination which nothing could break! How many have felt an invisible influence chaining them to a spot, where they have sacrificed every hope for this world, and for that which is to come! Poor, infatuated, ruined youth! You have nothing left but unceasing remorse, and nothing in reserve but irretrievable misery.

We cannot but hope that the pictures we have drawn of the dangers to which young men are exposed, may serve to deter those from vice who are comparatively moral. To recover those whose habits of vicious indulgence are confirmed, is beyond our expectations. The intemperate are seldom reclaimed. It has generally been found a hopeless effort to attempt to bring back the drunkard to the respectability he has forfeited. As much as it may wring the heart of benevolence, we are obliged to leave him to his destiny. All that we can do for him is to commend him to the mercy of God. So also is it with the confirmed profligate. Passion has so long domineered over reason and conscience, that hope, in his case, borders on despair. We cannot convince him, for his mind is brutalized. We cannot alarm him, for he acknowledges that even hell itself has less misery than is contained in his own bosom. We cannot rouse his sensibilities, for they have been drowned in the frequent and infamous debauch. He is an unhappy, devoted sensualist, over whom affectionate kindred must weep; and in whose behalf a virtuous community can do little more than pray.

But our hope is, to hold up to the minds of all who have been mercifully preserved from these extremes of wickedness, the danger to which they are exposed. We would take our stand between you youthful reader, and these scenes of horror and wretchedness : and by all that is sacred in religion, and desirable in " the life that now is," warn you to avoid them. We would post a sentinel at every passage of death, to cry in your ears, Beware, beware ! we would throw in the pathway to these haunts of pollution, every obstacle to impede your course ; and hang upon their door-posts the skeleton vestiges of those who have died within their precincts. We would invoke the ghosts of those unhappy wretches who have gone, to come back and hover around the scenes of their profligacy, to admonish you not to be allured to the same degradation and ruin. We would, were it possible, give them a voice that should curdle your blood, and dismay your soul, and save you from the anguish and the misery which they have gone to inherit.

ON THE PLEASURES OF THE UNDERSTANDING

In the savage man the intellectual faculties sleep. As soon as his appetites are satisfied, he sees neither pleasures to desire, nor pains to fear. He lies down and sleeps again. This negative happiness would bring desolation to the heart of a civilized man. All his faculties have commenced their development. He experiences a new craving, which occupations, grave or futile, but rapidly changed and renewed, can alone appease. If there occur between them intervals which can be filled neither by remembrances, nor by necessary repose, lassitude and ennui intervene, and measure for him the length of these chasms in life by sadness

The next enemy to happiness, after vice, is ennui

Some escape it without much seeming calculation
My neighbor every morning turns over twenty ga-
zettes, the state articles of which are copied the one
from the other. Economizing the pleasure of this
reading, and gravely reposing in the intervals, he
communicates, sometimes with an oracular tone,
sometimes with a modest reserve, his reflections
to those who surround him; and, at length, leaves
the reading room with the importance of one who
feels that he has discharged a debt to society.

In public places, it is not the spectacles, but the
emotions of the common people who behold them,
that are worthy of contemplation. In the murder
of a poor tragedy by poorer actors, what transports
from this enthusiastic mass of the audience, when
a blow of the poniard, preceded by a pompous
maxim, lays the tyrant of the piece low! What
earnest feeling, what sincere tears do we witness!
How much more worthy of envy these honest
people, who lose their enjoyment neither by the
revolting improbability of the situations, nor by
the absurdity of the dialogue, nor by the mouthing
of the rehearsal, than those fastidious critics who
exalt their intellectual pride at the expense of these
cheap enjoyments!

From the moment in which a man feels sincere
pleasure in cultivating his understanding, he may
date defiance to the fear of the weight of time. He
has the magic key, which unlocks the exhaustless
treasury of enjoyments. He lives in the age and
country which he prefers. Space and time are no
longer obstacles to his happiness. He interrogates
the wise and good of all ages and all countries;
and his conversations with them cease, or change
object, as soon as he chooses. How much gratitude does he owe the author of nature, for having

U

impressed on genius so many different impulses!
With Plato, he is among the sages of Greece, hearing their lessons, and associating his wishes with
theirs for the happiness of his kind. In the range
of history, he ascends to the infancy of empires
and time. Does he court repose? Horace bids
him gather the roses before they fade; or Shakspeare reminds him, when illusions will vanish like
the baseless fabric of a vision.

If a man has powers and acquirements, it is a
great evil, if he is disposed to fatigue others with
his self-love. If we could number all the subjects
of which the most accomplished scholar is ignorant, we should perceive that the interval between
him and a common person is not so immense as
he may imagine. Ought he to be astonished if
the real friends of the Muses tire of his declama-
tions, his recitations, and occupancy with himself?

To attain truth should be the real end of all
study. In such researches the mind kindles, as
by enchantment, at every step! The desire to
succeed, produces that noble emotion, which is always developed by ardent zeal and pure intentions.
Success, although we were to think nothing of its
results, inspires a kind of pleasure; because truth
comports with our understanding, as brilliant and
soft colors agree with the eye, or pleasant sounds
with the ear. This enjoyment naturally associates
with another, still more vivid. The effect of truth
is universally salutary; and every instance in
which our feeble intellect discovers some gleams,
elevates the spirit, and intimately penetrates it with
a high degree of happiness.

One of the chief advantages of study is, that it
enfranchises the mind from those prejudices that
disturb life. How many, and what agonizing

torments have been caused by those which are associated with false ideas of religion! After those great calamities in the dark ages, which destroyed the traces of the sciences and arts, men, pursued by terror, seemed to imagine that they constantly saw malevolent spirits flying among the clouds, or wandering in the depth of woods. The sound of strong wind and thunder came to their ears as the voice of infernal divinities; and, prostrate with terror, they sought to appease their angry gods by bloody sacrifices. In process of time, a small number of men, enlightened by observation, dared to raise the veil by degrees, and succeeded in dissipating these terrors, by tracing the seeming prodigies to some of the simplest laws of physics. The phantoms of superstition vanished, and, in the light of reason, revealed a just and beneficent Divinity, presiding over obedient nature.

We think, in our pride, that an immense interval separates us from those times of disaster, ignorance, and alarm. How many of our kind, unhappy by their intellectual weakness, still tremble before the jealous and implacable god of their imaginations, who enjoins hatred and wrath; and punishes even the errors of opinion by the most horrible torments! The man who is exempt from prejudices, is alone capable of prostrating himself before the divinity from a feeling of love, and whose prayer, alike confident and resigned, is addressed to his noble attributes of power, justice, and clemency.

There are other errors which study dispels. The student who is charmed with communion with the muses, does not consume his best years in gloomy intrigues: nor do you meet him pressing forward in the path which ambition has traced. The Greeks, fertile in significant allegories, supposed the same divinity to preside over the sciences and wisdom.

The habit of living in converse with the noblest works of mind and art, produces elevation of soul; and he who has an elevated mind must be intrinsically good and happy. Exempt from the weaknesses of vanity, free from the tumultuous passions, he cultivates the noble and generous virtues, for the pleasure of practising them. Disdaining a mass of objects of desire which disturb the vulgar, he offers a small mark to misery. Should adversity strike him, he has resources so much the more sure, as he finds them in himself.

No one can ever taste the full charm of letters and the arts, except in the bosom of retirement. If he reads and meditates only for the pursuit of fame, amusements change to labors. If we propose to enter the lists, outstrip rivals, and direct a party, we are soon agitated with little passions, but great inquietudes. Heaven, sternly decreeing that no earthly felicity shall be unalloyed, has placed a thirst for celebrity as a drawback upon the love of study.

But ought the ardor to render immortal services—ought the noble ambition to be useful, to be stifled? Are not these the source of pleasures as pure as they are ravishing? We contemplate an immense and indestructible republic, composed of all those men, who devote themselves to the happiness of their kind. Occupied without relaxation or abatement, in continuing the works which their predecessors have begun, they bequeath to their successors the care of pursuing and crowning their labors. Men of genius are the chiefs of this republic. As they have talents which separate them from the rest of the human race; they have also pleasures reserved for themselves alone. What a sublime sentiment must have elevated the spirit of Newton, when a part of the mysterious laws of the universe first dawned upon his mind ! A glow still more delightful must have pervaded the bosom of Fenelon, when meditating the most beautiful lessons which wisdom ever announced to the powerful and the rulers of the people. To these privileged beings it belongs, to give a powerful impulse to minds, and to trace a new path for the generations to come.

JUSTICE.

There is one virtue, of which the general rules determine, with the greatest exactness, every external action which it requires. This virtue is justice. The rules of justice are accurate in the highest degree, and admit of no exceptions or modifications, but such as may be ascertained as accurately as the rules themselves, and which generally, indeed, flow from the very same principles with them. If I owe a man ten pounds, justice requires that I should precisely pay him ten pounds, either at the time agreed upon, or when he demands it. What I ought to perform, how much I ought to perform, when and where I ought to perform it, the whole nature and circumstances of the action prescribed, are all of them precisely fixed and determined. Though it may be awkward and pedantic, therefore, to affect too strict an adherence to the common rules of prudence or generosity, there is no pedantry in sticking fast by the rules of justice. On the contrary, the most sacred regard is due to them; and the actions which this virtue requires are never so proper performed as when the chief motive for performing them is a reverential and religious regard to those general rules which require them. In the practice of the other virtues, our conduct should rather be directed by a certain idea of propriety, by a certain taste for a particular tenor of conduct, than by any regard to a precise maxim or rule; and we should consider the end and foundation of the rule, more than the rule itself. But it is otherwise with regard to justice: the man who in that refines the least, and adheres with the most obstinate stedfastness to the general rules themselves, is the most commendable, and the most to be depended upon. Though the end of the rules of justice be, to hinder us from hurting our neighbor, it may frequently be a crime to violate them, though we could pretend, with some pretext of reason, that this particular violation could do no hurt. A man often becomes a villain the moment he begins, even in his own heart, to chicane in this manner. The moment he thinks of departing from the most staunch and positive adherence to what those inviolable precepts prescribe to him, he is no longer to be trusted, and no man can say what degree of guilt he may not arrive at. The thief imagines he does no evil, when he steals from the rich, what he supposes they may easily want, and what possibly they may never even know has been stolen from them. The adulterer imagines he does no evil, when he corrupts the wife of his friend, provided he covers his intrigue from the suspicion of the husband, and does not disturb the peace of the family. When once we begin to give way to such refinements, there is no enormity so gross of which we may not be capable.

The rules of justice may be compared to the

rules of grammar; the rules of the other virtues,
to the rules which critics lay down for the attainment of what is sublime and elegant in composition.
The one, are precise, accurate, and indispensable.
The other, are loose, vague, and indeterminate,
and present us rather with a general idea of the
perfection we ought to aim at, than afford us any
certain and infallible directions for acquiring it.
A man may learn to write grammatically by rule,
with the most absolute infallibility; and so, perhaps, he may be taught to act justly. But there
are no rules whose observance will infallibly lead
us to the attainment of elegance or sublimity in
writing: though there are some which may help
us, in some measure, to correct and ascertain the
vague ideas which we might otherwise have entertained of those perfections. And there are no
rules by the knowledge of which we can infallibly
be taught to act upon all occasions with prudence,
with just magnanimity, or proper beneficence:
though there are some which may enable us to
correct and ascertain, in several respects, the imperfect ideas which we might otherwise have entertained of those virtues.

ON REVERENCING THE DEITY.

In many persons, a seriousness and sense of
awe overspread the imagination, whenever the idea
of the Supreme Being is presented to their thoughts.
This effect, which forms a considerable security
against vice, is the consequence not so much of
reflection as of habit; which habit being generated
by the external expressions of reverence which we
use ourselves, or observe in others, may be de

stroyed by causes opposite to these, and especially
by that familiar levity with which some learn to
speak of the Deity, of his attributes, providence,
revelations, or worship.

God hath been pleased (no matter for what reason, although probably for this,) to forbid the vain
mention of his name :—" Thou shalt not take the
name of the Lord thy God in vain." Now the
mention is *vain* when it is useless ; and it is useless when it is neither likely nor intended to serve
any good purpose ; as when it flows from the lips
idle and unmeaning, or is applied, on occasions
inconsistent with any consideration of religion and
devotion, to express our anger, our earnestness,
our courage, or our mirth ; or indeed when it is
used at all, except in acts of religion, or in serious
and seasonable discourse upon religious subjects.

The prohibition of the third commandment is re-
cognized by Christ in his sermon upon the mount ;
which sermon adverts to none but the moral parts
of the Jewish law : " I say unto you, Swear not at
all : but let your communication be Yea, yea ;
Nay, nay : for whatsoever is more than these com-
eth of evil." The Jews probably interpreted the
prohibition as restrained to the name JEHOVAH, the
name which the Deity had appointed and appro-
priated to himself ; Exod. vi. 3. The words of
Christ extend the prohibition beyond the *name* of
God, to every thing associated with the idea :—
" Swear not, neither by heaven, for it is God's
throne ; nor by the earth, for it is God's footstool ;
neither by Jerusalem, for it is the city of the Great
King." Matt. v. 35.

The offence of profane swearing is aggravated
by the consideration, that in *it* duty and decency are
sacrificed to the slenderest of temptations. Sup-

pose the habit, either from affectation, or by negligence and inadvertency, to be already formed, it must always remain within the power of the most ordinary resolution to correct it; and it cannot, one would think, cost a great deal to relinquish the pleasure and honor which it confers. A concern for duty is in fact never strong, when the exertion requisite to vanquish a habit founded in no antecedent propensity is thought too much or too painful.

A contempt of positive duties, or rather of those duties for which the reason is not so plain as the command, indicates a disposition upon which the authority of revelation has obtained little influence.—This remark is applicable to the offence of profane swearing, and describes, perhaps pretty exactly, the general character of those who are most addicted to it.

Mockery and ridicule, when exercised upon the Scriptures, or even upon the places, persons, and forms set apart for the ministration of religion, fall within the meaning of the law which forbids the profanation of God's name; especially as that law is extended by Christ's interpretation. They are moreover inconsistent with a religious frame of mind: for, as no one ever either feels himself disposed to pleasantry, or capable of being diverted with the pleasantry of others, upon matters in which he is deeply interested; so a mind intent upon the acquisition of heaven rejects with indignation every attempt to entertain it with jests, calculated to degrade or deride subjects which it never recollects but with seriousness and anxiety. Nothing but stupidity, or the most frivolous disposition of thought, can make even the inconsiderate forget the supreme importance of every thing which re-

lates to the expectation of a future existence.
Whilst the infidel mocks at the superstitions of
the vulgar, insults over their credulous fears, their
childish errors, or fantastic rites, it does not occur
to him to observe, that the most preposterous device by which the weakest devotee ever believed
ne was securing the happiness of a future life, is
more rational than unconcern about it. Upon
this subject nothing is so absurd as indifference;
no folly so contemptible as thoughtlessness and
levity.

Finally; The knowledge of what is due to the
solemnity of those interests, concerning which
Revelation professes to inform and direct us, may
teach even those who are least inclined to respect
the prejudices of mankind, to observe a decorum
in the style and conduct of religious disquisitions,
with the neglect of which many adversaries of
Christianity are justly chargeable. Serious arguments are fair on all sides. Christianity is but ill
defended by refusing audience or toleration to the
objections of unbelievers. But whilst we would
have freedom of inquiry restrained by no laws but
those of decency, we are entitled to demand, on
behalf of a religion which holds forth to mankind
assurances of immortality, that its credit be as-
sailed by no other weapons than those of sober discussion and legitimate reasoning;—that the truth
or falsehood of Christianity be never made a topic
of raillery, a theme for the exercise of wit or eloquence, or a subject of contention for literary fame
and victory;—that the cause be tried upon its
merits;—that all applications to the fancy, passions, or prejudices of the reader, all attempts to
preoccupy, ensnare, or perplex his judgment, by
any art, influence, or impression whatsoever, ex-

trinsic to the proper grounds and evidence upon
which his assent ought to proceed, be rejected from
a question which involves in its determination the
hopes, the virtue, and the repose of millions;—that
the controversy be managed on both sides with
sincerity; that is, that nothing be produced, in the
writings of either, contrary to or beyond the writer's
own knowledge and persuasion;—that objections
and difficulties be proposed, from no other motive
than an honest and serious desire to obtain satisfaction, or to communicate information which may
promote the discovery and progress of truth;—
that, in conformity with this design, every thing
be stated with integrity, with method, precision,
and simplicity; and above all, that whatever is
published in opposition to received and confessedly
beneficial persuasions, be set forth under a form
which is likely to invite inquiry and to meet examination. If with these moderate and equitable
conditions be compared the manner in which hos-
tilities have been waged against the Christian religion, not only the votaries of the prevailing faith,
but every man who looks forward with anxiety to
the destination of his being, will see much to blame
and to complain of. By *one unbeliever*, all the follies which have adhered, in a long course of dark
and superstitious ages, to the popular creed, are
assumed as so many doctrines of Christ and his
Apostles, for the purpose of subverting the whole
system by the absurdities which it is *thus* represented to contain. By *another*, the ignorance and
vices of the sacerdotal order, their mutual dissen-
sions and persecutions, their usurpations and encroachments upon the intellectual liberty and civil
rights of mankind, have been displayed with no
small triumph and invective; not so much to guard

the Christian laity against a repetition of the same injuries (which is the only proper use to be made of the most flagrant examples of the past,) as to prepare the way for an insinuation, that the religion itself is nothing but a profitable fable, imposed upon the fears and credulity of the multitude, and upheld by the frauds and influence of an interested and crafty priesthood. And yet, how remotely is the character of the clergy connected with the truth of Christianity! What, after all, do the most disgraceful pages of ecclesiastical history prove, but that the passions of our common nature are not altered or excluded by distinctions of name, and that the characters of men are formed much more by the temptations than the duties of their profession? A *third* finds delight in collecting and repeating accounts of wars and massacres, of tumults and insurrections, excited in almost every age of the Christian era by religious zeal; as though the vices of Christians were parts of Christianity; intolerance and extirpation precepts of the gospel; or as if its spirit could be judged of from the counsels of princes, the intrigues of statesmen, the pretences of malice and ambition, or the unauthorized cruelty of some gloomy and virulent superstition. By a *fourth*, the succession and variety of popular religions; the vicissitudes with which sects and tenets have flourished and decayed; the zeal with which they were once supported, the negligence with which they are now remembered; the little share which reason and argument appear to have had in framing the creed, or regulating the religious conduct of the multitude; the indifference and submission with which the religion of the state is generally received by the common people; the caprice and vehemence with which it is sometimes opposed; the frenzy with which men have been brought to contend for opinions and ceremonies, of which they knew neither the proof, the meaning, nor the original: lastly, the equal and undoubting confidence with which we hear the doctrines of Christ or of Confucius, the law of Moses or of Mahomet, the Bible, the Koran, or the Shaster, maintained or anathematized, taught or abjured, revered or derided, according as we live on this or on that side of a river; keep within or step over the boundaries of a state; or even in the same country, and by the same people, so often as the event of a battle, or the issue of a negotiation, delivers them to the dominion of a new master;— points, we say, of this sort are exhibited to the public attention, as so many arguments against the *truth* of the Christian religion;—and with success. For these topics being brought together, and set off with some aggravation of circumstances, and with a vivacity of style and description familiar enough to the writings and conversation of free-thinkers, insensibly lead the imagination into a habit of classing Christianity with the delusions that have taken possession, by turns, of the public belief; and of regarding it as, what the scoffers of our faith represent it to be, *the superstition of the day.* But is this to deal honestly by the subject, or with the world? May not the same things be said, may not the same prejudices be excited by these representations, whether Christianity be true or false, or by whatever proofs its truth be attested? May not truth as well as falsehood be taken upon credit? May not a religion be founded upon evidence accessible and satisfactory to every mind competent to the inquiry, which yet, by the greatest part of its professors, is received upon authority?

But if the *matter* of these objections be repre hensible, as calculated to produce an effect upon the reader beyond what their real weight and place in the argument deserve, still more shall we discover of management and disingenuousness in the *form* under which they are dispersed among the public. Infidelity is served up in every shape that is likely to allure, surprise, or beguile the imagination; in a fable, a tale, a novel, a poem; in interspersed and broken hints, remote and oblique surmises; in books of travels, of philosophy, of natural history; in a word, in any form rather than the right one, that of a professed and regular disquisition. And because the coarse buffoonery and broad laugh of the old and rude adversaries of the Christian faith would offend the taste, perhaps, rather than the virtue, of this cultivated age, a graver irony, a more skilful and delicate banter is substituted in its place. An eloquent historian, beside his more direct, and therefore fairer, attacks upon the credibility of Evangelic story, has contrived to weave into his narration one continued sneer upon the cause of Christianity, and upon the writings and characters of its ancient patrons. The knowledge which this author possesses of the frame and conduct of the human mind must have led him to observe, that such attacks do their execution without inquiry. Who can refute a *sneer*? Who can compute the number, much less, one by one, scrutinize the justice of those disparaging insinuations which crowd the pages of this elaborate history? What reader suspends his curiosity, or calls off his attention from the principal narrative, to examine references, to search into the foundation, or to weigh the reason, propriety, and force of every transient sarcasm and sly allusion, by which the Christian testimony is depreciated and traduced; and by which, nevertheless, he may find his persuasion afterwards unsettled and perplexed?

But the enemies of Christianity have pursued her with poisoned arrows. Obscenity itself is made the vehicle of infidelity. The awful doctrines, if we be not permitted to call them the sacred truths, of our religion, together with all the adjuncts and appendages of its worship and external profession, have been sometimes impudently profaned by an unnatural conjunction with impure and lascivious images. The fondness for ridicule is almost universal; and ridicule to many minds is never so irresistible as when seasoned with obscenity, and employed upon religion. But in proportion as these noxious principles take hold of the imagination, they infatuate the judgment; for trains of ludicrous and unchaste associations, adhering to every sentiment and mention of religion, render the mind indisposed to receive either conviction from its evidence, or impressions from its authority. And this effect, being exerted upon the sensitive part of our frame, is altogether independent of argument, proof, or reason; is as formidable to a true religion as to a false one; to a well-grounded faith as to a chimerical mythology, or fabulous tradition. Neither, let it be observed, is the crime or danger less, because impure ideas are exhibited under a veil, in covert and chastised language.

Seriousness is not constraint of thought; nor levity freedom. Every mind which wishes the advancement of truth and knowledge, in the most important of all human researches, must abhor this licentiousness, as violating no less the laws of rea soning than the rights of decency. There is but one description of men, to whose principles it ought to be tolerable; I mean that class of reasoners who can see *little* in Christianity, even supposing it to be true. To such adversaries we address this reflection :--Had Jesus Christ delivered no other declaration than the following, " The hour is coming, in the which all that are in the grave shall hear his voice, and shall come forth; they that have done good unto the resurrection of life; and they that have done evil unto the resurrection of damnation;"—he had pronounced a message of inestimable importance, and well worthy of that splendid apparatus of prophecy and miracles with which his mission was introduced and attested; a message, in which the wisest of mankind would rejoice to find an answer to their doubts, and rests to their inquiries. It is idle to say, that a future state had been discovered already:—it had been discovered, as the Copernican system was—it was one guess among many. He alone discovers who *proves;* and no man can prove this point but the teacher who testifies by miracles that his doctrine comes from God.

CONCLUSION.

HAVING thus completed the task which we had proposed to ourselves—having offered advice towards improving the mind, elevating the morals, refining the manners, and forming the whole character of a young man—such as we would give to our own brother or son: it only remains that we should take leave of our readers; which we now do with the most cordial wishes for their unlimited progress in all that is noble and excellent—for their success in all that insures a happy life and a blessed immortality.

THE END.

www.ingramcontent.com/pod-product-compliance
Lightning Source LLC
LaVergne TN
LVHW091213080426
835509LV00009B/974